Other titles in the Cognitive Strategy Training Series

Cognitive Strategy Instruction for Middle and High Schools

Eileen Wood
Wilfrid Laurier University
Vera Woloshyn
Brock University
Teena Willoughby
University of Waterloo

Editors

B r o o k l i n e   B o o k s

Library of Congress Cataloging-in-Publication Information

    Cognitive strategy instruction for middle and high schools / Eileen
      Wood, Vera Woloshyn, Teena Willoughby, editors.
          p. cm. -- (Cognitive strategy training series)
      Includes bibliographical references and index.
      ISBN 1-57129-007-9 (paper) : $26.95
        1. Thought and thinking--Study and teaching (Secondary)
    2. Cognitive learning. 3. High school teaching. 4. Learning,
    Psychology of. I. Wood, Eileen, 1960- . II. Woloshyn, Vera.
    III. Willoughby, Teena, 1955- . IV. Series.
    LB1590.3.C647 1995
    373.11'02--dc20   95-2144
                                     CIP

Printed in the United States by Thomson-Shore, Inc., Dexter, Michigan.
10 9 8 7 6 5 4 3 2

Part of the Cognitive Strategy Training Series
Series Editor: Michael Pressley, SUNY–Albany

ISBN 1-57129-007-9

Brookline Books

P.O. Box 1047
Cambridge, Massachusetts 02238-1047

We dedicate this book to our families
John, Joyce, and Steven
Bob and Raymond
Kim, Karen and Mark

We thank Dr. Mustaq Khan for sharing his expertise in cognitive psychology and providing helpful comments for the chapters. We would also like to thank Rod Balsom and Michelle Kalra for their assistance in the construction of the indexes and proofreading of the chapters, respectively. All three authors acknowledge the support of the Social Sciences and Humanities Research Council whose funding allowed for the preparation and research time required for the construction of this book. Finally, we would like to acknowledge the financial support offered by Wilfrid Laurier University for the preparation of this book.

Contents

Series Preface

This volume is one of a series of short paperbacks published by Brookline Books on the topic of cognitive strategy instruction. The goal of the series is to provide the very best and most up-to-date information about strategy instruction and related topics to the educator community.

Two types of books are featured in the series:

(a) Most are written by educational researchers who are doing work that directly relates to school performance. Their work is reviewed by the general editor, Michael Pressley, before an invitation to submit a book is delivered to them. The editor only provides invitations to scholars whose research is sound methodologically and unambiguously relevant to education. One clear goal of the series is to make the very best research on cognitive strategy instruction more readily available to teachers. Pressley and Milton Budoff, the publisher of Brookline Books, are proud that the series has attracted, and continues to attract, outstanding scholars and educators.

(b) A few books in the series are by scholars who are supervising outstanding demonstration projects in strategy instruction or who have done outstanding integrative work. A few well-known schools and institutes have or will contribute. Bibliographic scholars who can provide definitive commentary on how to do strategy instruction or who can provide input about changes in curriculum or educational practices that foster better information processing in children will also appear in the series.

All those involved with the series are extremely excited about bridging the gap between the researcher/scholar community and the teaching profession. The contributors to this series are all committed to make high quality work accessible to teaching professionals who can translate research findings into telling educational practices.

Because strategy instruction is particularly appropriate for intellectually handicapped populations, and because of the commitment of the publisher to provide materials to educators servicing students who experience difficulties in school, the series especially features outstanding contributions to the learning disabilities literature. But strategy instruction is highly appropriate for normal learners, especially inner city and minority children. The series will focus on conveying these methods for use with those students. Special education is not the exclusive focus of the series.

It is our strong desire to publish books about a variety of cognitive strategy interventions that are worthwhile for children—handicapped, average, and gifted. Authors who feel they might contribute to this effort should contact Milton Budoff at Brookline Books or Michael Pressley at the Department of Educational Psychology and Statistics, University at Albany, State University of New York, Albany, NY 12222.

CHAPTER 1

An Introduction to Cognitive Strategies in the Secondary School

Eileen Wood · Wilfrid Laurier University
Teena Willoughby · University of Waterloo
Vera Woloshyn · Brock University

Adolescents experience significant changes in expectations, goals, and educational format when they make the transition from elementary to secondary school. The altered structure of the secondary school environment sets the context for the many changes. For example, secondary schools generally run on a semester system, where students rotate through a series of classes taught by a different teacher who is specialized in that particular subject matter. This differs from the elementary school, where typically one teacher provides instruction across a variety of subjects for one group of students.

This change in structure brings the student new responsibilities. Because one single teacher is not always responsible for observing a particular student throughout the curriculum, the student must become more sophisticated at monitoring her own progress and responsible for her own learning. She now has more leeway in selecting the courses she wishes to take, even the choice of selecting her program (e.g., general or college track; vocational, commercial or academic, etc.). Such dramatic changes in the educational environment bring a greater sense of autonomy if the student can manage her learning.

To be effective self-directed learners, students must, first, have a wide array of learning strategies at their disposal and, second, know where, when, and how to use these strategies (Ghatala, 1986). Recent research in educational psychology has focused on helping students learn to be more involved and responsible for their own education (Zimmerman & Schunk, 1989). From a cognitive perspective, this entails an ability to monitor their performance as they pursue problems and tasks, an awareness of their relevant existing knowledge, and a repertoire of effective learning strategies which they can employ appropriately (Pressley, Borkowski, & Schneider, 1987).

The purpose of this book is to identify and explain the array of cognitive strategies which help students to actively organize the information they are expected to learn. The chapters also provide explicit examples of when and in what circumstances they can use each of the strategies. In addition, all of the strategies presented in this book have been *empirically validated*; that is, their positive effects on students' learning have been demonstrated experimentally, clearly identifying them as effective procedures.

All the learning strategies we present, whether general or subject-specific, are based on a model of memory suggesting that learning is enhanced when new material is made *meaningful* to the student. In other words, students must integrate new information with their existing knowledge. On those occasions when students have limited or no prior knowledge to draw upon, we have presented alternate strategies that allow students to establish a foundation of knowledge for subsequent use.

This model of learning is based upon information processing principles. In short, information processing models assume that information is manipulated by the learner as it passes through a series of learning operations. The level of *processing*, or manipulation of information, depends on the mechanisms that are involved, ranging from very simple processing at a perceptual level to deeper conceptual processing. The level of processing can be affected by the type of strategy the learner uses; generally, the more elaborate the strategy, the deeper the processing associated with it. All chapters in this book allude to the exchange of information within an information processing model. In addition, the model is diagrammed or described in Chapters 3 and 10.

The common theme across all the chapters is the relation between cognitive theory and strategic intervention. The chapters make explicit the cognitive demands students face within the specific domain, for given tasks, and with the recommended strategy. Similarly, readers have an opportunity to review the general model because a theoretical rationale is provided at the onset of each chapter, with a subsequent discussion of the unique features relevant to the domain.

Each chapter introduces a range of strategies. Some strategies are simpler (i.e., less sophisticated); others involve more cognitive effort. Teaching a range of strategies is important to ensure that students use the most efficient strategic intervention that matches the demands of the task. Additionally, a range of strategies is needed to reflect the diversity of students' interests and abilities. Larger classes, destreamed programs, and other initiatives aimed at inclusive classrooms make it necessary to provide a wide array of strategies to support the needs of all students.

Regardless of type of strategy or student experience, all newly presented strategies require training and practice for students (and often for the teachers as well). The chapters outline the instruction of strategies through examples, so that the sequence of steps of each strategy is conveyed accurately, and so that educators and learners can see the strategy appropriately applied in a 'real-world' learning context. Correct implementation of the strategies is critical in order to maximize learning.

Some of the strategies will appear more complex and cumbersome when first encountered. This is to be expected. Like learning to drive a car, complex strategies at first require much effort, but with repeated practice and experience they become relatively automatic and easy to execute.

However, it is also important to keep in mind that not all strategies can be used by all learners. If, after a period of practice, a strategy remains difficult to execute, it may be that the strategy involves demands that are too challenging for the learner. For instance, some younger and less academically successful learners have experienced difficulty with some strategies (Hidi & Anderson, 1986), most notably with imagery-based strategies (Schneider & Pressley, 1989). These problems can often be alleviated by providing illustrations and other visual supports to help these learners while using the strategies (Mastropieri, Scruggs, & Levin, 1987). If students experience difficulties with specific strategies, they can be guided to other strategies that do not share the same cognitive demands, or they can be provided with supports that moderate the demands of the strategies. In some cases, chapters highlight possible modifications of individual strategies.

The structure of the book is such that each chapter can be read independently. Although reference may be made to related information in the other chapters, each chapter is designed to stand on its own. It is important to remember that, although the strategies are presented independently, they can often be used in more than one subject setting. We also recommend that strategy instruction be integrated within the curriculum rather than taught as a separate unit or perceived merely as a tool to correct problems. Only when strategies are integrated within the curriculum will adolescents gain the experience needed to become effective self-regulated learners.

REFERENCES

Ghatala, E.S. (1986). Strategy-monitoring training enables young learners to select effective strategies. *Educational Psychologist, 21*, 43-54.

Hidi, S., & Anderson, V. (1986). Producing written summaries: Task demands, cognitive operations, and implications for instruction. *Review of Educational Research, 56*, 473-493.

Mastropieri, M.A., Scruggs, T.E., & Levin, J.R. (1987). Learning-disabled students' memory for expository prose: Mnemonic versus nonmnemonic pictures. *American Educational Research Journal, 24*, 505-519.

Pressley, M., Borkowski, J.G., & Schneider, W. (1987). Cognitive strategies: Good strategy users coordinate metacognition and knowledge. In R. Vasta and G. Whitehurst (Eds.), *Annals of Child Development, Vol. 5* (pp. 89-129). New York: JAI Press.

Schneider, W., & Pressley, M. (1989). *Memory development between 2 and 20*. New York: Springer.

Zimmerman, B.J., & Schurk, D.H. (Eds.) (1989). *Self-regulated learning and academic achievement: Theory, research, and practice*. New York: Springer.

CHAPTER 2

Mnemonic Strategies

Teena Willoughby • University of Waterloo
Eileen Wood • Wilfrid Laurier University

Most adults can remember being taught to use some type of memory "trick" during their high school years to help them learn difficult or unfamiliar material. For example, music teachers often instruct students to use the word *FACE* to help them remember the notes for the spaces of the treble clef. In math, a student might be taught the expression *SOHCAHTOA is a tribe of Indians that live in triangular teepees* to remember how to calculate the angles of a triangle (sine = opposite/hypotenuse, etc.). Similarly, students in a geography class might be given the phrase *Brap is a cold bowl of vin and chile peu and 3 little guyanas* to remember the names of the countries in South America in order of size (Brazil, Argentina, Peru, Columbia, Bolivia, Venezuela, Chile, Paraguay, Ecuador, Uruguay, Guyana, Suriname, French Guiana). All of these memory "tricks" are called *mnemonics*. There are a wide variety of mnemonic techniques that can be taught to secondary school students. Even though there is a great deal of research supporting the effectiveness of mnemonic strategies, few are taught in the classroom. This is especially true of some of the more elaborate mnemonic strategies. In this chapter, we will identify and describe a range of effective mnemonic techniques as well as discuss when and where these techniques facilitate learning.

WHAT ARE MNEMONIC TECHNIQUES?

Mnemonics are structured ways to help us *remember*. Most often, mnemonic strategies pair familiar information with unfamiliar to-be-learned information in order to make the new material more memorable. Mnemonic strategies are not just "tricks" to help students learn. These techniques are based on well-established principles of learning and memory (Higbee, 1977). Learning is greatest when new to-be-learned information is meaningful, concrete, and elaborated (Scruggs & Mastropieri, 1990). Mnemonics provide a structured system to make new, unfamiliar, abstract, and unelaborated material more meaningful, familiar, and concrete. For example, when a student is required to learn an unfamiliar word and its definition, they could first *recode* the unfamiliar word as a familiar one by associating it with a word that sounds the same (e.g., recode *coati* as "coat"). The student could then *relate* the new *keyword* "coat" to the definition of *coati* through the use of a mental picture (i.e., imagery). At *retrieval*, when the student needs to remember the definition, the student would think about the picture that had been created and use the keyword to get back to the unfamiliar word. These 3 R's—recoding, relating, and retrieving—are essential components of mnemonic techniques (Levin, 1983).

Students who use mnemonics remember more than students who are not trained to use these techniques (Bellezza, 1981; Higbee, 1979; Mastropieri, Scruggs, & Levin, 1987; Pressley, Levin, & McDaniel, 1987). Mnemonics can be used in a large number of domains: biology, geography, history, geology, etc. (e.g., Higbee, 1977; Pressley, Levin, & Delaney, 1982; Yates, 1966). For example, mnemonic strategies have facilitated students' memory for definitions (e.g., Pressley, Levin, & McDaniel, 1987), for distinctions among technical terms (e.g., *monocotyledons* = parallel veins; *dicotyledons* = branching veins; Rosenheck, Levin, & Levin, 1989) and the paintings of different artists (Carney, Levin, & Morrison, 1988). These findings are important because they suggest that mnemonic techniques can be taught in a number of different classes. It also means that once instructed, students can apply these techniques on their own in many of their different courses.

MNEMONIC TECHNIQUES

Mnemonics vary in their complexity and in their cognitive demands. Some mnemonics involve only one or two steps. Others involve more elaborate sequences. Similarly, some mnemonics require more cognitive effort, for example, requiring the construction of both images and verbal cues. Imagery is an important component of many mnemonic strategies because the process of creating unique mental pictures to represent new information makes that material more *distinctive* and, therefore, more memorable (Willoughby, Wood, & Khan, 1994). The first two mnemonic strategies listed below are verbal techniques; the remaining involve both imagery and verbal components.

Rhymes

Researchers have suggested that when trying to recall a word, other words that rhyme with it may be effective cues to help recall (Higbee, 1977). Many examples of rhyming mnemonics can be found in phrases that were learned in school and are now fairly common. For example, the phrase "Thirty days hath September..." uses rhyme to help students remember the number of days in each month. To remember when Columbus discovered America, a student can be taught the rhyme "In

1492, Columbus sailed the ocean blue." Other examples include "A pint's a pound the world around" and "Cooking rice—Water's twice." Constructing rhymes for students, or having students construct their own rhymes, can facilitate memory for words and facts.

First-letter mnemonics

Most students are familiar with the strategy of using the first letter of a list of unfamiliar words to create a meaningful work or phrase. For example, to help you remember the Great Lakes, you can use the word *HOMES* (for the lakes Huron, Ontario, Michigan, Erie, and Superior). The name *Roy G. Biv* can be used to remember the colors of the visible spectrum (red, orange, yellow, green, blue, indigo, and violet). First-letter mnemonics can be either acronyms or acrostics. An acronym is a word formed from the first letters of other words. An acronym to help a French student remember most of the verbs that are conjugated with the helping verb "to be" is the name of a lady, "Mrs. Vandertramp" (*monter, rester, sortir, venir, aller, naitre, descendre, entrer, rentrer, tomber, revenir, arriver, mourir, partir*). Another example is the word *FOIL*, used in math classes to help students remember the sequence of operations in multiplying two binomials $(a + b)(c + d)$: *f*irst terms, *o*uter terms, *i*nner terms, *l*ast terms. An acrostic uses the first letters of other words to spell a word or phrase. For example, an acrostic for remembering the order of planets from the sun is *Men Very Easily Make Jugs Serve Useful Nocturnal Purposes* (Mercury, Venus, Earth, Mars, Jupiter, Saturn, Uranus, Neptune, Pluto).

The first-letter mnemonic strategy helps memory because it makes the to-be-learned material meaningful, it chunks the information, and it changes a rote retrieval task to an aided retrieval task by providing cues to help the student retrieve the items. One major concern with first-letter mnemonics, however, is that the first letter may not give enough information to the student at retrieval to remember the word (Levin, 1993). For example, if a student has to remember a series of unfamiliar words for which they have no referent, (e.g., sine, cosine, etc.), then providing a mnemonic such as *SOHCAHTOA* would not necessarily facilitate learning. When the student has a basic understanding of the terms *sine, cosine* and so forth, then the mnemonic will help them to recall the equations for the triangle. First-letter mnemonics are most beneficial when the to-be-learned material has some meaning so that knowing the first letter facilitates remembering the remainder of the word.

Method of Loci

Almost everyone who claims to have new "tricks" for better memory will encourage the use of an imagery mnemonic, such as the method of loci. The method of loci is the oldest mnemonic system, dating back to the ancient Greeks. According to Yates (1966), the method of loci got its name when a poet named Simonides was delivering a speech at a banquet and was called outside. While Simonides was outside, the banquet hall roof collapsed, crushing the people inside beyond recognition. Simonides was able to identify each person by thinking of the places where they had been sitting at the banquet table. Because Simonides used location to remember the information, this memory technique became known as the "method of loci."

Before the invention of the printing press, the method of loci was used by Greek and Roman orators to memorize speeches. Orators created mental pictures of objects that represented the topics they were going to cover in their speeches, and then mentally placed these objects in different locations—usually in different rooms of a building or along a well- travelled road. While giving their speech, they mentally walked through the building or along the road, retrieving the images of the objects, and thus the topics, from each location.

The method of loci involves two steps. First, the student would picture a well-known series of locations, such as the rooms in their house or landmarks that they see on their way to school. Second, the student would place each item in the order that they are to be remembered with one of the locations. At retrieval, the student would take an imaginary walk past the locations and retrieve the items. The advantages of locations are that they exist in a natural serial order and are concrete and easy to picture. With this method, a retrieval test becomes an aided retrieval test because there are cues available to prompt memory (Higbee, 1977).

An important goal is to form a strong association between each of the to-be-remembered items and their corresponding locations. It is important to make each image vivid and to have each item *interacting* with its corresponding location. For example, rather than imagining two objects sitting beside one another, it is better to picture them intermingled or actively engaged with one another. A number of studies have demonstrated the effectiveness of using the method of loci strategy (e.g., Ross & Lawrence, 1968; Snowman, Krebs, & Lockhart, 1980). The method of loci is particularly good for learning lists of items, especially if the list has to be remembered in a particular order (Herrmann, 1987). There also is some support for using the method of loci to help remember a prose passage. Snowman, Krebs, and Lockhart (1980) found that freshmen who used the method of loci to learn the main themes in a passage remembered more than students who did not use this technique.

One common concern about using this technique is whether learners might experience problems with interference. In other words, can a student get lists mixed up so that they remember something from a previous list rather than what they have to learn now? To avoid interference, it is possible to use different sets of locations. However, it is not a problem to use just one set of locations unless the student has to remember two lists in a short period of time. Most often, when a learner places a new list in the locations, their memory for previous items will weaken. It is also possible to place more than one item with each location. In this case, all of the items placed in one location should be pictured interacting with each other in *one* image. For example, a student could learn a list of 30 items by placing 3 items in each of 10 locations. The disadvantage, however, is that the student may not remember the order of the 3 items (Higbee, 1977).

Pegwords

If a student wanted to find the tenth item in a list, the method of loci would require them to go through all the ten locations before it could be found. The pegword method is a strategy that is designed to get around this problem by including the actual number in the association in the picture so that you can go right to it. Numbers are abstract, however, so it is important to create pegwords to represent the numbers so that they become more concrete. The following list includes the typical pegwords used for the numbers one through ten:

Number	Peg
one	bun
two	shoe
three	tree
four	door
five	hive
six	sticks
seven	heaven
eight	gate
nine	pine
ten	hen

These pegwords are often chosen because they rhyme with their respective number and therefore, are easy to remember. In addition, the pegwords are concrete and easy to picture. In order to learn new material, the student using the pegword method must link the new material with each of the pegwords in order. Students use imagery to create this association. For example, if the first item that the student has on a to-be-remembered list is shoes, they would create an interactive image of the shoes with the bun, for instance, a picture of the shoes sandwiched between a hamburger bun. Later, when the student needs to remember the first item on their list, they call up the number one, which leads to the peg "bun," which then yields the image of the shoes sandwiched within the bun. Pegwords are very effective as long as the student has time to make a vivid image (Paivio, 1971).

The pegword and method of loci strategies have several advantages. According to Higbee (1977):

First, the learner has a definite and consistent learning strategy. They know what to do with each item as they study it. Second, they have definite pigeonholes (pegwords or locations) that they can use to "store" the items. Third, they have a systematic retrieval plan telling them where to begin recall, how to proceed systematically from one item to the next, and how to monitor how they are doing, for example, how many items they have forgotten and which ones. So both mnemonic methods overcome one of the major problems in trying to remember—how to remind yourself of all the things you are supposed to recall. The direct advantage of the pegword method is that you can have direct retrieval—if you need the eighth item, you don't have to go through the whole system. The advantage of the method of loci, however, is that a large number of mental images can be made. There really is no limit on the number of locations you can use, while it is difficult to find a large number of pegwords that rhyme or look like the numbers larger than 20 (p. 126).

Keywords

One of the most extensively tested mnemonic techniques is the keyword method (Atkinson, 1975; Pressley, Levin, & Delaney, 1982)). Similar to the method of loci and the pegword method, the keyword strategy involves the use of imagery. The strategy consists of two steps, an acoustic link and an imagery link. In vocabulary learning, the first step would require the student to associate the unfamiliar foreign word with a familiar English word that sounds the same, called the keyword (e.g., "coat" for *coati*). Keywords should sound as much as possible like part of or all of the unfamiliar word. In the second step, an association is made between the keyword and the definition for the unfamiliar word. For example, since the coati is a type of raccoon, a picture could be created of a raccoon wearing a bright yellow coat sneaking around at night. The keyword strategy has been used extensively for foreign language vocabulary learning (Atkinson, 1975; Mastropieri, Scruggs, Levin, Gaffney, & McLoone, 1985) and pairings between facts and their referents. For example, Pressley and Dennis-Rounds (1980) taught junior high and high school students to use the keyword method to associate the names of cities with the names of their products (for example, Deerfield (*deer*) = wheat (*deer eating wheat*). In addition, McCormick and Levin (1987) report the effectiveness of training second-ary school and college students to use the keyword method to remember the main ideas of a prose passage. However, keywords also can be used to teach scientific terms (Veit, Scruggs, & Mastropieri, 1986) and complex scientific concepts (Scruggs & Mastropieri, 1992). See Figure 2-1 for an example of an illustration using the keyword strategy to teach students the meaning of radial symmetry.

CONSIDERING WHEN AND WHERE TO USE MNEMONICS

Although mnemonic techniques have a strong and consistent history for improving performance across a wide variety of domains (Higbee, 1977; Pressley, Levin, & Delaney, 1982; Yates, 1966), there are a number of teachers who hesitate to use them. The concerns expressed by educators range from worries about whether mnemonics promote meaningful learning to whether learning is maintained. The following section outlines concerns raised by educators and empirical research that validates when and where mnemonics are most effective.

1. Mnemonic techniques are sometimes perceived as unnatural or "artificial" memory strategies (Levin, 1988). But as Bellezza (1987) has argued, mnemonic strategies share many characteristics with natural memory structures or "schemata." *Schemata* are organized knowledge structures in memory. These structures consist of interrelated pieces of information about objects, persons, situations, events, etc. Once activated, the schema influences the processing of new information by providing a context for the information.

Information can be stored hierarchically, or by association to a

---

Figure 2-1
Keyword reconstruction of "radial symmetry = similar body parts extending out from the center, as a starfish".

From Scruggs & Mastropieri (1992).

related concept. For example, a student studying facts about the Swift Fox could organize the information under the general heading "Swift Fox," or they may tie the information to their more general schema about mammals. In either case, this type of organization will provide the student with access to more than one piece of information. Access to schemata is more of a problem when students are faced with unfamiliar material. Mnemonics can provide a cue for students to attach new information to these existing schemata or provide a general concept to organize the information. In the example mentioned above, the term "coat" served as a general concept to organize the information about the animal "coati." In general, mnemonic strategies enable learners to create a schema for those situations when an existing schema is not readily available (Levin, 1988).

2. It is sometimes thought that mnemonics may be useful for the learning of factual content but not very effective for the learning of principles, rules, and operations (Levin, 1988). Not true. Mnemonic strategies have been created for the learning of principles: most notably, the Japanese Yodai system, which uses verbal mediators to spell out rules for solving problems. For example, to teach kindergarten children how to do fractions, a fraction is called a bug with a head and a wing. The head is the numerator and the wing is the denominator. Words such as fraction, denominator and so on are not used. Higbee and Kunihira (1985) have reported a great deal of success with this method, although to date the Yodai method needs to be more adequately tested.

Adaptations of this method could be used to teach adolescents as well. For example, students learning algebra can be taught the rules for multiplying binomials $(a + b)(c + d)$ by thinking of sumo wrestling with West and East teams. The wrestlers on the West team wrestle each wrestler on the East team, with the result that $(a + b)(c + d) = ac + ad + bc + bd$ (Higbee, 1987). Both simple and complex procedures in mathematics, as well as in the sciences, have been successfully taught mnemonically. In science, for example, mnemonic taxonomies have been created to show hierarchical relations among concept families (Levin & Levin, 1990). Levin and Levin found that scientific mnemonomies enhanced undergraduates' recall and conceptual understanding of a hierarchical plant classification system to a greater extent than figural taxonomies (See Figure 2-2).

3. One reason cited for dismissing mnemonic strategies is that they produce "rote" learning rather than "comprehension" (Levin, 1988). This issue is a critical one because in fact mnemonics do provide verbatim information. However, it is information that the student needs in order to execute higher level functions, such as comprehending, inferencing, etc. In other words, mnemonics serve as a effective means to acquire knowledge which then can be used and expanded for the purpose of using that information to comprehend, make inferences, and solve problems (Levin & Levin, 1990). For example, Mastropieri,

Figure 2-2
A figural and mnemonic taxonomy to show hierarchical relations among plant groups.

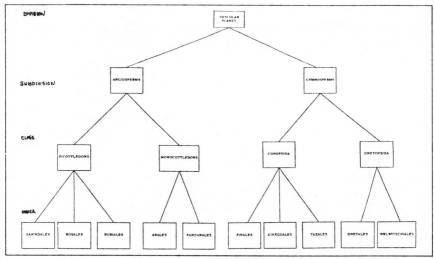

Figural taxonomy for the plant classification system

To remember that the subdivision angiosperms includes the class dicotyledons, which in turn includes the three orders rubiales, sapindales, and rosales, study the picture of the angel with the pet dinosaur that is walking up the Rubik's cubes so that he can lick the sweet sap that drips down from the rose tree.

To remember that the subdivision angiosperms includes the class monocotyledons, which in turn includes the two orders arales and pandanales, study the picture of the angel with the pet monkey that is shooting arrows into a pan.

To remember that the subdivision gymnosperms includes the class conopsida, which in turn includes the three orders ginkgoales, pinales, and taxales, study the picture of the swinging gymnast with the ice cream cone in his hand. The ice cream is about to splat in the face of the king who is leaping from the bench of his royal piano after sitting on some tacks.

To remember that the subdivision gymnosperms includes the class gnetopsida, which in turn includes the two orders welwitschiales and gnetales, study the picture of the fallen gymnast holding his sore knee tops. He is being treated (or tricked!) by a witch doctor who is sticking a very long needle into his injured knee.

Pictorial mnemonomy for the plant classification system

From Levin & Levin (1990).

Scruggs, and Fulk (1990) found that training students with learning disabilities in mnemonic techniques facilitated rather than diminished comprehension. According to Mastropieri and Scruggs (1991), mnemonic systems enhance the meaningfulness of new information, and therefore facilitate comprehension. By using mnemonics, students can remember the factual routine things more efficiently, allowing them more time to spend on tasks that involve understanding and reasoning. It is important to understand that mnemonics are good for *remembering* information. Once students remember, they then have the opportunity for higher-order thinking.

4. Another concern is that with mnemonic strategies, the student has more to remember (Higbee, 1977). Most mnemonic systems do add to the material that students have to remember. However, it is important to note that mnemonics do not necessarily make remembering any easier, just more effective. Using mnemonic techniques effectively is a skill which requires practice, much like typing. At first you are much slower at typing than you are at writing but with practice, typing is much faster and more efficient than writing. The same is true for mnemonic techniques. With repeated practice, the strategy becomes automatic and requires minimal effort to execute.

Teacher-Provided or Student-Generated Mediators?

There are three alternatives for teaching mnemonic strategies: (1) all of the materials, such as keywords and pictures for the keyword strategy, can be constructed by the teacher and then provided to the student; or (2) teachers may provide the basic structure but require the students to create their own images or cues; or (3) students instead may be encouraged to be responsible for creating their own mnemonic materials. Researchers investigating the comparative benefits of teacher-provided versus student-generated materials have suggested that although memory performance may not always be higher when students construct their own materials as when teachers provide them, even young and less-skilled learners can enhance their learning when generating their own mnemonic materials (Mastropieri, Scruggs, Levin, Gaffney, & McLoone, 1985; Pressley, Levin, & McCormick, 1980). In addition, Levin, Levin, Glasman, and Nordwall (1992) found that students enjoyed working collaboratively to create mnemonic materials.

One drawback of providing mnemonic materials for students is that they take time to create. Encouraging students to create their own images obviously saves time for the teacher. However, another concern is students' skill at creating images. Many students are not familiar with using imagery, and a few may require a lot of training in order to make effective images. In this case, the best strategy may be to generate the image yourself as a teacher and provide your image to the student.

Alternatively, McCormick and Levin (1984) have suggested that an effective "compromise" found to be successful with secondary school students is to have them generate their own images in response to a scene described by the teacher. In this case, the teacher does not have to physically provide the picture. Teachers must decide whether their focus in any specific situation is the content or the strategy. If the strategy is more important than the content being used to teach the strategy, then training students to self-generate materials is advisable. If, on the other hand, the content is of the most importance, then teacher-provided mnemonics may be the most expedient (Scruggs & Mastropieri, 1990). When students become experienced at generating the materials, they can be expected to construct their own materials more effectively. The amount of training varies across students and across strategies. As with all strategies, mnemonics require practice before students can use them effectively.

Special Populations

A great deal of research has been conducted demonstrating the effectiveness of mnemonic techniques with children who have learning disabilities (e.g., Fulk, Mastropieri, & Scruggs, 1992; McLoone, Scruggs, Mastropieri, & Zucker, 1986; Scruggs, Mastropieri, Brigham, & Sullivan, 1992). For more detail on these populations, see Mastropieri and Scruggs (1989) and Chapter 12 of this volume.

SUMMARY

Mnemonic techniques can be useful ways to help students *remember*. Mnemonics are most effective when students encounter novel information for which they have limited prior knowledge. It allows them to construct knowledge and retrieve that knowledge intact at a later date. Mnemonics might best be perceived as a stepping stone for higher-order thinking. Once students are given techniques that allow them to remember, they can be expected to engage in inferencing, problem solving, etc. The goal of teachers should be to use mnemonic techniques as a way for students to establish a schema—then build on this foundation using other more elaborative techniques (e.g., *coati* should be attached to existing knowledge about raccoons).

More recently, researchers have paid attention to whether material learned through mnemonic techniques is maintained over time. According to Wang, Thomas and Ouellette (1992), in classroom situations where students typically realize that they will be tested later on the material, material learned mnemonically will be practiced. In this case, memory performance should persist over time (for an example using the keyword approach for vocabulary learning, see McDaniel, Pressley,

& Dunay, 1987). However, if the information is not studied again, material learned mnemonically may be susceptible to forgetting (Wang, Thomas, & Ouellette, 1992). It is important then, that students be given an opportunity and be encouraged to practice their mnemonic strategy once it is introduced.

RECOMMENDED READINGS

Higbee, K.L. (1977). *Your memory: How it works and how to improve it.* New Jersey: Prentice Hall.

Levin, J.R. (1993). Mnemonic strategies and classroom learning: A twenty-year report. *The Elementary School Journal, 94,* 235-244.

Mastropieri, M.A., & Scruggs, T.E. (1991). *Teaching students ways to remember: Strategies for learning mnemonically.* Cambridge, MA: Brookline Books.

REFERENCES

Atkinson, R. C. (1975). Mnemotechnics in second language learning. *American Psychologist, 30,*821-828.

Bellezza, F.S. (1981). Mnemonic devices: Classification, characteristics, and criteria. *Review of Educational Research, 51,* 247-275.

Bellezza, F.S. (1987). Mnemonic devices and memory schemas. In M.A. McDaniel and M. Pressley (Eds.) *Imagery and related mnemonic processes: Theories, individual differences, and applications* (pp. 34-55). New York: Springer-Verlag.

Carney, R.N., Levin, J.R., & Morrison, C.R. (1988). Mnemonic learning of artists and their paintings. *American Educational Research Journal, 25,* 107-125.

Fulk, B.M., Mastropieri, M.A., & Scruggs, T.E. (1992). Mnemonic generalization training with learning disabled adolescents. *Learning Disabilities Research and Practice, 7,* 2-10.

Herrmann, D.I. (1987). Task appropriateness of mnemonic techniques. *Perceptual and Motor Skills, 64,* 171-178.

Higbee, K.L. (1977). *Your memory: How it works and how to improve it.* New Jersey: Prentice Hall.

Higbee, K.L. (1979). Recent research on visual mnemonics: Historical roots and educational fruits. *Review of Educational Research, 49,* 611-629.

Higbee, K.L. (1987). Process mnemonics: Principles, prospects, and problems. In M.A. McDaniel and M. Pressley (Eds.), *Imagery and related mnemonic processes: Theories, individual differences, and applications* (pp. 407-427). New York: Springer-Verlag.

Higbee, K.L., & Kunihira, S. (1985). Cross-cultural applications of yodai mnemonics in education. *Educational Psychologist, 20,* 57-64.

Levin, J.R. (1983). Pictorial strategies for school learning: Practical illustrations. In M. Pressley & J.R. Levin (Eds.), *Cognitive strategy research: Educational applications* (pp. 213-237). New York: Springer-Verlag.

Levin, J.R. (1988). Elaboration-based learning strategies: Powerful theory = powerful application. *Contemporary Educational Psychology, 13,* 191-205.

Levin, J.R. (1993). Mnemonic strategies and classroom learning: A twenty-year report. *The Elementary School Journal, 94,* 235-244.

Levin, M.E., & Levin, J.R. (1990). Scientific mnemonomies: Methods for maximizing more than memory. *American Educational Research Journal, 27,* 301-321.

Levin, J.R., Levin, M.E., Glasman, L.D., & Nordwall, M.B. (1992). Mnemonic vocabulary instruction: Additional effectiveness evidence. *Contemporary Educational Psychology, 17,* 156-174.

Mastropieri, M.A., & Scruggs, T.E. (1991). *Teaching students ways to remember: Strategies for learning mnemonically.* Cambridge, MA: Brookline Books.

Mastropieri, M.A., Scruggs, T.E., & Fulk, B.J.M. (1990). Teaching abstract vocabulary with the keyword method: Effects on recall and comprehension. *Journal of Learning Disabilities, 23,* 92-96.

Mastropieri, M.A., Scruggs, T.E., & Levin, J.R. (1987). Mnemonic instruction in special education. In M.A. McDaniel & M. Pressley (Eds.), *Imagery and related mnemonic processes: Theories, individual differences, and applications* (pp 358-376). New York: Springer-Verlag.

Mastropieri, M.A., Scruggs, T.E., Levin, J.R., Gaffney, J., & McLoone, B. (1985). Mnemonic vocabulary instruction for learning disabled students. *Learning Disability Quarterly, 8,* 57-63.

McCormick, C.B., & Levin, J.R. (1984). A comparison of different prose-learning variations of the mnemonic keyword method. *American Educational Research Journal, 21,* 379-398.

McCormick, C.B., & Levin, J.R. (1987). Mnemonic prose-learning strategies. In M.A. McDaniel & M. Pressley (Eds.), *Imagery and related mnemonic processes: Theories, individual differences, and applications* (pp. 392-406). New York: Springer-Verlag.

McDaniel, M.A., Pressley, M., & Dunay, P.K. (1987). Long-term retention of vocabulary after keyword and context learning. *Journal of Educational Psychology, 79,* 87-89.

McLoone, B.B., Scruggs, T.E., Mastropieri, M.A., & Zucker, S.F. (1986). Memory strategy instruction and training with learning disabled adolescents. *Learning Disabilities Research, 2,* 45-53.

Paivio, A. (1971). *Imagery and verbal processes.* New York: Holt.

Pressley, M., & Dennis-Rounds, J. (1980). Transfer of a mnemonic keyword strategy at two age levels. *Journal of Educational Psychology, 72,* 575-582.

Pressley, M., Levin, J.R., & Delaney, H.D. (1982). The mnemonic keyword method. *Review of Educational Research, 52,* 61-91

Pressley, M., Levin, J.R., & McCormick, C.B. (1980). Young children's learning of foreign language vocabulary: A sentence variation of the keyword method. *Contemporary Educational Psychology, 5,* 22-29.

Pressley, M., Levin, J.R., & McDaniel, M.A. (1987). Remembering versus inferring what a word means: Mnemonic and contextual approaches. In M.G. McKeown & M.E. Curtis (Eds.), *The nature of vocabulary acquisition* (pp. 107-127). Hillsdale, NJ: Erlbaum.

Rosenheck, M.B., Levin, M.E., & Levin, J.R. (1989). Learning botany concepts mnemonically: Seeing the forest and the trees. *Journal of Educational Psychology, 81,* 196-203.

Ross, J., & Lawrence, K.A. (1968). Some observations on memory artifice. *Psychonomic Science, 13,* 159-160.

Scruggs, T.E., & Mastropieri, M.A. (1990). The case for mnemonic instruction: From laboratory research to classroom applications. *The Journal of Special Education, 24,* 7-32.

Scruggs, T. E., & Mastropieri, M.A. (1992). Classroom applications of mnemonic instruction: Acquisition, maintenance, and generalization. *Exceptional Children, 58,* 219-229.

Scruggs, T.E., Mastropieri, M.A., Brigham, F.J., & Sullivan, G.S. (1992). Effects of mnemonic reconstructions on the spatial learning of adolescents with learning disabilities. *Learning Disability Quarterly, 15,* 154-162.

Snowman, J., Krebs, E.W., & Lockhart, L. (1980). Improving recall of information from prose in high-risk students through learning strategy training. *Journal of Instructional Psychology, 7,* 35-40.

Veit, D., Scruggs, T.E., & Mastropieri, M.A. (1986). Extended mnemonic instruction with learning disabled students. *Journal of Educational Psychology, 78,* 300-308.

Wang, A.Y., Thomas, M.H., & Ouellette, J.A. (1992). Keyword mnemonic and retention of second-language vocabulary words. *Journal of Educational Psychology, 84,* 520-528.

Willoughby, T., Wood, E., & Khan, M. (1994). Isolating variables and impact on or detract from the effectiveness of elaboration strategies. *Journal of Educational Psychology, 86*(2), 279-289.

Yates, F. (1966). *The art of memory.* Chicago: University of Chicago Press.

CHAPTER 3

Cognitive Strategies for Learning from Direct Teaching

Alison King • California State University, San Marcos

Teacher presentation of information, often called *direct teaching, direct instruction,* or *classroom teaching,* is the most commonly-used teaching method in middle school and high school classes (Kennedy, 1991). Such presentations are generally made to the entire class at once and can take the form of a full-blown lecture or lesson, a shorter "mini-lecture", an extended explanation, or a more interactive whole-class discussion. Because such forms of direct teaching are so prevalent, if they are going to succeed in school young people need to be able to understand and remember material presented to them during this type of classroom discourse.

DIRECT TEACHING

A major advantage of direct teaching is that it provides a means of efficiently communicating large amounts of information in a short period of time (Gage & Berliner, 1992). At the same time, these methods have been criticized for putting learners in a passive role (Gage & Berliner, 1992). Indeed, direct teaching forms of instruction are said to be based on the outdated *transmission model* of teaching and learning which views knowledge as something that can be transmitted from the teacher to the student, much in the same way that liquids can be poured from one container into another. The effectiveness of the transmission approach is dependent on rote memorization of the presented material rather than on genuine understanding of it. Although direct teaching may not always be as appropriate in middle school and high school classrooms as problem-based learning, case studies, independent projects, class discussion, simulations, cooperative learning, and other approaches that require the learner to be more active; nevertheless, direct teaching is a reality and is probably here to stay, at least for the foreseeable future, in part because of the need to maintain large classes in these times of scarce resources.

Teachers can make direct teaching more effective as a method of instruction if they deliver the material in a well-organized manner, provide opportunities for students to actively process the information throughout the presentation, use techniques to prompt students to pay attention during instruction, and periodically check for students' understanding during the presentation (see discussion later in this chapter). However, students can do much on their own to enhance their learning from teacher presentations. Students can be taught cognitive strategies that they can use on their own to help them to actively process the material being presented as well as reformat and review that material later on.

Constructivist Theory of Learning

In contrast to the transmission model of teaching and learning, constructivist theories of learning maintain that knowledge is actively constructed by each individual and therefore cannot be transmitted from one person to another in a passive manner. In the constructivist view, when individuals are presented with new information they use their own existing knowledge and previous experience to help them understand it (Resnick, 1987). In essence, they use their prior knowledge and experience to *interpret* the new material in personally meaningful ways. They make inferences, elaborate on the new information by adding details, and generate relationships among the new ideas and between the new material and information already in memory (Brown & Campione, 1986; Brown, Bransford, Ferrara, & Campione, 1983; Thomas & Rhower, 1986; Wittrock, 1990). Through this active process of constructing meaning for themselves, they generate new knowledge or modify their existing knowledge.

According to connectionist theories and network models of memory (e.g., Anderson, 1976; Baddeley, 1976; Rumelhart & McClelland, 1986; Schank, 1986), the structure of memory is associative, and that structure is altered during learning. When individuals engage in constructing new knowledge or reformulating given information, new links (associations) are formed and old ones altered within the individual's knowledge networks. The links connect the new ideas together and integrate them into that individual's existing cognitive representations of the world. As more and better links are created, more richly integrated structures evolve in long-term memory. This process facilitates understanding of the new material and makes it easier to remember and apply.

The Need for Student Strategies

According to futurists such as Toffler (1990), today's students face a very challenging future. Passive transmission-reception of information and memorization of facts are not the kinds of learning that will be required of them for success in the 21st Century. Computers can be used to transmit, "memorize," store, and retrieve information far more quickly and accurately than humans can. In the future, different forms of knowledge will be emphasized, as will different cognitive skills. Emphasis will be placed, not on memorizing and repeating details and ideas, but on the integration of information. Individuals will be expected to think critically about what they have heard and read, identifying relationships among ideas, integrating ideas across topics, synthesizing concepts into something new. They will be expected to solve challenging problems, engage in complex decision making, and create new ideas. The focus, both in school and in the workplace, will be on the production of knowledge rather than the reproduction of information—on constructing knowledge not transmitting information (King, 1994b). Therefore, students need to be taught how to construct knowledge effectively and how to think about information and knowledge in new and creative ways.

Chapter Overview

Within such a constructivist context, this chapter examines some ways that young people can be taught to engage in constructing meaning from their teachers' classroom presentations. In order to learn from direct-teaching forms of instruction, students need to engage in a number of different cognitive tasks. They must focus and maintain their attention on the presentation, interpret the new information to construct their own meaning from the ideas presented, organize and store their newly-constructed knowledge in memory, and be able to recall

Figure 3-1
Cognitive activities in learning from direct teaching.

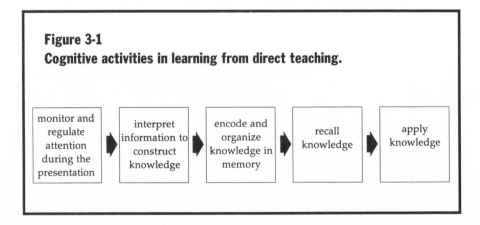

and use that knowledge when needed in new situations (see Figure 3-1). This chapter first addresses how students can prepare themselves to learn from teacher presentations. That section is followed by general principles of strategy instruction that should be followed in teaching the cognitive strategies to be covered later on. The remainder of the chapter focuses on a variety of different cognitive strategies that students can use to help them construct and organize their understanding of material presented by their teachers. Both individual and group-based strategies are included. Information on how to teach each strategy is included as are findings from research on that strategy.

STRATEGIC PREPARATION FOR LEARNING FROM DIRECT TEACHING

Metacognition and Learning

Metacognition refers to awareness and conscious regulation of one's own thinking and learning. Thus metacognitive strategies are ones that students use to plan, monitor, and control their learning (Flavell, 1981; Palincsar & Brown, 1989; Pressley, Borkowski, & O'Sullivan, 1984). Metacognitive knowledge includes knowing what one knows and what one does not know, knowledge of the learning process, knowledge of the task, knowledge of one's self as a learner, knowledge of planning and study strategies, and how these factors interact with each other. Metacognitive skills include planning how to study for an exam, setting goals for learning, allocating time for study, being aware of one's level of attention during a learning task, selecting strategies to use in learning and problem solving, monitoring strategy use and change of strategy when necessary, monitoring comprehension during learning, planning how to repair comprehension deficits, and evaluating the effectiveness of strategies, goals, and plans. Learners are engaging in metacognitive self-monitoring activity when, during learning, they ask themselves questions such as: "What am I trying to do here? What is my plan?" or "How am I doing? Should I revise my strategy?" (King, 1991a). Useful metacognitive behaviors for learning from direct teaching include activating prior knowledge, keeping attention focused on what the teacher is saying, and self-checking understanding during the presentation.

Activating Prior Knowledge

Before instruction begins students can prepare for the teacher's presentation by activating prior knowledge about the topic to be covered. Questions such as "What do I already know about this topic?", "What do I want to know?", "How does this topic relate to what we've already learned in this class?", "What questions do I have about this particular topic?", and "What am I curious about?" help to access any material already known about the topic and set a context for the new information (King, 1991b). This provides mental anchors to which the new ideas can be readily attached.

Monitoring and Regulating Attention During the Presentation

Self-talk (Table 3-1) can also be used to regulate attention during instruction. Self-reminders such as "Pay attention!" and questions such as "How does this idea relate to the ones just presented?" (King, 1992a) help to focus attention. The act of taking notes also helps to maintain concentration (Kiewra, 1989).

GENERAL PRINCIPLES OF STRATEGY INSTRUCTION

Explaining the Strategy and Providing a Rationale for its Use

The instructional method used to teach cognitive strategies is very important. In teaching such strategies, it is useful to begin with a brief explanation of the strategy followed immediately by an explanation of the rationale for using that strategy. A complete rationale includes both where the strategy can be used and why it is effective. When students can see that strategies are ways that they can gain control over their own learning, they are likely to become more motivated to use those strategies.

Table 3-1
Example of Cognitive Modeling to Access Prior Knowledge

"Let's see—today's lesson is on the respiratory system. I know that *respiratory* means breathing, so it's going to be about how we breathe and the parts of the body involved. What do I already know about that? Well, I know that we all have lungs that fill up with air when we breathe in and empty when we breathe out. I've often wondered why during a physical exam, the doctor always has me take a deep breath and hold it while he taps on my back. It must have something to do with the lungs. Maybe I'll find out in today's lesson. If not, I must remember to ask. I also know that air gets into the blood but I have no idea how. Now that I think about it, I saw a diagram of the respiratory system that shows some kind of connection between the lungs and the heart. I expect that the teacher will explain that in her presentation today."

Cognitive Modeling

The strategy itself must be presented through teacher modeling of the strategy. This obviously has to be in the form of "cognitive" modeling. In cognitive modeling, the teacher demonstrates use of the strategy while "thinking aloud" to show the thoughts and reasoning that accompanies the strategy (Meichenbaum, 1977). Modeling the strategy while "thinking aloud" allows students to observe the strategy in action. Cognitive modeling is doing the strategy—not simply explaining it, but actually doing it. Thus cognitive modeling provides students with a complete model of strategy use for them to imitate. When using cognitive modeling of problem-solving strategies, it is important to incorporate errors and "wrong turns" into the thinking aloud to help students see the benefits of detecting and analyzing errors during learning and problem solving. Incorporating self-reinforcing statements (e.g., "Good for me.") into the modeling process shows students with low self confidence a way to monitor and reward their own successes. Table 3-1 is an example of cognitive modeling to show how a sixth grader might prepare for a teacher's presentation on the respiratory system.

Cognitive Coaching

Cognitive coaching is a training procedure that incorporates cognitive modeling and collaborative practice in a scaffolded context. The cognitive coaching sequence in strategy instruction exemplifies a gradual shift of strategy execution from the teacher to the student. This gradual shift begins with the teacher modeling the strategy while students observe, and it ends with students doing the strategy on their own. During coaching, responsibility for effective use of the strategy is gradually given up by the teacher and assumed by the students. During this transition the teacher provides help in the form of scaffolds (hints,

Figure 3-2
Cognitive Modelling/Coaching Sequence

TEACHER DOES IT

TEACHER DOES IT—STUDENTS HELP

TEACHER AND STUDENTS DO IT TOGETHER

STUDENTS DO IT—TEACHER HELPS

STUDENTS DO IT

sentence starters, leading questions) for the students, to support them in using the strategy. As the students become more proficient with the strategy the teacher gradually withdraws the supporting scaffolds until the students can manage on their own. This cognitive coaching sequence is depicted in Figure 3-2. Cognitive modeling of the strategy is the "TEACHER DOES IT" step, the first step in the cognitive coaching process. Following teacher modeling the teacher performs the strategy again, this time with student input and assistance. Then the teacher and students work together to use the strategy. The "STUDENTS DO IT—TEACHER HELPS" step usually extends over several trials and constitutes a gradual fading of teacher assistance, scaffolding, and feedback as students assume increasingly more responsibility for their use of the strategy. Finally, students use the strategy independently. Figure 3-2 shows the gradual nature of this shift from teacher to student. Peer feedback and help can also be incorporated into the coaching process.

Monitoring Strategy Use and Effectiveness

Ongoing monitoring and regulation of strategy use should be part of any overall plan for strategy instruction. Monitoring can be the responsibility of both teacher and student, but methods of doing so, as well as opportunities, must be provided. Long-term use of any strategy, and the benefits that accrue, will only result from such ongoing attention to classroom strategy use.

Teacher Monitoring

It is very important for the teacher to keep track of each individual student's ability to use the strategy appropriately, as well as each student's success (improvement) from using the strategy. Teachers can check to see whether students continue to be aware of the strategy's benefits—why it should be useful and when to use it. Corrective feedback and reinforcement should be provided by the teacher accordingly. Reminders can be used as needed.

Student Self-Monitoring

Students need to be taught to monitor their own progress with any strategy they are using. They can be encouraged to notice if the strategy is working for them; that is, whether they are doing better by using the strategy than they were before using it. Rating scales and self-questioning are excellent ways for students to monitor and regulate their use of a strategy. (Examples of these methods can be found in later sections of this chapter.)

THE GUIDED PEER-QUESTIONING STRATEGY

Question-asking can be an important skill for enhancing thinking and learning in a number of contexts. In fact, several contemporary models of learning claim that question asking is a critical mechanism in comprehension, problem solving, creativity, and intelligence (Collins, Brown & Larkin, 1980; Schank, 1986; Sternberg, 1987). Individuals who question what they read and see and hear in the world around them tend to understand their world better. Such individuals are constantly asking "What does this mean?", "What is the nature of this?", "Is there another way to look at it?", "Why is this happening?", "What is the evidence for it?" and "How can I be sure?" (King, 1994b).

A large number of research studies have been conducted on question asking in school-related contexts. That research has generally found that generating one's own questions about material to be learned improves comprehension of that material (see reviews by Haller, Child & Walberg, 1988; Rosenshine, Chapman & Meister, 1992; Wong, 1985). Most of this work has been done in the area of reading from text (e.g., Billingsley & Wildman, 1988; Davey & McBride, 1986; Graesser, 1992; Palincsar & Brown, 1984; Paris, Cross, & Lipson, 1984; Pressley, Symons, McDaniel, Snyder, & Turnure, 1988). However, researchers have also found that question generation improves learning in a tutoring context (Graesser & Person, in press), facilitates problem solving (Graesser & McMahen, 1993; King, 1991a), and enhances learning from lectures and direct instruction (King, 1989, 1990a, l991b, 1992).

Guided Questioning

Guided Peer Questioning is a question-asking strategy designed for learning from direct instruction and other types of teacher presentation. Guided Peer Questioning is a general cognitive strategy that can be used with any presentation regardless of subject matter. This strategy is appropriate for use by students from middle elementary grades to college. It has been used by fourth- and fifth-graders to help them learn material presented in science lessons (King, 1994c; King & Rosenshine, 1993), by ninth-graders to learn from teacher presentations in history classes (King, 1991b), and by university students to learn from lectures in psychology, anthropology, political science, and education (e.g., King, 1989, 1990a, 1992b, 1994a).

To use the Guided Peer Questioning strategy for learning from direct teaching and other types of teacher presentation, students first individually generate two or three thoughtful questions following the presentation. Then they work cooperatively in pairs or small groups to take turns asking and answering each others' questions in a reciprocal manner. The questions they generate may or may not be ones they are able to answer. To guide them in formulating their thought-provoking questions, students are provided with a set of generic questions such as "What are the strengths and weaknesses of ...?" and "What do you think would happen if ...?" These general questions are content-free so that they can be used with any subject matter. Students are trained to use these general questions as a model of inquiry, to guide them in creating their own specific questions on the material presented. To do so, they fill in the blanks with relevant content from the presentation. Table 3-2 shows a list of such generic questions. These exemplary generic questions are the key component to the Guided Peer Questioning strategy because using them ensures that the specific questions will be thought-provoking ones. If their partners cannot answer a question, or if the answer is incorrect, students are taught to drop back and ask a related (but easier) comprehension question and then build up to the incorrectly answered question once more. If an answer is not complete, the others in a group should ask probing questions. The set of generic thought-provoking questions can be made available to students by printing them on index cards to be distributed so that each student has one, or they can be displayed to the class on a chart or overhead projector. Table 3-3 shows the steps of the Guided Peer Questioning strategy.

The questions in Table 3-2 are designed to induce critical thinking in the questioner as well as the responder. They require students to use such thinking skills as analysis, prediction, comparison and contrast, application, inference, evaluation, and the like. These thinking skills include those outlined in Bloom's (1956) *Taxonomy of Thinking*. Table 3-4 shows the same set of questions as Table 3-2, with the corresponding

---

Table 3-2
Generic Thought-Provoking Questions

Explain why ... (Explain how ...)
What is the main idea of ...?
How would you use ... to ...?
What is the significance of ...?
What is the difference between ... and ...?
How are ... and ... similar?
What is a new example of ...?
What do you think would happen if ...?
What conclusions can you draw about ...?
Compare ... and ... with regard to ... .
What do you think causes ...? Why?
How does ... affect ...?
What are the strengths and weaknesses of ...?
Which ... do you think is best and why?
How is ... related to ... that we studied earlier?
Do you agree or disagree with this statement: ...?
And what evidence is there to support your answer?

thinking skills those questions are designed to activate in students during questioning and answering. The Guided Peer Questioning strategy also serves a metacognitive role. Asking and answering those thoughtful questions functions as a self-testing experience, giving students the chance to check their understanding of the material covered.

Research on Guided Peer Questioning

Several research studies have been conducted using this questioning strategy with students in regular classroom settings (King, 1989, 1990a, 1991b, 1992a, 1994a; 1994c; King & Rosenshine, 1993). Results of those studies have shown that students using the Guided Peer Questioning strategy to learn from lectures or teacher-led lessons: performed better on comprehension of the presented material than did comparison students who simply discussed the material (King, 1989); used the same guiding questions in an individual learning context (King, 1989, 1991a, 1991b); used cooperative questioning without the guidance of the generic questions (King, 1990a); used similar questions generated by other students using the same generic questions to guide them (King, 1994a); or used cooperative questioning with less-elaborated question prompts such as "Why...?" and "How...?" (King & Rosenshine, 1993). Furthermore, analysis of the tape-recorded student interaction during the dyadic or small-group discussions revealed that the guiding questions consistently elicited elaborated explanations, inferences, justifications, speculations, and the like from students (King, 1989, 1990a, 1991; 1994c; King & Rosenshine, 1993).

It became clear from those analyses that the effectiveness of the guided questioning strategy can be attributed to the format of the guiding questions. The format of those questions helped students to

---

Table 3-3
The Guided Peer Questioning Strategy: Steps

1. teacher provides students with a set of generic thought-provoking questions

2. following the teacher's presentation, students choose several appropriate questions to use as a guide to create their own specific questions on the material presented

3. students individually generate two or three thoughtful questions on material from the presentation

4. students work cooperatively in pairs or small groups to take turns asking and answering each others' questions in a reciprocal manner

Table 4
Generic Questions with Corresponding Cognitive Processes the Questions are Intended to Activate

Generic question	Cognitive Processes
Explain why ... (Explain how ...)	**analysis** of processes and concepts—explicit or implicit in the presentation; **inference**—if implicit—**translating** terms into different vocabulary
What is the main idea of ...?	**analysis**—indentification of central idea explicit or implicit in presentation **inference**—if implicit
How would you use ... to ...?	**application** of information in another context—perhaps relating to prior knowledge or experiences—also **creative thinking**
What is the significance of ...?	**analysis**—identification of central idea explicit or implicit in presentation **inference**—if implicit
What is the difference between ... and ...?	**analysis** of two concepts—**comparison and contrast of concepts**
How are ... and ... similar?	**analysis** of two concepts—**comparison and contrast of concepts**
What is a new example of ...?	**application**—generation of novel examples of a concept or procedure—perhaps involving relating to prior knowledge or experience
What do you think would happen if ...?	**prediction/hypothesizing**—retrieval of background knowledge and integration with new material to make predictions—**creative thinking**
What conclusions can you draw about ...?	**drawing conclusions** based on the content presented
Compare ... and ... with regard to ...	**comparison-contrast** based upon criteria
What do you think causes ...? Why?	**analysis** of relationship (cause-effect)—**supporting an argument**
How does ... affect ...?	**analysis** of cause-effect relationships
What are the strengths and weaknesses of ...?	**analysis/inference** and **integration** of concepts
Which ... do you think is best and why?	**evaluation** of ideas based on criteria and evidence—**supporting an argument**
How is ... related to ... that we studied earlier?	**activation of prior knowledge** and **integration** with new information
Do you agree or disagree with this statement? And what evidence is there to support your answer?	**evaluation** and provision of evidence—**supporting an argument**

Adapted from King (1992b).

generate specific kinds of questions that prompted them to think about and discuss the presented material in specific ways such as comparing and contrasting, inferring cause and effect, noting strengths and weaknesses, evaluating ideas, explaining, and justifying. As a result, during discussion, the learners tended to make those same kinds of connections among ideas. Presumably, in true constructivist fashion, the mental representations they constructed reflected those same precise and explicit links between and among the ideas. Such highly-elaborated and richly-integrated mental representations would provide more cues for recall and would be more stable over time. This would account for strategy users' improved comprehension of the material and for their enhanced ability to remember it later on.

A Classroom Example (from King, 1990b)

Mr. Jones instructed his high school World Cultures class for 20 minutes on the topic "culture and language." Then he paused, signaled to the class, and the students turned to their neighbors to form groups of three. Mr. Jones flipped on the overhead projector to display the list of generic questions in Table 3-2, which he referred to as "thinking" questions. Within two minutes, each student in the class (working individually), using the generic questions as a guide, had selected appropriate question starters and had written down at least two specific questions on the topic presented. At another signal from Mr. Jones, the small groups began questioning and responding. Table 3-5 shows the beginning portion of one group's discussion.

The students continued asking and answering each other's questions until Mr. Jones signaled that their discussion time was over. He then brought the class together to share and discuss inferences, examples, and explanations generated, and to clarify any misunderstandings that the students might have had regarding culture and language.

During this sequence of guided peer-questioning and responding, Mr. Jones's students were engaged in several different cognitive activities. To begin with, they were actively involved in processing the information during Mr. Jones' presentation. Because this was not the first time these students had used this question-asking approach to learning, they knew that they would be required to generate questions during the questioning session immediately following the presentation; therefore, they paid closer attention to the presentation. Most of them even began to formulate their questions while listening to the presentation, and some actually jotted down a question or two in their notes. This would definitely enhance their initial understanding of the presented material. Also, Mr. Jones' students had to think critically about the presented content just to be able to formulate relevant thought-provoking questions. To generate their specific questions, the students had to identify the main ideas presented, then consider how those ideas relate to one another and to their own existing knowledge. In order to answer those questions, the students had to be able to analyze and evaluate ideas presented, apply the information in new situations, make inferences from the new material (see Table 3-4), and then construct explanations and other elaborated responses and communicate those to the questioner.

This process of explaining is crucial to the effectiveness of the Guided Peer Questioning strategy. Explaining something to someone else often requires the explainer to think about and present the material in new ways, such as relating it to the questioner's prior knowledge or experience, translating it into terms familiar to the questioner, or generating new examples (Bargh & Schul, 1980). Such cognitive activities force the explainer to clarify concepts, elaborate on them, reorganize thinking, or in some manner reconceptualize the material. Webb's (1989) extensive research on interaction and learning in peer groups indicates that giving such explanations improves comprehension for the individual doing the explaining (see also Pressley, Wood, Woloshyn, Martin, King, & Menke, 1992). To illustrate from the dialogue shown in Table 3-5, Sally asked for the definition of a term, and Jim, in the first

---

Table 3-5
Guided Reciprocal Peer Questioning in the Classroom

Sally starts her group off by reading her question, "What does culture mean?"

Jim explains, "Well, Mr. Jones said in the presentation that a culture is the knowledge and understandings shared by members of a society. I guess it's all the things and beliefs and activities that people in a society have in common. It includes things like religion, laws, music, medical practices, dance, art, family roles, ... stuff like that."

Barry points out, "Knowledge includes language. So, I guess culture includes language too."

"I guess so." answers Jim and then he asks, "How does a culture influence the language of a society?"

Barry replies, "Well, for one thing, the language is made up of words that are important to the people of that culture. Like, the words name things that the people care about, or need, or use. And so, different cultures would have different vocabularies. Some cultures may not even have a word for telephone. But phones are important in *our* culture, so we have lots of different words for phones—like cellular phone, desk phone, wall phone, cordless phone, phone machine, and ..."

Jim laughs, "I'll bet desert cultures don't have *any* words for snow or skiing."

Sally chuckles, and then, turning to Barry, she asks, "What's your question?"

Barry replies enthusiastically, "I've got a great question! You'll never be able to answer it. What would happen if there was a tribe somewhere without any spoken language? Maybe they were all born not being able to speak—or something like that. How would that affect their culture, or

part of his response, parroted Mr. Jones' definition; however, Jim also went on to explain the term by restating the definition in his own words. Jim's ability to paraphrase the material in this way suggests that he had reorganized his thinking by incorporating the concept into his own knowledge structures. Similarly, Barry's inclusion of language as a new example of culture was an indication of reconceptualization on his part. Barry's explanations of how culture influences language also showed concept clarification; and his own example of the relationship between culture and language (the various words for telephone) was an elaboration of that concept. In the discussion precipitated by Barry's "What would happen if...?" question, the three students together explored the relationship between culture and language by speculating about what culture would be like without language. In so doing, they undoubtedly forged new links among the ideas presented and between those ideas and their own prior knowledge. For example, Sally integrated the new information with such cultural concepts as "status," which she had learned a few weeks earlier. Thus, asking and answering questions based on Mr. Jones's presentation enhanced Sally, Jim, and Barry's understanding of culture because it stimulated them to think about how culture and language are related in ways that were not covered in the

---

Table 3-5 continued
Guided Reciprocal Peer Questioning in the Classroom

could there even *be* a culture?"

After a short pause, Sally remarks, "Well, it would mean they couldn't communicate information very clearly."

"And they wouldn't have any music!" exclaims Jim.

Sally continues, "Maybe they would develop a non-verbal language system—you know—the way people use hand signals."

Barry adds, "Yes, but it would be difficult for them to communicate with anyone who was out of their line of sight, like if they had their backs turned."

Sally replies, "Well, not if they could hear. Just because they couldn't *speak* doesn't mean they couldn't *hear*. If they were able to hear, they could communicate with drums or clackers of some sort. But, they'd have to carry their drums around with them all the time so they could 'talk' to each other. Then maybe drums would become very important to them—and some people would have bigger, louder, or more decorated drums than others. The drums might even become a status symbol, a way to tell who were the important people in the society and who were not so important."

Barry adds, "Maybe they'd clap their hands in a lot of different ways to communicate with each other. Then they wouldn't have to carry the drums around!"

Jim interjects, "Well, if they could hear, then they *could* have music after all, but they still wouldn't be able to *sing* to their music." ....

From King (1990b).

---

presentation and that were based on their own knowledge.

The kind of group discussion promoted by Guided Peer Questioning facilitates learning beyond what any individual could achieve alone. According to theories of the *social construction of knowledge* (e.g., Bearison, 1982; Damon, 1983; Mugny & Doise, 1978, Perret-Clermont, 1980; Vygotsky, 1978), during peer interaction individuals' misconceptions about a topic are revealed and differences arise in their perceptions of ideas, their factual information, assumptions, values, and general understandings. Peer interaction is also the process through which those conceptual discrepancies can be resolved. Reconciling those *socio-cognitive conflicts* (see Mugny & Doise, 1978) generally occurs when individuals explain concepts and defend their own views to each other. Guided Peer Questioning promotes this process of exposing and reconciling socio-cognitive conflict, because when students ask and answer thought-provoking questions such as "What do you think would happen if ...?", they tap in to each others' different views on the matter. Once these differing views or conflicting facts are exposed, individuals are called upon to engage in elaborating, explaining, justifying, and other socio-cognitive behaviors, which may lead to reconciling those differences to achieve some agreed-upon meaning. As Cobb (1988) pointed out, individuals engaged in such meaning-negotiation are continually restructuring their own thinking.

The peer group can also be a source for models of good questioning-and-responding behavior. These modeling opportunities may be particularly beneficial for less able students who are provided with the opportunity to model their questions and responses on those of their more able peers. Modeling of thoughtful questioning can be further promoted by teachers when they use the generic question stems format to pose questions to students during instruction.

Because the Guided Peer Questioning strategy is structured so that students take turns asking and answering questions, each individual is obligated to contribute questions and answers. This gets everyone actively participating, thus reducing the likelihood of socio-cognitive loafing on the part of any individual learner. Socio-cognitive loafing occurs when individuals in a discussion or problem-solving group shirk their share of the thinking and discussion, leaving others to carry the burden. Although they do not contribute ideas, they benefit from the group efforts. Guided Peer Questioning strategy is also particularly beneficial for students who are reluctant to participate in class for fear of asking the teacher "stupid" questions, but less hesitant about posing such questions to their peers in a small group setting.

How to Teach the Guided Peer Questioning Strategy

Essentially there are three phases to teaching the strategy: explaining the question-answering strategy, training students to generate thought-provoking questions (see Table 3-6), and providing lots of guided practice of the strategy in conjunction with classroom presentations. The steps in the question-training process follow the general cognitive coaching sequence and are detailed in Table 3-6. Training may take anywhere from half an hour to an hour, depending on the students. Prior to beginning training, it is very important to tell students that research has shown that asking thought-provoking questions improves learning because it makes them think intensely and in a number of different ways about the ideas presented; in particular, making connections among ideas within the presentation and between the presentation and prior knowledge. Throughout the strategy training it is important to remind students of the reasons why the questioning strategy works. Demonstrating to students the value of using a particular strategy to help them learn has been shown to improve the effectiveness of that strategy (e.g., Pressley et al., 1984).

Although not absolutely necessary, it is beneficial, particularly with less academically able students, to begin the questioning training by differentiating between "memory" questions (those requiring one to simply remember and repeat what has been heard and memorized from the presentation) and "thinking" questions (those that require one to not only remember the presented information, but also think about that information in some way, such as explaining, comparing and contrasting with something else, analyzing, justifying, making up an example, etc.). Table 3-7 shows the difference between these two types of questions.

During training, direct explanation, modeling, cognitive coaching, scaffolding, and feedback are used as indicated in Table 3-6. For the development of each questioning skill it is important to follow the general cognitive coaching sequence shown in Figure 3-2. Initial teacher modeling is followed by a gradual shifting of responsibility to the students as in the following four steps: teacher models thinking aloud and how to generate a question; teacher generates a question with student input; students generate several questions with teacher help; students generate questions independently. An example of the first step, teacher modeling of question generation, is shown in Table 3-8.

When students have become proficient in generating thought-provoking questions individually, they are ready to work in pairs or small groups to engage in reciprocal questioning and answering. They should be reminded to work together to answer each other's questions fully. Sometimes students become so intent on asking their question that they answer others' questions in a rote and superficial manner rather than responding thoughtfully and completely. Students should be reminded that it sometimes takes several minutes of back and forth discussion to "answer" one thoughtful question. Discussions can be extended when students are taught to use probing questions and comments such as "Why?", "Tell me more about that," "That doesn't make sense to me. Why do you think so?" and "I still don't understand."

Student Self-Monitoring of Strategy Use

After each of the first few sessions of using the Guided Peer Questioning strategy, it is important to have students evaluate the quality of the questions they generate and the answers they construct. For example, students could be shown how to use a scale such as the one in Figure 3-3 to rate how well they performed in both questioning and answering. Immediately after their first use of the strategy, students individually complete the rating scale. It is useful to follow up with a brief whole-class sharing and discussion of difficulties experienced with the strategy and suggested remedies. This self-monitoring process can be followed after each use of the strategy until students are using the strategy well. The rating scale should be used periodically thereafter. Research has shown that when students monitor their use of a strategy in this manner, their performance with the strategy is improved (Davey & McBride, 1986; Pressley, Goodchild, Fleet, Zajchowski, & Evans, 1989). Another useful technique for self-monitoring is to have individual groups listen to a playback of their previously tape-recorded question-and-answer discussion. When listening to their discussion in this way, students often realize the need to ask probing questions to promote more thorough responses.

GUIDED SELF QUESTIONING

The Strategy

Guided Self Questioning is a solo version of the Guided Peer Questioning strategy. In this version of the strategy, students work independently to learn from teacher presentations. They use the same generic question stems to guide them in generating their own specific questions on the material presented. Then they write answers for their own questions. The procedure used for teaching question generation for Guided Self Questioning is the same as that presented in Table 3-6 for the Guided Peer Questioning strategy.

Of course this independent use of guided questioning has the same metacognitive benefits as the group-based version of the strategy. Asking and answering one's own thoughtful questions functions as self-testing, providing students the chance to monitor their comprehension of the new material as they are studying. It can also be important to have students ask metacognitive self-questions such as "What do I still not understand about ...?" after their question-answering session.

Table 3-6
Training Students to Generate Questions

1. Inform students that making up their own "thinking" questions and answering their own and each others' questions will help them to learn.

2. Explain and show the difference between memory questions and "thinking" questions.

3. Show students examples of each type of question (see Table 3-7 for examples).

4. Have students explain why each question is a memory or thinking type.

5. Provide students with a copy of the generic questions shown in Table 3-2 (or a subset of those).

6. Point out that for every memory question, a thinking question could be made up. Demonstrate how to do so using the generic questions as a guide. Point out that all of the thinking questions in Table 3-7 use the generic questions as "starters," and then "fill in the blanks" with material from the presentation. Use modeling, coaching, and feedback as needed (see Figure 3-2) to have the class generate several thinking questions.

7. Explain that some thinking questions are called comprehension questions—they check how well you understand something presented. Other thinking questions link two ideas from the presentation together—these can be called connection questions.

8. Using material from a recent lesson, model for students how to generate comprehension questions and connection questions using the generic questions as a guide. Provide examples and modeling for each generic question stem.

9. Work with class as a whole to walk through generating thinking questions using the modeling and scaffolding sequence outlined in Figure 3-2. Provide individual student practice with sharing and corrective feedback as needed.

10. Explain that some thinking-type connection questions link ideas from the presentation with ideas outside of the presentation—that is things already known about (prior knowledge or experience). Point out questions from Table 3-7 that require prior knowledge to answer. Model generating those kinds of questions. Work with class as a whole to walk through generating these types of questions using the modeling/scaffolding sequence outlined in Figure 3-2.

Table 3-7
Differentiating between Memory Questions and Thinking Questions

Memory Questions	Thinking Questions
What are the main parts of the digestive system?	How are the *digestive system* and the *respiratory system* similar?
Where does food go when it leaves the stomach?	What do you think would happen if *our intestines were shorter*?
	What is the difference between the *small intestine* and the *large intestine*?
What is the covering of the body called?	Explain why the *skin is so important*.
What is the purpose of the circulatory system?	Which *body system is most essential* and why?
What are the tubes that carry the blood?	How are *veins* and *arteries* similar?
	Explain how the *circulatory system is like a tree*?
List the systems of the body.	Explain how *our body systems might be different if we lived in the water*.
	How does the *respiratory system* affect the *circulatory system*?

From King (1994c).

Table 3-8
Teacher Cognitive Modeling of Question Generation

(Following a presentation on migration)

Let's see, I guess I'll start by listing some of the things covered in the presentation. Of course, one thing was migration—and that whales and birds and some butterflies migrate; and so do some people. A question might be "What animals migrate?", but that's too easy. And it's just a memory question. I want to make up *thoughtful* questions—like "Explain why monarch butterflies migrate." That's a good one because I want to be sure that I really understand that in the way it was explained *first* before I go any further. Now I'll look at the question stems again for ideas about another question. What I still wonder about, and we didn't already cover this, is what happens to the land and the animals in the areas where the birds migrate to—they must have some effect on it in terms of the ecology—for example, some effect on the insects and other food that they eat. And also when they leave an area, it must change the ecology of that area too. So my next question will be "How does migration affect the ecology of the area left and area migrated to?"

Research on Guided Self Questioning

Research has shown that Guided Self Questioning is more effective in promoting learning from teacher presentations than is summarizing (King, 1992b) and independent review (King, 1989, 1991b). However, it is not as effective as the group version of the strategy. Guided Self Questioning is not as powerful a cognitive strategy as Guided Peer Questioning because, in self-questioning, knowledge is independently constructed rather than socially constructed. Although cognitive conflict can still occur in the solo version of the strategy, in that discrepancies and contradictions can arise between what an individual "knows" and what is presented by the teacher, the emergence and resolution of socio-cognitive conflict (Mugny & Doise, 1978)–and the resulting learning benefits–cannot occur in the absence of interaction with others. Nor is there, in Guided Self Questioning, the opportunity for students to model their thinking and discussion skills on that of their peers.

Advantages of Guided Self Questioning over Peer Questioning

There are, however, several advantages to the independent version of guided questioning over the cooperative version. Guided Self Questioning can be used by the students anywhere, anytime: at home when studying alone, in class after the teacher's presentation, in any other location and under any conditions. This can be particularly important when a study partner is not available and for students who prefer to work independently.

Guided Self Questioning can even be used during direct teaching to facilitate encoding. In such cases, the questions may be written down as a form of note taking. Guided Self Questioning can also be used prior to instruction. Such pre-instruction questions as "What do I already know about ...?" help activate background knowledge about the topic to be covered. Accessing prior knowledge helps students make connections between the new information and what they learned previously, thus helping them remember the new material. Also, questions such as "Why are we learning about ...?" can help students establish a purpose for learning about a particular topic and may improve motivation to attend to instruction. Thus pre-instruction, student-generated questioning can enhance students' motivation as well as promote their understanding of the new material.

SCRIPTED COOPERATION IN DYADS

Scripted Cooperation in Dyads (Dansereau, 1988; O'Donnell & Dansereau, 1992) is another strategy that provides students with an

Figure 3-3
Self-Monitoring Rating Scale

How well did I do in making up **comprehension** questions?
1=======2=======3=======4=======5
not very   extremely
well   well

How well did I do making up **connection** questions?
1=======2=======3=======4=======5
not very   extremely
well   well

How well did I **probe** for more complete answers?
1=======2=======3=======4=======5
not very   extremely
well   well

How well did I **explain** to others?
1=======2=======3=======4=======5
not very   extremely
well   well

From King (1994c).

opportunity to cooperatively process material presented during lectures and other types of direct teaching. Scripted cooperation differs from peer tutoring in that neither partner is an expert on the material being studied or the task being learned (O'Donnell & Dansereau, 1992).

The Strategy

Dansereau (1988) developed scripted cooperation as a method to specify and direct the processing activities that students engage in during learning. Script is used here as the term is used in the theatre. The two members of a dyad each have specific roles and activities to carry out; the script is used to direct the performance of those roles and activities. When students lack adequate learning skills and strategies, scripting their learning activities ensures that meaningful processing takes place and, at the same time, provides a way of training them in effective skills (O'Donnell & Dansereau, 1992).

The roles that learners assume in the Scripted Cooperation in Dyads strategy are *summarizer* (recaller) and *listener*. First, both partners in the dyad listen to the teacher's presentation and take notes. Then the summarizer orally recalls the main ideas of the presentation while the partner listens and checks for errors and omissions. During this part of the strategy, the summarizer does not look at his or her notes, but the listener may do so to facilitate the error-detection process. The listener does not interrupt the recaller but waits until the summary is completed. When the summarizer has finished summarizing the presentation from memory, the listener provides feedback to the recaller on material missed and on errors in the material summarized. Then both partners together elaborate on the material by adding details, generating examples, developing images, and generally relating the new material to what they already know and to their personal experience. Table 3-9 outlines the roles and activities of the script for the strategy. Members of a dyad alternate the listener and recaller roles when they use the strategy on multiple occasions.

Scripted Cooperation in Dyads has been used for various learning tasks such as writing, performing concrete procedures, processing text, and learning from direct instruction and lectures. O'Donnell and Dansereau (1992) claim that this strategy is effective because it facilitates several activities that previous research has shown to enhance learning: summarization, elaboration, metacognitive monitoring, cross-modeling, and multiple passes through to-be-learned material. Summarization, elaboration, and making multiple passes through the material provide opportunities for students to reformulate the new material and consolidate and extend their learning through further encoding. Such activity makes the new material more memorable to students. Partners in a dyad are also able to improve their skills in summarizing, error detection, and elaboration through observation and imitation of each others' behavior. Such cross-modeling is presumably more likely to

Table 3-9
Script for Scripted Cooperation in Dyads

· Both partners listen to the presentation and take notes

· One partner plays the role of *recaller*

· The other partner plays the role of *listener*

· The recaller summarizes the presentation orally without looking at any notes (recalls out loud from memory all the things that can be remembered from the presentation)

· The listener listens carefully to discover any errors or omissions (the listener can use his or her notes when listening to the summary)

· When the recaller is finished the listener provides feedback to the recaller on errors, distortions, and material omitted

· Together partners elaborate on the material presented (e.g., develop analogies, generate images, relate the new information to prior knowledge, reformat the material)

occur when neither member of a dyad is designated as the "expert." Also, summarizing as well as providing and receiving error feedback are metacognitive activities, and such comprehension monitoring is an important aspect of this strategy. During summarizing, students are doing a self-check on how well they understand the presented material. For the summarizer, inability to summarize signals a lack of understanding, and errors or omissions suggest inaccurate or incomplete comprehension; then, when the listener provides feedback, this allows the recaller to pinpoint the specific nature of any comprehension problems. There are metacognitive benefits for the listener, too, through the continuous process of monitoring the summarizer's comprehension and detecting errors.

Research on Scripted Cooperation

Over the past ten years, numerous studies have been conducted to assess the effectiveness of scripted cooperation. O'Donnell and Dansereau (1992, 1993) reported that the strategy has been effective for comprehending text, learning concrete procedures, writing, and learning from lectures. Students who use scripted cooperation consistently outperform those who work alone (e.g., Larson, Dansereau, O'Donnell, Hythecker, Lambiote, & Rocklin, 1985). Some studies have focused on the effects of particular roles and various scripts, as well as on the interaction of scripts with tasks and learners' individual differences. In terms of roles, in general, recallers learn more than listeners (Dansereau, 1988); however, when scripted cooperation was used for learning from lectures, there were no differences between recallers and listeners in free recall of lecture material (O'Donnell & Dansereau, 1993). Externally-imposed scripts were found to be more effective than student-generated scripts (Larson et al., 1985). When the basic script has been modified to emphasize either its cognitive activity (e.g., elaboration) or its metacognitive activity (e.g., error detection), the metacognitive script resulted in better content-dependent learning, while the cognitive script led to better content-independent transfer (Larson, et al., 1985). In using scripted cooperation, dyads that are heterogeneous in ability and cognitive style seem to perform better than dyads that are homogeneous on these learner characteristics (Larson, Dansereau, Goetz, & Young, 1985; Larson et al., 1985), probably because heterogeneous dyads give low-ability students more opportunities to model cognitive skills after those of the high-ability students. Under scripted cooperation in such pairings, the performance of low-ability students improves, while that of high ability students does not appear to suffer (O'Donnell & Dansereau, 1992). O'Donnell and Dansereau (1992) conclude that scripted cooperation is effective in part because it stimulates active processing of material (rehearsal, reorganization, elaboration), it allows for comprehension monitoring, and, in general, students find the strategy motivating.

How to Teach Scripted Cooperation in Dyads

Some training and practice with scripted cooperation is necessary to gain proficiency with the strategy. First the teacher describes the scripted cooperation strategy, including the roles and activities outlined in Table 3-9. The teacher and a student then model how to use the strategy to study material from previous instruction. When summarizing, it is helpful if the teacher deliberately makes an error and omits some material so that the listener can model detecting errors and providing feedback. After the roles of summarizer and listener have been demonstrated, the class should practice in dyads on this part of the strategy before going on to the elaboration step. After each student has had a chance to practice being a summarizer and a listener, the teacher and a student can model working together to elaborate. Students find this the most difficult part of the strategy because of their lack of experience with elaboration techniques (O'Donnell, 1993a); therefore, it is important to model a variety of ways of doing this. Following each practice session, partners should assess their use of scripted cooperation by using a strategy rating scale similar to the one in Figure 3-3.

A Classroom Example (Adapted from O'Donnell, 1993b)

Ms. McGillicuddy was teaching her 9th-grade ancient history class about early medical practices. One section of her presentation was on *trephining*, a form of "psychiatry" used by Stone Age men some half-million years ago. Ms. McGillicuddy explained that for certain forms of mental illness (probably severe headache with convulsions, which were thought to be caused by evil spirits in the head), early medicine men used an operation called trephining: chipping a round hole (a trephine) in the head to allow the evil spirit to escape. This hole may also have relieved pressure on the brain that may have been causing the problems. Some trephined skulls of early men show healing around the opening, indicating that the individual survived trephining to live for many years afterward.

Following Ms. McGillicuddy's description of trephining and explanation of its use, she had students pair up and designate one partner as the summarizer and the other the listener. The students knew their roles from previous use of scripted cooperation. After the summarizers completed their summaries, the listeners told them any details or facts they had missed or gotten wrong. Then partners worked together to elaborate the material. One pair did so by reorganizing the material into four steps one might go through in trephining: find someone with a severe headache; chip a hole in the person's skull; the evil spirit escapes; the person's headaches stop. Another pair related the trephining information to a television show they had seen on archaeologists digging among the remains of early man. To help them remember about trephining, they pictured those same archaeologists examining a skull with a trephine in it. Partners in another pair made up a rhyme to help them remember trephining:

> "When a caveman with convulsions made a scene,
> Along came his buddy to do a trephine."

Other students found that what worked well for them was simply creating an image of the trephine being chipped away with a sharp stone, the chips falling to the ground, and the evil spirit crawling out of the hole. To assess how well they used their strategy, Ms. McGillicuddy had each student complete a rating scale.

Student Self-Monitoring of Strategy Use

After their initial use of the scripted cooperation strategy, students should assess how well they performed their roles in the strategy. To do so, they can complete a rating scale attached to the following questions (adapted from O'Donnell, 1993b):

- How well did the summarizer use his/her own words in summarizing the presentation?
- How well did the listener detect any errors or omissions by the summarizer?
- How well did you and your partner discuss any information that was left out and correct any information that was recalled incorrectly?
- How well did you and your partner elaborate on the new material, add to it, make up images, reorganize the material, or tie it to what you already knew to help you remember it?

Such a rating scale can be used in an ongoing manner after each session of scripted cooperation, until students become very proficient in the strategy; thereafter, the rating scale can be used occasionally.

SMALL-GROUP GENERATIVE SUMMARIZING

Generative summarizing is another cooperative learning strategy for learning from direct teaching. Summarizing has been found to enhance comprehension and recall for content of text passages read by students at various academic levels (e.g., Brown & Day, 1983; Reinhart, Stahl & Erickson, 1986; Ross & DiVesta, 1976). In order to end up with a much-shortened version of the passage, but one that captured all the main ideas, the summaries in those studies were produced by selecting, deleting, and modifying existing sentences in the passage. However, according to Wittrock (1990; Wittrock & Alesandrini, 1990), effective summarization is generative in nature. For a summary to be generative, a learner's own words and experiences should be used to construct novel sentences (ones that do not appear in the presented material), and those sentences should make connections among the presented concepts and relate the new information to the learner's prior knowledge and experience. According to this line of thinking, when learners use their own words to summarize, connections between the new material and each learner's existing knowledge are automatically constructed because those words are associated with information stored in that learner's memory. Wittrock's research has shown that this form of summary is highly successful in promoting comprehension and recall when reading from text (e.g., Wittrock & Alesandrini, 1990). Generative summarizing of this sort has also been used successfully as a strategy for learning from lectures (King, 1992b). The same approach can be used for learning from any kind of teacher presentation.

The Strategy

In this strategy, summarizing occurs following the presentation and serves the purpose of organizing and encoding the new information by reformatting it into a summary. These generative summaries are first constructed by students individually; later, they are synthesized into a group summary (King, 1992b). The summarizing should take place as soon as possible after the teacher's presentation. First, each student constructs a summary of the presentation by linking presented ideas together using only that student's own words to do so. For each individual student, the process of constructing such a summary results in that student's own personal and unique representation of the presentation in long-term memory. The first step in summarizing is to review notes taken during instruction to identify the topic of the presentation. The student then composes a sentence to reflect that topic only. Based on the notes and memory of the presentation, the student next identifies a subtopic or main idea and related facts from the material presented, and creates a sentence linking them to each other. All sentences must be in the student's own words. A second main idea and related facts are then identified and a sentence written to combine them. Additional sentences are written in this same manner. These several sentences constitute the summary of the presentation. The steps in this summarizing process are outlined in Figure 3-4.

Summaries constructed this way are truly generative in nature, because students write original sentences which paraphrase the ideas presented by the teacher and relate those ideas to each other; they use their own words in place of words and expressions used by the teacher. This approach can be distinguished from approaches in which summarizers simply modify sentences they remember from the material

Figure 3-4
Scheme for Summarizing a Presentation

Identify:		Write (USING YOUR OWN WORDS)
The TOPIC of the presentation	→	Turn topic into a sentence about the main idea of the presentation
One SUBTOPIC (or MAIN IDEA) and RELATED IDEAS	→	Link together to write a second sentence
A second SUBTOPIC (or MAIN IDEA) and RELATED IDEAS	→	Link together to write a third sentence
A third SUBTOPIC (or MAIN IDEA) and RELATED IDEAS	→	Link together to write a fourth sentence
A fourth SUBTOPIC (or MAIN IDEA) and RELATED IDEAS	→	Link together to write a fifth sentence
A fifth SUBTOPIC (or MAIN IDEA) and RELATED IDEAS	→	Link together to write a sixth sentence
etc.		
etc.		

Adapted from King (1992b).

presented (a standard practice in many text-summarizing studies, e.g., Brown & Day, 1983). Generative summarizing is effective because it allows students to monitor their comprehension during classroom instruction, and because inventing sentences for the summaries helps them construct their own more-memorable cognitive representations of the material.

When students have completed their individual summaries, they read them aloud to their small group to jointly construct a group summary. In doing so, the group decides what to select and modify from each individual summary. This cooperative approach to summarizing provides students opportunities for modeling their summarizing skills on those of their peers, thereby improving their summarizing. Further, observing others and practicing the strategy in cooperative groups helps individual students to internalize the generative summarizing skills (Brown & Palincsar, 1989; Vygotsky, 1978).

How to Teach the Strategy

The teacher begins by describing the strategy and how it works. This should include an explanation of why the strategy is effective in learning from teachers' presentations. The explanation should stress that generating a summary makes the material understandable and easier to remember in two ways. First of all, paraphrasing ideas into students' own words automatically connects the new material to something they already know—at least in terms of vocabulary; and during the act of connecting ideas together into sentences, corresponding links are created in students' mental representations of the new material. Together these various links provide numerous ways to recall the information.

Using cognitive modeling, the teacher demonstrates the generative summarizing procedure, as outlined in Table 3-10, with material previously taught. The usual cognitive coaching sequence (see Table 3-2) should be followed to effect a gradual shift of responsibility for summarizing from the teacher to the students. Scaffolding with feedback must be continued over several practice sessions. In this strategy, peer modeling comes into play also. Individual self-monitoring of strategy use should follow each practice session. Figure 3-5 shows examples of rating scales that can be used for that purpose. Once students are able to summarize individually, they work in small groups to develop a joint summary of the teacher's presentation. Students in a group select the best sentences from the members' summaries, modify them, and integrate them into a group summary. The steps in this latter process can be modeled by the teacher with one or two student volunteers.

Figure 3-5
Self-Monitoring Rating Scale for Summarizing

How well did I identify important information?
1==========2==========3==========4==========5
not very   extremely
well   well

How well did I link information together?
1==========2==========3==========4==========5
not very   extremely
well   well

How well was I able to use my own words rather than the exact words from the presentation?
1==========2==========3==========4==========5
not very   extremely
well   well

How well did I summarize?
1==========2==========3==========4==========5
not very   extremely
well   well

From King (1992b).

Research on Generative Summarizing

Although generative summarizing has been found effective with text material (Wittrock, 1990, Wittrock & Alesandrini, 1990), the empirical evidence for the effectiveness of generative summarizing with orally-presented material is limited to one research study (King, 1992b). Participants in that study were under-prepared college students in their freshman year who listened to videotaped lectures in political science. Findings from that study may not generalize to younger students. This is a limitation that should be kept in mind when using this strategy.

STRATEGIES FOR NOTE TAKING REVIEW

The strategy that most students use for learning from direct teaching, lectures, and other kinds of teacher presentations is taking verbatim notes during the presentation (Bretzing & Kulhavy, 1981; Kiewra & Fletcher, 1984; Peper & Mayer, 1986), and then rereading those notes at a later time (Kiewra, 1989). Clearly this "strategy" is based on the transmission view of learning; it assumes that material will be memorized and retained through this writing and rereading process. Essentially, there are two ways to encode information: *rote memorization* or *meaningful learning*. Rote memorization can be achieved through repetition of the information several times, whereas meaningful learning requires acting upon the information in some thoughtful way, such as elaborating it, making mental images, or generating analogies, to construct knowledge. Rote memorization of an entire presentation is an inefficient and unreliable approach. As the previous part of this chapter has shown, to really understand and remember the content of a presentation, learners must actively process the presented material in some meaningful way.

As Kiewra (1989) pointed out, researchers have distinguished between two functions of note taking: *storage* and *encoding*. In the *storage* function, notes are taken in order to store the information for later review. Presumably, that review should facilitate meaningful learning by helping learners consolidate information, reconstruct details left out during note taking, relearn forgotten information, or elaborate on the material. The *encoding* function suggests that simply recording notes enhances learning by increasing attention, facilitating elaboration of ideas, and improving organization of the presented material (Einstein, Morris, & Smith, 1985). Although taking notes is said to help the note taker somewhat in encoding the new information, any kind of note taking per se is relatively ineffective as a learning strategy when used alone (Kiewra, 1989). The real value of note taking is as a form of external storage of ideas for later review. To make note taking effective, the learner must combine it with active review of those notes. Generally, active review can be achieved by reorganizing the notes taken or reformulating the information in some other manner after the lecture or presentation. All of the strategies presented earlier in this chapter are ways for students to actively process orally-presented material. Other strategies that can be used in conjunction with note taking are presented in this section of the chapter.

Unfortunately, researchers have found that students take incomplete notes, capturing an average of less than 40% of the ideas presented (e.g., Hartley & Cameron, 1967). Researchers have also found that when students take notes during teacher presentations, they are far more likely to record bits and pieces of the material verbatim or simply paraphrase information, rather than organize the presented material into some sort of conceptual framework or relate the new information to what they already know (Bretzing & Kulhavy, 1981; Kiewra & Fletcher, 1984). Actually, such verbatim note taking may be all that can be expected of students, because trying to listen to a presentation, record the information, and at the same time integrate and reformulate the material may place an unrealistic cognitive burden on any learner. Nevertheless, some researchers (e.g., Peper & Mayer, 1986) claim that note taking is a generative activity, in that during note taking, connections should be automatically created between the new material and the learner's prior knowledge. However, no clear evidence for generative processing has been found, and no attempts have been made to actually train students in such generative note taking (Kiewra, 1989), although results of the King (1992b) study on generative self-questioning or summarizing as review strategies did show that these strategies improved encoding during a lecture, at least to some extent. Given the incompleteness of notes students generally take, the lack of organization of those notes, the cognitive burden of the note taking task, and the lack of evidence to support training in generative note taking, Kiewra (1989) has concluded that during a lecture it might be best for students to concentrate their efforts on recording complete and accurate notes rather than on trying to encode the information through some form of on-line generative activity; and then, after the presentation when time is not a constraint, they can review those notes to integrate ideas and relate them to prior knowledge.

Teachers can help students to increase the quantity and quality of their notes through purely instructional means such as presenting the material at a slow enough rate, reducing the amount of material presented, and providing cues for note taking (Kiewra, 1989). These approaches, however, are entirely teacher-dependent ones and do not lead to student responsibility and self-regulation in learning. (Additional teaching suggestions are presented in a later section of this chapter.) Within that context, the following section deals with note taking strategies that students can use on their own (or with little teacher direction) to increase the quantity and accuracy of the notes they take.

Note Taking Review

Regardless of how well a teacher organizes and presents material, or the amount and quality of notes taken, students must still review those notes. As mentioned previously, the purpose of taking notes is primarily to store the information; the purpose of review is to encode or learn the material (steps 2 and 3 in Figure 3-1). During review, the volume of notes is reduced and notes are consolidated. Indeed, for real learning to take place, it is critical that students reorganize and integrate their notes in some manner. This is often referred to as *reformatting* notes. During reformatting, information is actively processed by the student. That is, the information is interpreted and organized for efficient storage in long-term memory and to facilitate recall from memory later on (refer to Figure 3-1).

Most of the note taking strategies covered in this section also include a component targeted specifically at reviewing notes already taken. Although most strategies provided here emphasize both note taking and review, some (e.g., mapping and outlining) can be used only for reformatting notes in ways that help students to improve their review of those notes. Nevertheless, all are referred to as note taking review strategies.

Because the value of notes is primarily in the external storage of ideas for later review (Kiewra, 1989), and the more complete the notes the more effective such review will be (Kiewra & Benton, 1988), note taking strategies should focus first of all on enhancing the completeness and accuracy of notes taken. A number of general tips for taking notes can be helpful for use with any note taking review strategy. These tips are summarized in Table 3-10.

Outline Methods of Note Taking

One method for improving the quantity and quality of notes that students take is to provide them with a structure for their notes, in the form of a skeletal outline or matrix listing ideas to be covered (Risch & Kiewra, 1989). Such a framework lists the topic and subtopics and leaves space for students to take notes.

Linear outlines

A linear framework lists the topics and subtopics in traditional outline form, leaving room between for note taking. Unlike ordinary note taking, where students generally list only those relationships that the teacher makes explicit during instruction, an outline automatically makes certain relationships obvious. For example, in an outline, topic-subtopic relationships are apparent because subtopics appear below

Table 3-10
General Tips for Notetaking

· Don't write down everything—concentrate on getting the main ideas and supporting ideas and only *relevant* details.

· Listen for summary statements—write those down. Good teachers summarize key points, concepts, etc.

· When possible take notes in your own words—except for technical terms (don't change them).

· Use abbreviations whenever possible—leave space behind each one and fill in complete word later.

· Use symbols (∴ for therefore, + for and, w/ for with, arrow —> to show cause-effect).

· Write down anything written on the chalkboard or overhead projector—this material is generally important.

· Listen for signal words. Words such as "next ...", "in addition ...", "The following ...", signal a change in topic. Words such as "first, ...", "second, ...", "There are four reasons ...", signal that a list is about to be presented. "Therefore ...", "since ...", "because ..." indicate cause-effect relationships.

· Write clearly so notes can be read later.

topics and are indented; also, the spaces provided under topics and subtopics allow the note taker to connect each point recorded to a specific topic and subtopic on the outline (Kiewra, DuBois, Christian, McShane, Meyerhoffer, & Roskelley, 1988). Making these kinds of connections among ideas in the presentation enhances understanding and recall. In comparison to ordinary note taking, use of a linear outline has been found to increase the number of ideas recorded by students and to facilitate the development of internal connections among ideas in the presentation (Kiewra et al, 1988).

Matrix outlines

A matrix presents the topics across the top of a page and the subtopics down the left margin; this forms internal cells that are used for note taking. Like the linear outline, the matrix also increases the number of ideas recorded; and, in addition, it facilitates the making of connections among the topics and subtopics (Kiewra et al., 1988). First of all, like the linear outline, a matrix makes topic-subtopic relationships evident and connects all recorded ideas to a topic and subtopic. Also, it provides room for notes on the relationships among ideas across topics and thus allows the student to synthesize material across topics. These latter kinds of connections are usually not evident in either the linear-outline method or standard note taking.

Research on Outline Methods of Note Taking

Although research on outline methods of note taking indicate that both linear and matrix formats are effective (Kiewra et al., 1988), the matrix is particularly effective when integration of ideas and relationships are stressed, since the matrix format facilitates such connections. For example, in a study conducted by Risch and Kiewra (1989), eighth-graders viewed an 8-minute videotaped lecture describing four theories of personality in turn. For each personality theory, the lecturer pre-sented the same seven subtopics (e.g., definition, founder, early influences, example, treatment). Some students received a linear framework on which to record notes, while others received a matrix. As described by Risch and Kiewra (1989), the linear framework listed the four theories one after another on three sheets of paper with the same seven subtopics listed in the same order and indented under each theory. Space was left for taking notes under each. The matrix outline was a two-dimensional chart on one large piece of paper. The four theories were listed across the top of the matrix, and the seven subtopics were listed once along the left margin. Lines were drawn so that the topics became columns and the subtopics appeared as seven rows.

This created 28 boxes for note taking. Figure 3-6 shows an example of a linear outline of such material and the same material presented in matrix form. In that study Risch and Kiewra (1989) found that the matrix format facilitated concept learning because students could easily look across the cells of the matrix to compare definitions of the four theories, examples, and the like, at a glance.

Following note taking in an outline format, students should review the material using those outlines. During review, connections not noted previously can be added to the linear or matrix outline, and the material can be further consolidated through reflection about the connections generated.

Matrix and linear outlines can also be used as a strategy for reviewing notes taken in a conventional way. Reorganizing a set of notes into an outline or matrix can help students identify internal connections among ideas in their notes, as well as generate connections across topics.

The Cornell System of Note Taking

Probably the most commonly-used formal note taking procedure is the Cornell System (Pauk, 1974), often referred to as the Split Page method. In this system, a line is drawn down the page about a third of the way

Figure 3-6
Matrix and Linear Outlines

Theories of Personality	Freudian	Jungian	object-relations	social cognitive
definition				
founder				
early influences				
example				
treatment				

Matrix

<u>Theories of personality</u>

    Freudian Theory

Definition

Founder

Early Influences

Example

Treatment

Linear Outline

across to make two columns. The right column is used to record notes during the presentation (see Figure 3-7). As soon as possible after the presentation the notes are reviewed; any information missed can be added and main ideas underlined. The left side of the page, called the *recall column*, is used to fill in key words and phrases that can serve as recall cues for remembering the ideas recorded in the notes in the right-hand column of the page. To study, the notes can be covered up and the key words used to help recall the material. The Cornell System is considered simple, efficient, logical, and easy to use; and it can be adapted for use with almost any presentation.

Teaching the strategy

There are three stages to this system: preparation, recording, and review. The steps in these three stages are outlined in Table 3-11.

Research

Although intuitively the Cornell System seems well-designed and is considered effective, research on this approach is limited to evaluation studies which did not use a control or comparison group (Pauk, 1974). It should be noted that no empirical research on the Cornell approach

Figure 3-7
The Cornell System Format for Notetaking

-----------2-1/2"-----------	-----------------------------------6"-----------------------------------
Recall column	*Notetaking column*
Key words	Presentation notes

Table 3-11
The Cornell System of Notetaking

Preparation for notetaking
· use a large loose-leaf notebook to allow room to insert any handouts
· use a separate page for each day—date it and write topic at top
· prepare the notebook by drawing the recall column from top to bottom of page—one third of the distance from left edge of page; leave the right two thirds of the page for notetaking—see Figure 4
· review previous presentation to make connections—do this by overlapping each page so only the recall column can be seen

Recording notes during presentation
· keep notes simple
· paraphrase
· record main ideas
· link supporting details
· use key words and phrases only—to abbreviate
· listen for clues and signal words in what the teacher says about important points to come
· listen for repetition of points—these are important
· listen for comparison-contrast statements
· if the teacher summarizes—use this time to fill in material missed the first time
· teacher's gestures can be clues to what is important
· changes in voice—a raised voice or a whisper—can indicate an important point
· a pause may indicate an important point is going to be made
· write down anything the teacher has written on the board during the presentation

Review
· as soon as possible after the presentation, review notes, underlining key ideas and adding any material missed while taking notes
· use the recall column at the left to fill in key words and phrases to serve as cures for recalling the ideas in the notes on the right-hand side of the page—these key words help jog the memory
· cover up the notes and use the key words to help recall the presented material aloud
· uncover the notes to check for accuracy

Adapted from Pauk (1974).

could be found, and this limitation should be kept in mind when making decisions about selecting note taking strategies to teach to students in middle school and high school.

Mapping Strategies

Maps are a useful way to graphically represent information. Mapping uses hierarchical structure and a minimum of words. A map can display the ideas presented as well as the relationships among those ideas. Because maps are hierarchical in nature, the important ideas are generally written down first, with related ideas then placed underneath and connected to the previous level. Tree diagrams, flow charts, and concept webs are all examples of maps, as are elaborate knowledge maps. Knowledge maps are more complex than tree diagrams and other forms of graphic reformatting, since knowledge maps can represent multiple relationships among ideas simultaneously and at a glance. Examples of knowledge maps and tree diagrams are shown in Figures 3-8 and 3-9. Knowledge mapping has been found to be an effective strategy for reformatting and reviewing material presented by the teacher (Lambiote, Peale, & Dansereau, 1992).

There are several reasons for using mapping as a strategy for review and for reformatting notes taken. First of all, a map provides a way to graphically show how main ideas relate to the topic of the presentation, to each other, and to supporting ideas and details. In addition, the map produced condenses the material (the map becomes a graphic summary). Mapping calls for critical thinking to identify main ideas, then analyze and make judgments about the relationships among those ideas and the presented material in general. Thus, the process of mapping forces the mapper to actively think about the new material, identify those main ideas and relationships, and determine how best to display them.

How to Teach Mapping

When teaching mapping it is useful to start out with an example of a map based on previous instruction (see sample maps in Figures 3-8 and 3-9). It is important to explain to students why maps are useful as a strategy for reorganizing their notes. This explanation can be followed by modeling how to construct such a map from a previous presentation. Steps used in the mapping strategy are shown in Table 3-12. As usual, cognitive modeling should be followed by scaffolded practice with the class as a whole. The most difficult aspect of the strategy is identifying hierarchical relationships among ideas and depicting relationships accurately (Jones, Pierce, Hunter et al., 1988-1989).

Research on Knowledge Mapping

A number of studies (King & Rosenshine, 1993; Leinhardt & Smith,

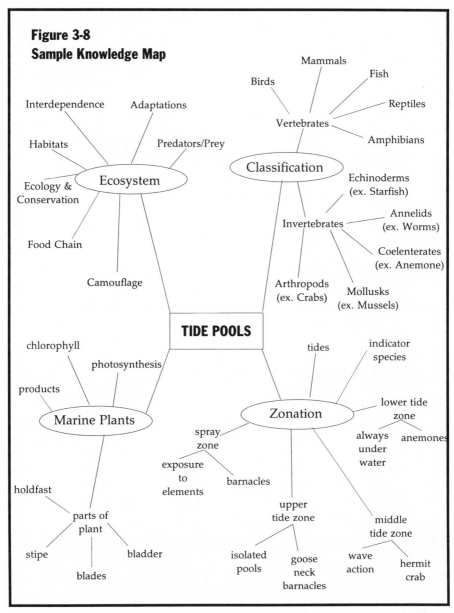

Figure 3-8
Sample Knowledge Map

1985; Leinhardt, 1987; Naveh-Benjamin, McKeachie, Lin, & Tucker, 1986) have used knowledge mapping as a way of monitoring children's understanding of lesson content following classroom lessons on that material, and as a technique for children to check their own level of comprehension. Those studies have found that children benefit from the opportunity to organize their knowledge graphically into a map format. From a constructivist point of view, during the process of developing their concept maps, students are identifying and labeling

Table 3-12
Steps in Knowledge Mapping

1. Identify the topic of the presentation and write it in the middle of a page. Draw a circle or square around it.

2. Identify the main ideas or subtopics and link each of them to the topic by branching lines.

3. Add the important facts to the map by attaching them to the ideas they belong with. This will make a secondary category and a second set of branching lines. A third and fourth set of branching lines may be necessary if the presented material can be broken down further.

4. Show relationships among ideas with lines and/or arrows. Words can be used to label the kind of relationship being shown (e.g., cause and effect, is part of, etc.)

The one-page map is a graphic summary of the presentation.

Figure 3-9
Sample Tree Diagram

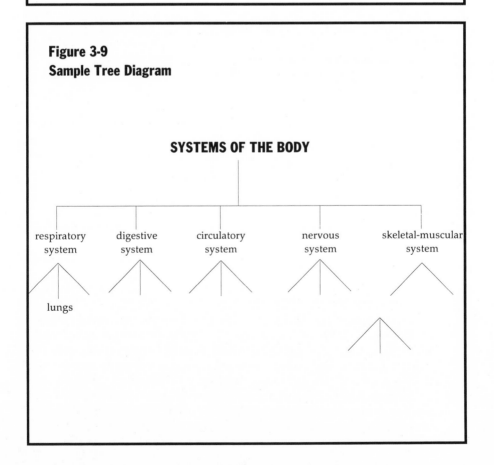

main ideas and subordinate ideas and making connections among those ideas. The knowledge maps themselves thus become external manifestations of students' mental representations of the material and indicate what knowledge they have constructed from a lesson or presentation.

Such maps can be very useful, both as a method of reorganizing material from notes taken and for subsequent review of that material (Lambiote et al., 1992). In their investigation of the use of knowledge maps as post-lecture organizers for review of lecture material, Lambiote et al. (1992) found that students who reviewed using maps of the lecture material, with ideas connected in link-node format, performed better on application of the lecture content than students who reviewed the lecture using the same content in a list format. Although the maps did not lead to better recall of the material, they did facilitate higher-level thinking, in that map reviewers were better able to generate examples and apply them in problem-solving scenarios.

Recognizing and Using Expository Frameworks

Many people feel that the most important skill for taking notes during instruction is the ability to recognize the organizational form that the speaker is using for the presentation or for parts of the presentation. These organizational forms are called *discourse patterns* or *expository frameworks* (*expository* means to "set forth," and during instruction what the teacher does is set forth information; Farnam-Diggory, 1994). Teaching students to recognize particular organizational forms being used by the teacher can greatly enhance learning. The framework that the teacher has in mind (that is, the teacher's conceptual framework) is guiding what the teacher says next. Once students can identify the underlying framework of pieces of the presentation as they are being presented, and can detect the underlying framework of the presentation as a whole, they can use that framework to guide their own understanding. Then, later on, when they want to remember the information, the framework guides their recall of that information. For example, the underlying framework in a particular history presentation might be a timeline. That timeline could serve to organize the events into chronological order so they could be related to each other and remembered in that order (Farnam-Diggory, 1994). Students could actually draw a timeline in their notes and, as the teacher presents material, mark dates and events on the timeline. Thus the timeline guides what students write down as well as their understanding of that material. In this way, the teacher's expository framework becomes the students' conceptual framework for understanding and remembering the material.

Based on Van Dijk and Kintch's (1983) work on text structures and McNeil's (1984) work on patterns in expository text, Farnam-Diggory (1992) describes several expository frameworks that commonly appear in lectures and other sorts of direct teaching: definition; description or listing of features; comparison-contrast; time ordering (chronological order/sequence of events); explanation (cause and effect); principle, rule, or generalization (with example); and problem-solution. Other frequently-used discourse patterns include: argument followed by support, establishing context, background, or perspective. Table 3-13 lists these frameworks.

When teachers make those patterns clear in the delivery of the presentation, it helps students to see them and take notes in those same formats, as well as review material accordingly. Cueing by the teacher during the presentation can help students identify these patterns. For example, when two ideas or items are to be compared, it is useful to point this out by saying, "Now I'm going to compare ... and ...." Listing the items on the board as headings for two columns with a line drawn down between them makes the comparison-contrast pattern even clearer, and allows students to replicate that format in their notes to facilitate recording similarities and differences as they are presented. When a particular expository framework is identified, it may be useful if students flag it in their notes with a key word in the margin (e.g., DEFN for definition, EXPLN for explanation, an arrow —> to show cause and effect, RULE-ex for a rule followed by an example, PROB/SOLN to indicate a problem and its solution).

Reformatting notes into expository frameworks and diagrams.

Teaching students to reformat their notes according to these common discourse patterns is also important. When summarizing a definition, for example, it may be beneficial to attach the features and examples of the term to a central node (the term being defined); when the teacher

---

Table 3-13
Common Expository Frameworks

· context or perspective

· definition

· description

· comparison-contrast

· ordering

· explanation (cause-effect)

· rule-example or principle-example

· problem-solution

· argument-support

is presenting the evolution of a problem and the steps to its solution, a flowchart might be most helpful (Farnam-Diggory, 1992). Although reformatting material graphically has very powerful recall effects, reformatting does not have to be graphic. Features of a definition can be listed (rather than mapped), steps in a procedure can be numbered (rather than flow-charted), and events can be numbered or listed by date (rather than time-lined). When students reformat their notes into the same discourse pattern used by the teacher when presenting the material, they are much more likely to be replicating the original conceptual framework that the teacher had in mind. This pattern then becomes the student's own conceptual framework for thinking about the material, for organizing the material in memory, and for recalling the material later on (refer to Figure 3-1); thus assuring a closer match between what the teacher is teaching and what the student is learning.

Developing an Individual Style of Note Taking

Although students may learn several strategies for taking notes, they should be encouraged to develop their own individual style of note taking. One way to encourage personalizing a note taking style is to have students share their notes with each other. By looking at a variety of sets of notes from the same presentation, students become more acutely aware of the benefits of different approaches and can better synthesize those approaches into a personal style.

TEACHING HINTS FOR WHOLE CLASS PRESENTATIONS

Although the emphasis of this chapter has been on strategies that students can be taught to help them learn from direct teaching, students' learning from such presentations is also affected by the ways in which teachers deliver those presentations. And, as Gage and Berliner (1992) have pointed out, lecturing and other forms of direct teaching can be very effective as an instructional method for particular learning objectives when the presentations are well-organized and delivered. Teachers can make learning easier by delivering well-organized presentations, activating students' prior knowledge, using relevant examples, promoting student attention, cueing students to important ideas and transitions, and by providing opportunities for students to actively process the presented material. A few selected ideas are provided in this section, but these are only suggestions and are just a sampling. These suggestions should not be considered prescriptive nor exhaustive.

Improving Attention During the Presentation

Although the primary responsibility for paying attention during instruction should ideally rest with each individual student (refer to Figure 3-1), there are numerous things that a teacher can do to promote student attention. For example, when a teacher informs students at the beginning of a presentation that they will be required to summarize to their partners the 3 or 4 most important things covered, the students are likely to attend more closely. Similarly, attention to the presentation can be improved if the teacher does not allow students to take notes during instruction but lets them do so immediately after. To illustrate, Ms. Glarnk is explaining a physics principle to her students and has told them not to take notes. After 15 minutes she stops and tells students to take notes, make diagrams, or do whatever they need to do to get the main points down. After note taking, she shows them a brief summary on the overhead, or students exchange notes to check how well they captured the main ideas. Knowing they will have to remember the material well enough to take notes from memory later on not only promotes better attention, it also assures learning during the presentation (because if they don't understand an idea, students will ask questions so that they can construct meaning well enough to summarize it later).

Organization and Delivery

As Figure 3-1 shows, a major aspect of learning from direct teaching is being able to organize and store the newly-constructed knowledge into memory so that it can be recalled and used later on as needed. When the teacher's presentation is well organized and delivered, this facilitates the student's organization and encoding.

Not only does an oral presentation need to be well organized, that organization needs to be made clear to the students. Along those lines, it is best to begin a presentation by announcing the topic. The main subtopics could also be listed on the board, or on an overhead projector, to be revealed as the presentation proceeds. This provides students with a conceptual framework to help them take notes and to organize their thinking about the presentation as a whole. At this point it is important to link the topic to something students already know about, such as previous instruction or something common to their everyday experience. This is consistent with the notion of network models of memory, as successful encoding of information into long-term memory depends on making connections with networks already there. Brief statements or questions before beginning (such as "What do you already know about ...?" as described earlier) can provide opportunities for students to access their existing knowledge. Activating their prior knowledge in this way helps students connect the new ideas to material already in memory and makes it easier to remember it later on.

Graphic organizers can make relationships among ideas clear. As described previously, tree diagrams and charts, such as those in Figures 3-8 and 3-9, help students organize the information and make additional connections. When appropriate, such organizers can be displayed on an overhead and developed as the points are made during the presentation.

Providing Opportunities for Active Processing During Instruction

Providing students with opportunities to actively process the new material during instruction enhances learning enormously, because such active processing facilitates students' knowledge construction. There are numerous activities that can be easily and quickly incorporated into a typical teacher presentation to make it a more active and interactive learning experience. For each major concept or principle presented, an activity that requires students to generate meaning about that concept or principle can be built into the instructional sequence. One such activity is "think-pair-share" (see King, 1993, for numerous other examples). For example, Mr. Zonk is expounding to his ninth-grade social studies class on the relationship between the geography of a region and patterns of settlement, transportation, and economics. After several minutes, he poses the question: "What do you think would have happened differently if Columbus had landed halfway up the St. Lawrence River instead of in the Caribbean? Think about that for a minute." After a minute he continues, "Now pair up with the person beside you and share your ideas." "Think-pair-share" can be accomplished during a two-minute pause in the presentation.

Other activities can be accomplished by students working independently. For example, Mr. Zonk could have stopped talking and asked students to quickly list the three main points he had made in the first part of his presentation. For these active-processing activities to be effective, students must use their own words and experiences—not regurgitate material verbatim from the presentation. Short sessions of Guided Peer Questioning and pair summarizing can also be incorporated into teacher presentations.

Checking for Understanding During the Presentation

Checking to see how well students understand the material being presented can facilitate student learning, in that misunderstandings can be flagged early on before they are encoded into memory, and gaps in knowledge can be filled before additional related material is covered. Such feedback can help a teacher direct the remainder of the presentation. All teachers are familiar with methods for monitoring their students' understanding "on line" during instruction, such as having them signal "yes-no" in response to a question, writing instant quizzes on the overhead, listing the several main ideas of the presentation (see "Improving Attention during the Presentation" above), etc. Checking for understanding at the end of a presentation in preparation for the next instructional session can be accomplished by asking students to quickly jot down an answer to the question "What do I still not understand fully?" (see King, 1992a, 1992b).

CONCLUSION

The cognitive strategies presented here are effective ways for students to enhance their learning from direct teaching, lectures, and other forms of teacher presentation. Not all students will be equally comfortable with all strategies, and it is expected that most students will favor one or two strategies for learning from such teacher presentations. Students should take a flexible attitude toward strategy use. Usually they will adapt and modify strategies and even combine strategies to come up with what works for them. It is beneficial to stress that students should try to select and use strategies that match their own preferred learning styles.

It is important for students and teachers to remember that a great deal of practice with any strategy is necessary before significant learning gains will be evident. In addition, monitoring and regulating strategy use and effectiveness needs to be an ongoing process. Such monitoring can be very effective when both teacher and students take responsibility for this aspect of cognitive strategy use.

REFERENCES

Anderson, J.R. (1976). *Language. memory and thought.* Hillsdale: Erlbaum.

Baddeley, A.D. (1976). *The psychology of memory.* New York: Harper & Row.

Bargh, J.A., & Schul, Y. (1980). On the cognitive benefits of teaching. *Journal of Educational Psychology, 72,* 593-604.

Bearison, D.J. (1982). New directions in studies of social interactions and cognitive growth. In F.C. Serafica (Ed.), *Social-cognitive development in context* (pp. 199-221). New York: Guilford.

Billingsley, B.S., & Wildman, T.M. (1988). Question generation and reading comprehension. *Learning Disability Research, 4,* 36-44.

Bloom, B.S. (Ed.) (1956). *Taxonomy of educa-tional objectives: The classification of educational goals. Handbook 1. Cognitive domain.* New York: McKay.

Bretzing, B.H., & Kulhavy, R.W. (1981). Note-taking and passage style. *Journal of Educational Psychology, 73,* 242-250.

Brown, A.L., Bransford, J.D., Ferrara, R.A., & Campione, J.C. (1983). Learning, remembering and understanding. In Flavell, J.H., and Markman, E.M. (Eds.), *Handbook of Child Psychology. Vol. III: Cognitive Development* (pp. 77-166). New York: Wiley.

Brown, A.L., & Campione, J.C. (1986). Psychological theory and the study of learning disabilities. *American Psychologist, 41,* 1059-1068.

Brown, A.L., & Day, J.D. (1983). Macrorules for summarizing texts: The development of expertise. *Journal of Verbal Learning and Verbal Behaviour, 22,* 1-14.

Brown, A.L., & Palincsar, A.S. (1989). Guided cooperative learning and individual knowledge acquisition. In Resnick, L.B. (Ed.), *Knowing, Learning, and Instruction* (pp. 393-451). Hillsdale: Erlbaum.

Cobb, P. (1988). The tensions between theories of learning and instruction in mathematics education. *Educational Psychologist, 23,* 78-103.

Collins, A., Brown, J.S., & Larkin, K.M. (1980). Inference in text understanding. In R.J. Spiro, B.C. Bruce, & W.F. Brewer (Eds.), *Theoretical issues in reading comprehension* (pp. 385-407). Hillsdale, NJ: Erlbaum.

Damon, W. (1983). The nature of social-cognitive change in the developing child. In W. F. Overton (Ed.), *The relationship between social and cognitive development* (103-142). Hillsdale, NJ: Erlbaum.

Dansereau, D.F. (1988). Cooperative learning strategies. In C. E. Weinstein, E.T. Goetz, and P.A. Alexander (Eds.), *Learning and study strategies: Issues in assessment. instruction and evaluation.* New York: Academic Press.

Davey, B., & McBride, S. (1986). Effects of question-generation training on reading comprehension. *Journal of Educational Psychology, 78,* 256-262.

Einstein, G.O., Morris, J., & Smith, S. (1985). Note taking: Individual differences, and memory for lecture information. *Journal of Educational Psychology, 77,* 522-532.

Farnam-Diggory, S. (1992). *Cognitive processes in education.* (2nd ed.). New York: HarperCollins.

Farnam-Diggory, S. (1994). *SkilMod: Study Skills.* Manuscript submitted for publication.

Flavell, J.H. (1981). Cognitive monitoring. In W.P. Dickson (Ed.), *Children's oral communication skills.* New York: Academic Press.

Gage, N.L., & Berliner, D.C. (1992). *Educational psychology* (5th ed.). Palo Alto, CA: Houghton Mifflin.

Graesser, A.C., & McMahen, C.L. (1993). Anomalous information triggers questions when adults solve quantitative problems and comprehend stories. *Journal of Educational Psychology, 85,* 136-151.

Graesser, A.C., & Person, N.K (in press). Question-asking during tutoring. *American Educational Research Journal.*

Graesser, A.C. (1992). Questioning mechanisms during complex learning. Technical report, Cognitive Science Program, Office of Naval Research, Arlington, VA.

Haller, E.P., Child, D.A., & Walberg, H.J. (1988). Can comprehension be taught?. *Educational Researcher, 17,* 5-8.

Hartley, J., & Cameron, A. (1967). Some observations on the efficiency of lecturing. *Educational Review, 20,* 3-7.

Jones, B.F., Pierce, J., & Hunter, B. (1988-9). Teaching students to construct graphic representations. *Educational leadership, 46*(4), 20-25.

Kennedy, M. (1991). Policy issues in teacher education. *Phi Delta Kappan* (May), pp. 661-666.

Kiewra, K.A. (1989). A review of note-taking: The encoding-storage paradigm and beyond. *Educational Psychology Review, 1,* 147-172.

Kiewra, K.A., & Benton, S.L. (1988). The relationship between information-processing ability and note taking. *Contemporary Educational Psychology, 13,* 33-44.

Kiewra, K.A., & Fletcher, H.J. (1984). The relationship between levels of note-taking and achievement. *Human Learning, 3,* 273-280.

Kiewra, K.A., DuBois, N.F., Christian, D., McShane, A., Meyerhoffer, M., & Roskelley, D. (1988). Theoretical and practical aspects of taking, reviewing, and borrowing conventional, skeletal, and matrix lecture notes. Paper presented at the annual meeting of the American Educational Research Association, New Orleans, 1988.

King, A. (1989). Effects of self-questioning training on college students' comprehension of lectures. *Contemporary Educational Psychology, 14,* 1-16.

King, A. (1990a). Enhancing peer interaction and learning in the classroom through reciprocal questioning *American Educational Research Journal, 27,* 664-687.

King, A. (1990b). Reciprocal peer-questioning: A strategy for teaching students how to learn from lectures. The *Clearing House, 64*(2), 131-135.

King, A. (1991a). Effects of training in strategic questioning on children's problem-solving performance. *Journal of Educational Psychology, 83,* 307-317.

King, A. (1991b). Improving lecture comprehension: Effects of a metacognitive strategy. *Applied Cognitive Psychology, 5,* 331-346.

King, A. (1992a). Facilitating elaborative learning through guided student-generated questioning. *Educational Psychologist, 27,* 111-126.

King, A. (1992b). Comparison of self-questioning, summarizing and note taking-review as strategies for learning from lectures. *American Educational Research Journal, 29(2),* 303-323.

King, A. (1993). Making a transition from 'Sage on the Stage' to 'Guide on the Side'. *College Teaching, 41(1),* 30-35.

King, A. (1994a). Autonomy and question asking: The role of personal control in guided student-generated questioning. *Learning and Individual Differences.*

King, A. (1994b). Inquiry as a tool in critical thinking. In Halpern, D. (Ed.), *Changing College Classrooms: New Teaching and Learning Strategies for an Increasingly Complex World.* San Francisco: Jossey-Bass.

King, A. (1994c). Guiding knowledge construction in the classroom: Effects of teaching children how to question and how to explain. *American Educational Research Journal, 31,* 338-368.

King, A., & Rosenshine, B. (1993). Effects of guided cooperative questioning on children's knowledge construction. *Journal of Experimental Education, 61,* 127-148.

Lambiote, J.G., Peale, J., & Dansereau, D.F. (1992). Knowledge maps as review devices: Like 'em or not. Presented at the American Educational Research Association Conference, San Francisco.

Larson, C.O., Dansereau, D.F., Goetz, E.T., & Young, M.D. (1985). Cognitive style and cooperative learning: Transfer of effects. Paper presented at the annual meeting of the Southwest Educational Research Association, Austin, TX.

Larson, C.O., Dansereau, D.F., O'Donnell, A.M., Hythecker, V.I., Lambiote, J.G., & Rocklin, T.R. (1985). Effects of metacognitive and elaborative activity on cooperative learning and transfer. *Contemporary Educational Psychology, 10,* 342-348.

Leinhardt, G., & Smith, D.A., (1985). Expertise in mathematics instruction: Subject matter knowledge. *Journal of Educational Psychology, 77,* 247-271.

Leinhardt, G., (1987). Development of an expert explanation: An analysis of a sequence of subtraction lessons. *Cognition and Instruction, 4,* 225-282.

McNeil, J.D. (1984). *Reading comprehension.* Glenview: Scott Foresman.

Meichenbaum, D. (1977). *Cognitive behaviour modification: An integrative approach.* New York: Plenum.

Mugny, G., & Doise, W. (1978). Socio-cognitive conflict and the structure of individual and collective performances. *European Journal of Social Psychology, 8,* 181-192.

Naveh-Benjamin, M., McKeachie, W.J., Lin, Y., & Tucker, D.G. (1986). Inferring students' cognitive structures and their development using the "Ordered Tree Technique". *Journal of Educational Psychology, 78,* 130-140.

O'Donnell, A.M., & Dansereau, D.F. (1992). Scripted cooperation in student dyads: A method for analyzing and enhancing academic learning and performance. In Hertz-Lazarowitz, R., & Miller, N. (Eds.), *Interaction in cooperative groups: The theoretical anatomy of group learning* (120-141). New York: Cambridge University Press.

O'Donnell, A.M., & Dansereau, D.F. (1993). Learning from lectures: Effects of cooperative review. *Journal of Experimental Education, 6,* 116-125.

O'Donnell, A. (1993a). Personal communication.

O'Donnell, A. (1993b). Cooperative Learning Strategy Instructions. Rutgers: Unpublished materials.

Palincsar, A.S., & Brown A.L. (1989). Instruction for self-regulated reading. In L.B. Resnick & L.E. Klopfer (Eds.), *Toward the thinking curriculum: Current cognitive research.* Alexandria, VA: Association for Supervision and Curriculum Development.

Palincsar, A.S., & Brown, A.L. (1984). Reciprocal teaching of comprehension-fostering and monitoring activities. *Cognition and Instruction, 1,* 117-175.

Paris, S.G., Cross, D., & Lipson, M. (1984). Informed strategies for learning: A program to improve children's reading awareness and comprehension. *Journal of Educational Psychology, 76,* 1239-1252.

Pauk, W. (1974). *How to study in college.* Palo Alto, CA: Houghton Mifflin.

Peper, R.J., & Mayer, R.E. (1986). Generative effects of note-taking during science lectures. *Journal of Educational Psychology, 78,* 34-38.

Perret-Clermont, A. (1980). *Social interaction and cognitive development in children.* New York: Academic Press.

Pressley, M., Goodchild, F., Fleet, J., Zajchowski, R., & Evans, E.D. (1989). The challenges of classroom strategy instruction. *Elementary School Journal, 89,* 301-342

Pressley, M., Borkowski, J.G., & O'Sullivan, J.T. (1984). Memory strategy instruction is made of this: Metamemory and durable strategy use. *Educational Psychologist, 19,* 94-107.

Pressley, M., Symons, S., McDaniel, M.A., Snyder, B.L., & Turnure, J.E. (1988). Elaborative interrogation facilitates acquisition of confusing facts. *Journal of Educational Psychology, 80(3),* 268-278.

Pressley, M., Wood, E., Woloshyn, V.E., Martin, V., King, A., & Menke, D. (1992). Encouraging mindful use of prior knowledge: Attempting to construct explanatory answers facilitates learning. *Educational Psychologist, 27,* 91-109.

Reinhart, S.D., Stahl, S.D., & Erickson, L.G. (1986). Some effects of summarization training on reading and studying. *Reading Research Quarterly, 22,* 422-438.

Resnick, L. (1987). *Education and Learning to Think.* Washington, DC: National Academy Press.

Risch, N.L., & Kiewra, K.A. (1989). Content and form variations in note taking: Effects among junior high students. *Journal of Educational Research, 83,* 355-357.

Rosenshine, B., Chapman, S. and Meister, C. (1992). Teaching Students to Generate Questions: A Review of Research of the Effectiveness of Different Concrete Prompts. Paper presented at the annual meeting of the AERA: San Francisco, CA: April, 1992.

Ross, S.M., & DiVesta, F.J. (1976). Oral summary as a review strategy for enhancing recall of text material. *Journal of Educational Psychology, 68,* 689-695.

Rumelhart, D.E., & McClelland, J.L. (1986). *Parallel distributed processing: Explorations in the microstructure of cognition.* Cambridge: MIT Press.

Schank, R.C. (1975). Conceptual information processing. North Holland: Amsterdam.

Schank, R. (1986). *Explanations patterns: Understanding mechanically and creatively.* Hillsdale, NJ: Erlbaum.

Sternberg, R. (1987). Questioning and intelligence. *Questioning Exchange, 1,* 11-13.

Thomas, J.W., & Rhower, W.D. (1986). Academic studying: The role of learning strategies. *Educational Psychologist, 21,* 19-41.

Toffler, A. (1990). *Powershift: Knowledge, wealth, and violence at the edge of the 21st century.* New York: Bantam.

Van Dijk, T.A., & Kintsch, W. (1983). *Strategies for discourse comprehension.* New York: Academic Press.

Vygotsky, L.S. (1978). Internalization of higher cognitive functions. In M. Cole, V. John-Steiner, S. Scribner, and E. Souberman (Eds. & Trans.), *Mind in society: The development of higher psychological processes* (pp. 52-57). Cambridge: Harvard University Press.

Webb, N.M. (1989). Peer interaction and learning in small groups. *International Journal of Educational Research,* 21-39.

Wittrock, M.C. (1990). Generative processes of comprehension. *Educational Psychologist,* 24, 345-376.

Wittrock, M.C., & Alesandrini, K. (1990). Generation of summaries and analogies and analytic and holistic abilities. *American Educational Research Journal, 27,* 489-502.

Wong, B.Y.L. (1985). Self-questioning instructional research: A review. *Review of Educational Research, 55,* 227-268.

CHAPTER 4

Cognitive Strategies for Reading Comprehension

Sonya Symons and Cathy Richards • Acadia University
Catherine Greene • University of Windsor

Although reading comprehension is often perceived as a critical part of the elementary school curriculum, it is also a prevalent component of successful learning in secondary school. Secondary school students are expected to read, understand, and expand upon narrative and expository text, write papers, and give oral presentations, all of which involve reading comprehension skills. Students who *actively* apply comprehension-based cognitive strategies are at a definite advantage compared to more passive students. The challenge for teachers is to encourage "passive" readers to take a more active role in their learning. In this chapter we describe specific strategies that promote active reading. To facilitate understanding of how strategies may affect performance, we will first describe some of the cognitive demands associated with reading to comprehend.

The skills associated with successful comprehension include semantic encoding, proposition assembly, integration, and text modeling (Perfetti & Curtis, 1986). *Semantic encoding* is the link between simply decoding words and giving meaning to words. Giving meaning includes interpretation of words within a context by using relevant prior knowledge. For example, the word *fair* would be interpreted differently in the sentence "The weather forecast calls for sunny and fair" than it would in the sentence "The weather was pleasant and sunny for the fair" (Perfetti & Curtis, 1986, p. 26). As a reader decodes words in context, propositions are assembled and integrated. A *proposition* is a relation between a predicate and one or more nouns which forms an elementary unit of meaning. For example, in the sentence "The automatic reel was too expensive, so Fred bought the manual one" (Perfetti & Curtis, 1986, p. 27), "manual [reel]" forms one proposition, "reel" being the noun and "manual" being the predicate. Word meaning and propositional processes help the reader to construct a *text model*: a set of higher-level propositions that summarize a larger number of text propositions. The text model can be likened to the "gist" or underlying meaning of the text. Construction of the text model also draws upon the reader's personal knowledge to help organize the text. This kind of personal knowledge is often referred to as *schemata*. For example, the reader who watches or plays a lot of baseball is likely to have a "baseball schema" that includes the rules and physical setup of the game. When these readers watch games or read about them, they are more likely to recall "schema-relevant" information about the game (e.g., that the bases were loaded) than "schema-irrelevant" information (e.g., there were a lot of fans in attendance). Knowledge about the structure of different types of text also helps in the construction of text models (e.g., knowing the difference between narrative and expository text).

In addition to the demands of reading to comprehend, students are faced with the tasks of reading to learn and to memorize. While learning and memorizing involve study skills in addition to the processes involved in reading to comprehend, study skills in the absence of comprehension will not facilitate learning. Thus, comprehension strategies may also be considered to be study strategies, since better comprehension will eventually translate into better learning and recall. Cognitive strategies can be useful in building the text model, or gist of the text: they help the reader organize information by deciding what is most important. Strategies can also help the reader relate the information to what they already know, thereby improving recall in the future. Attention is a limited resource, and if directed at irrelevant or distracting detail it is, in a sense, wasted. Directing attention to the most important aspects of text and away from less relevant information can maximize the learning that occurs during reading.

Pressley, Goodchild, Fleet, Zajchowski and Evans (1989) stressed that "good strategy users" possess metacognitive knowledge about strategies. Metacognitive knowledge includes an understanding of when, where, and how to apply the strategies, as well as assessing the success of the strategy. These researchers, therefore, advocate that teachers explain and model strategic procedures and provide guided practice and corrective feedback when students use strategies. It is important to provide students with knowledge of when and where to use specific strategies, and where appropriate, to have students activate prior knowledge about material that is to be read. Instructional recommendations from multi-strategy programs, such as reciprocal instruction (Palincsar & Brown, 1984), direct instruction of strategies (Duffy et al., 1987), and the strategies intervention model (e.g., Clark, Deshler, Schumaker, Alley, & Warner, 1984; Deshler & Schumaker, 1988), include introducing strategy use through teacher modeling, facilitating learning through discussion groups, and providing opportunities for students to take responsibility for their own strategy use in a gradual manner. The teacher who is able to incorporate effective strategy instruction will help students not only to learn specific procedures to attain academic goals but to become more actively engaged in their own learning (Harris & Pressley, 1991).

In this chapter, we describe some empirically-supported strategies that enhance reading comprehension in secondary school students. The bulk of the strategies reported here have been investigated individually. This reflects the difficulty in isolating the independent merits of strategies in multi-strategy programs and the fact that these intervention programs have been implemented largely with younger learners or adolescents with learning disabilities (e.g., Deshler & Schumaker, 1988). The reporting of individual strategies may be appropriate for teachers who are looking for one or two specific techniques to enhance targeted areas of reading/studying. Following a description of each strategy, we review some of the ways in which it has been instructed successfully. These descriptions are intended to serve as general guidelines. There is room left for individual interpretation and adaptation; teacher input and the design of strategy instruction has been associated with greater learning gains than experimenter-implemented instruction (Alvermann & Moore, 1991).

Prior Knowledge Activation

Encouraging students to use their background knowledge increases the likelihood that they will comprehend and recall text (Baldwin, Peleg-Bruckner, & McClintock, 1985; Recht & Leslie, 1988). It is believed that prior knowledge facilitates recall by drawing attention to the important parts of text and away from less important details. It also facilitates inferencing and provides a structure for recall. For example, when reading that "the car was stopped by the police after it sped through the YIELD sign," knowledge of driving rules and the concept "yield" would help the reader infer that the driver had broken the law in not slowing down at the YIELD sign. Similarly, knowledge of a "who-done-it" story structure implies the need to name a weapon and suspect when recalling the story.

One way to activate prior knowledge is to use small-group discussion prior to having students read. Schmidt, DeVolder, DeGrave, Moust, and Patel (1989) tested the effectiveness of small-group problem-solving discussion on the learning of biology concepts by ninth- and tenth-grade students. They had groups of six or seven students develop, with a teacher/facilitator, explanations of a natural phenomenon. Students were instructed to focus their discussion on explanation. For example, "A red blood cell is put into pure water under a microscope. The blood cell swells rapidly and eventually bursts. Another blood cell is added to a solution of salt in water and is observed to shrink. How can this phenomenon be explained?" The teacher acted as a chairperson, summarizing different points of view at regular intervals and terminating the discussion when no one wished to add any further clarifications of explanations. The discussions lasted approximately 10 minutes. Following this, some students also read a six-page passage on osmosis and diffusion. On a subsequent memory test where students were instructed to write all they could remember from the passage, students who had discussed the red blood cell problem recalled significantly more of the information presented in the text than students who discussed a problem unrelated to osmosis. Moreover, the discussions facilitated students' recall of information found in the text independent of the students' knowledge base. Discussion facilitated the learning of students who, prior to reading about osmosis, had no specific knowledge of osmosis. It is possible that the discussion activated the students' general knowledge related to cell structure, highlighted the lack of specific knowledge about osmosis, and facilitated incorporation of the new material with general concepts.

Another way to activate prior knowledge is through the use of *analogy*, or the process of reasoning from parallel cases. There is some support for the theory that providing students with familiar analogies prior to reading new information improves learning. Hayes and Tierney (1982) showed that analogies activate general knowledge as well as specific analogous knowledge. They provided eleventh- and twelfth-grade students with a passage about baseball prior to reading about cricket. Students who read about baseball remembered more of the cricket passage, and learned more about cricket from the passage, than did students who had not read an analogous passage. Moreover, recall was enhanced by making explicit the analogy between cricket and baseball. Analogies were more effective if the students had more knowledge of the topic. In this case, the baseball analogy was most beneficial to those students who were most knowledgeable about baseball.

Not all analogies are equally effective in promoting comprehension and recall of text. Analogies which have little surface resemblance to the to-be-learned content, and/or which are familiar and concrete, appear to promote recall and understanding of text. Research by Halpern, Hansen, and Riefer (1990) explored the differences between "near" and "far" analogies, where "near" analogies have high surface similarity (e.g., baseball and basketball) and "far" domains contain few obvious links between topics (e.g., baseball and mathematics). When presented with scientific passages to read, students reading passages with an accompanying "far" analogy recalled more facts than students who read passages with a "near" analogy. In addition, students with a far analogy gave correct answers to more questions that required inferences or comprehension of novel analogies. In fact, the near analogy did not promote learning more than did reading a passage with no analogy. These results suggest that, in some cases, far-domain analogies, but not near-domain analogies, may be useful in promoting comprehension and memory of science content.

An example from Halpern et al. (1990) of the difference between a near- and a far-domain analogy may prove useful in understanding why far-domain analogies promote comprehension of scientific text. The near analogy used for the lymph system was the movement of blood through veins; the far-domain analogy was the movement of water through the spaces in a sponge. Why did the sponge prove to be a better analogy for learning about the lymph system than did the movement of blood through veins? The most likely answer is that the near-domain analogy does not require as much effort on the part of the learner. The lymph and blood systems are alike both on the surface and in terms of function or structure, whereas the flow of water through the spaces in a sponge differs from the lymph system greatly in terms of surface similarity, but not in terms of function. With a far-domain analogy, the reader has to process the information at a deeper level to go beyond the surface differences to understand the structural similarities. This greater effort, or deeper processing, translates into better learning.

Halpern et al. (1990) further caution that analogies should also be *familiar* to the students and highly *imageable* (i.e., the analogy should easily elicit a mental image). The familiarity issue is probably obvious: if the learner is unfamiliar with the analogy, it is difficult to use it to understand something that is supposedly also unfamiliar to the learner. Analogies that are imageable are more effective than abstract ones because they create a stronger memory trace, one with both verbal and spatial components (Paivio, 1986). These studies suggest that prior knowledge can play a role in improving not only long- and short-term recall of related information, but comprehension as well, particularly when enriched by other strategies such as small-group discussion and problem analysis. Analogies work to activate the learner's prior knowledge, enhancing comprehension by providing a framework for understanding new information and integrating it with that which is already known.

There is a debate as to whether activating inaccurate prior knowledge can actually interfere with learning (Alvermann, Smith, & Readence, 1985). There is no instructional evidence that this is the case with secondary school students, but there is some research that suggests that interference can occur for elementary-school students if materials activate their previously held misconceptions (Woloshyn, Paivio, & Pressley, 1994). Alternatively, other research findings suggest that activating prior knowledge highlights the differences between new information and previously-held beliefs, and the process of changing those knowledge structures to accommodate the new information *promotes* learning (Schmidt et al., 1989).

Summarization

The ability to summarize text is a crucial reading and study skill. By reducing large amounts of information to more manageable units, summarization enables readers to learn in an economical fashion, extract important ideas, and recall text (Bretzing & Kulhavy, 1979). Kintsch and van Dijk's (1978) model of reading suggests that proficient readers extract a 'gist' of the text which can be considered a summary. Brown and Day (1983) identify six rules that readers utilize spontaneously when creating text summaries:

1. deletion of unimportant or trivial information;
2. deletion of redundant information;
3. substitution of superordinate terms for lists (e.g., if a list contains items such as chairs, tables, sofas, the term "furniture" could replace the individual items);
4. substitution of a superordinate action term for a list of actions (e.g., "John cooked dinner" for John fried fish, John boiled potatoes, John made a salad, etc.);
5. selection of a topic sentence for each paragraph from the text if one is provided by the author;
6. invention of a topic sentence if one did not appear in the text.

Brown and Day (1983) examined the use of these summarization rules by students in grades 5, 7, and 10 and in college. They found that students at all ages use deletion of trivial and redundant information effectively, but there were age differences in the use of a superordinate term for lists, with 10th-grade and college students more efficient in their use of superordination than the younger students. There was a similar age-related difference in the use of the selection of a topic sentence. The invention rule was the most difficult for the students, with 10th-grade students using the rule on only one-third of the occasions when it would be appropriate to do so. None of these students were experiencing academic difficulty or had been identified as having reading problems, and while they were using most of the rules some of the time, only the delete strategy was used very efficiently. There was a lot of room for improvement on the more sophisticated strategies of superordination and selecting or inventing topic sentences. This suggests that instruction in the rules of summarization may improve the note taking and study skills of all students.

Direct instruction has proven to be an effective way to teach students to use the Brown and Day (1983) summarization rules. Direct instruction involves both explicit process instruction and self-monitoring instruction so that students learn to use the strategy in a self-regulated manner. Strategy use is modeled, practice is guided, students are monitored with corrective feedback, and finally the acquired skills are practiced independently. The specific approach to summarization instruction outlined here is a summary of the approach described by Hare and Borchardt (1984).

The first step is to ensure that students understand the concept of "summary." Discussion of a "summary help sheet" like the one found in Table 4-1 can make the summarization rules explicit and clear. This help sheet is very similar to the one used by Hare and Borchardt (1984) and describes the delete strategy in steps 3a and 3c, the select and invent strategies in step 3b, and an integration strategy in step 3d. Discussion of the help sheet should include an explicit definition of what a summary is, a step-by-step description of the help sheet, and a model of the construction of a summary using the steps on the help sheet.

Table 4-1
Sample helpsheet for describing the summarization strategy.

Follow these Steps to Write a Summary

1. **Be sure that you have understood what you have read.**
   Ask yourself, "What was the general theme?" and "What did the author say?". Try to re-state the main idea in your own words.

2. **Look back to the text.**
   Reread the text to make sure that you got the main idea right. Also make sure you understand what the important parts of the text are. Mark the important points of the text.

3. **Write the summary following these suggestions.**
   a. *Collapse lists.* Try to replace a list with one word or phrase. For example, if you see "elms, oaks, birches, and spruce", replace it with "trees".

   b. *Use topic sentences.* A topic sentence is one that summarizes a paragraph. Some paragraphs will have a topic sentence in them. If there is one, include it in your summary. If a paragraph does not include a topic sentence you should write one yourself.

   c. *Get rid of unnecessary detail.* Some text contains unimportant or repetitive information. Get rid of unimportant or repetitive information, since a summary is meant to be short.

   d. *Collapse paragraphs.* Some paragraphs are more necessary than others. Sometimes the main ideas are summarized in one paragraph and the details filled in by other paragraphs. Decide which paragraphs are necessary for the summary and which ones you can get rid of.

4. **Check your summary.**
   Did you leave in any lists? If you did, replace it with one word or phrase. Did you repeat yourself? If you did, get rid of the repetition. Did you skip anything important?

5. **Polish the summary.**
   Read your summary to make sure that it flows well and doesn't sound unnatural. Fix this if it is a problem for your summary. You might insert connecting words like "and", "because", or "therefore". You may also need to write an introductory or concluding statement.

Adapted from Hare & Borchardt (1984).

Students should then be given an opportunity to create their own summaries. To ensure that summaries are concise, it is advisable to impose a limit on the number of words used in the summary. A general rule of thumb might be that the summary contain no more than 10% of the number of words in the original passage.

After this introduction to summary writing, the rules should be reviewed and the students provided with practice on more text passages, with longer text passages being used as the quality of students' summaries improves. Students should be provided feedback about the quality of their summaries, including specific statements about their application of the summarization rules. Hare and Borchardt (1984) used this direct instructional approach with a group of secondary school students and found improvement in summary writing after only three sessions of instruction, a learning gain that was also apparent in a two-week follow-up.

Given that a summary is an indication of text comprehension, this strategy is clearly an important one to incorporate into a strategy instructional repertoire. Summary writing gets students actively involved with reading and requires that students integrate what they are reading with their prior knowledge of the topic (e.g., in providing a superordinate term for a list of items, students are activating their background knowledge with the new material). Several studies suggest that direct instruction of summarization is also beneficial for students with learning disabilities (Gajria & Salvia, 1992; Malone & Mastropieri, 1992). Some of the rules may prove difficult for the students to implement such as inventing topic sentences and identifying implicit main ideas. This may be due to difficulty in deciding on relative importance of text, so discussing the relative importance of ideas in a passage may improve students' effectiveness at applying these rules.

Text Structure Instruction

Knowledge about the organization of text facilitates text comprehension and recall by giving students an appropriate frame of reference in which to incorporate new information (Slater, Graves & Piche, 1985). Models of text structure traditionally focus on two major types of texts: *expository texts* such as textbooks and training manuals, where the main purpose is to communicate information to a reader to learn something, and *narrative texts* such as stories, in which the main purpose is more to entertain or tell a story than to provide information (Weaver & Kintsch, 1991). Since expository and narrative text structures differ, suggestions for teaching the two types of text structure will be discussed separately.

Expository text structure

Expository texts are typically classified by their rhetorical structure, described in terms such as *classification, illustration, comparison/contrast, causal, collection, problem/solution,* and *procedural description* (Weaver & Kintsch, 1991). These types of expository text structures provide the reader with a systematic, organized strategy for encoding information from text and for retrieving it from memory.

Meyer, Brandt, and Bluth (1980) had teachers direct students' attention to the structure-relevant parts in expository passages. For example, in a passage with a problem/solution text structure, students would underline the parts of the text that were consistent with a main problem and a solution. Another example of text structure is the comparison/contrast format, which begins with the comparison of two concepts or ideas to determine their similarity. The discussion could begin with a broad description of each concept, working toward more specific attributes to explain how each concept is alike, then moving onto a description of how the two concepts differ. *Top-down* structure means that text propositions are represented in a hierarchical structure starting from the top and working downward.

An example of a top-down problem/solution structure describing oil spills and supertankers might include the following. The passage first starts with an abstract, general concept: *the need to prevent oil spills from supertankers.* Next, chunks of information are specified about the general concept: *a typical supertanker carries a half-million tons of oil and is the size of five football fields.* Then specific items relate back to the general concept: *a wrecked supertanker spills oil in the ocean.* Then more specific elaborations are given about the specific items: *this oil kills animals, birds and microscopic plant life.* Next the reader would start at the top again, stating a general concept about the solution to this problem, and work downward. To direct students to text structure, statements alerting students to the problem/solution structure in each passage were underlined. For example, the supertanker passage began with, '*A problem of vital concern* is the prevention of oil spills from super tanker,' and '*The solution to the problem* is not to immediately halt the use of tankers on the ocean' (p. 102). Directing students' attention to the parts of the text relevant to the problem/solution structure improved recall.

Teaching students to use a structural organizer is another way to improve comprehension of expository text. The approach described here is that used by Slater, Graves, and Piche (1985). Students were given eight 700-word passages of expository text taken from a junior high school history text. Teachers described the benefits of using a top-down structure as an aid for retaining information, defined the top-down organization, and provided a brief example of a passage and its organization. The passages were classified as one of these five text structures: problem–solution, cause–effect, claim–counterclaim, and claim support–conclusion. Students were taught to use the structural organizer with an outline grid, and to fill it in as they read the passages (see Figure 4-1). Structure instruction with all five organized types of text was found to equally facilitate students' comprehension and recall of expository text. The intent would be for students to internalize the knowledge they have gained from using the text structure prompts, so

Figure 4-1

Authors can organize their writing in several ways. One way of organizing a passage is to list causes and their effects. A cause and effect passage consists of a number of causes and their effects, with supporting information related to each pair. Additionally, a cause and effect passage may include related topics and supporting information for these topics. For example, you might read a passage about the causes and effects of the increase in fuel costs in the United States.

Blank Model   Completed Document

Rising Fuel Costs in the United States

Blank Model	Completed Document
1. Cause: _____	1. Cause: Greater demand for fuel
Support: _____ _____	Support: How much the demand for fuel has increased up to the present
Support: _____ _____	Support: How much the demand for fuel will increase in the future
2. Effect: _____	2. Effect: Increased fuel costs
Support: _____ _____	Support: How much fuel costs have increased
Support: _____ _____ _____	Support: How this increase in fuel costs reduces the distance people can afford to travel
3. Related Topics: _____ _____	3. Related Topics: How fuel increases are forecast
Support: _____ _____	Support: Details about how fuel increases are forecast for air transportation
Support: _____ _____	Support: Details about how fuel increases are forecast for ground transportation

Adapted from Slater, Graves, & Piche (1985).

that they develop their own cognitive structures to aid the recall and understanding of expository text.

Narrative text structure

Narrative text entertains, provokes arguments, and may simply make a point to the reader. Narrative text has a specific structure that can be anticipated by the reader. Narratives are expressions of event-based experiences described in terms of episodes of a story that can be anticipated by the reader (Graesser, Golding & Long, 1991). This structure is typically made up of:

a) a main character who has goals, motives, beliefs, attitudes, and emotions;
b) a time period or setting;
c) a major goal the main character attempts to achieve;
d) a plot unraveling how the character resolves a conflict to achieve the goal;
e) an outcome describing whether the character achieves the goal;
f) a moral and theme (such as perseverance or cooperation).

This narrative structure is commonly referred to as *story grammar*, since it assigns a hierarchical structure to the textual information. The structure of story grammar itself acts as a model which can be used as a strategy to improve both story comprehension and writing (Olson & Gee, 1988).

Narrative text instruction has proven to be particularly effective with younger and poorer readers (Short & Ryan, 1984). While research is scarce regarding instruction with average readers in secondary schools, narrative text instruction has been useful for secondary school students with learning disabilities. Story grammar training has been found to facilitate the processing of story elements and provides these students with techniques to improve their understanding of the story as a cohesive unit (Montague, Maddux & Dereshiwsky, 1990).

For example, Gurney, Gersten, Dimino, and Carnine (1990) implemented a story grammar strategy to teach special education secondary school students to comprehend short stories. The stories contained at least one discernible conflict or problem and had an identifiable main character. After students read a story aloud, teachers defined and explained four major story grammar components: 1) *identification of the main problem/conflict*, adding pertinent background information and new vocabulary; 2) *character clues*, clarifying major and minor problems, determining the source of the problem and the theme; 3) *resolution*, defining how the character solves—or fails to solve—a problem; and 4) *theme*, defining what the author is trying to tell the reader. The students were taught to determine the theme by: (a) naming the main character(s) and the major conflict problem; (b) reviewing the resolution and conclusion; (c) determining which character clues were related to the conflict problem; and (d) using this information to generate a statement about what the story meant to them and what the author was trying to say. The teachers modeled each of the steps, explaining how each character clue did or did not relate to the conflict, then stating and justifying the theme. Throughout training, teachers used story grammar note sheets (see Figure 4-2) that helped organize, outline, and reflect story grammar elements such as the main problem/conflict,

Figure 4-2
Student notesheet used during story grammar strategy instruction

NAME_____

STORY_____

1. Protagonist (main character):_____

2. Character clues: _____

_____

_____

3. Name the problem/conflict:

_____

_____

_____

4. How do the characters try to solve the problem?

_____

_____

_____

5. Tell how the problem gets solved or doesn't get solved:

_____

_____

_____

6. Conclusion: Is there an added twist or complication at the end of the story? Tell what happens at the end of the story if it is different from what you said in number 5.

_____

_____

_____

7. Theme: What is the author trying to say?

_____

_____

_____

_____

8. Important Events: (What you think would be important to remember.)

_____

_____

_____

_____

_____

Adapted from Gurney, Gersten, Dimino, & Carnine (1990).

character clues, resolution, and theme.

To summarize, text structure instruction is important because it specifies the logical connections among ideas in expository and narrative text. Recognizing and utilizing text structure is an important organizational strategy for remembering and recalling information (Meyer, Brandt & Bluth, 1980). The use of structural organizers with expository text highlights text structure. Narrative text instruction, or story grammar instruction, seems particularly successful for students with learning disabilities. The use of note sheets in story grammar training provides a framework to focus students' attention on story elements. However, teacher discussions of vocabulary and story elements, as well as modeled instruction with an interactive focus, seem to be important components that lead students to use this strategy independently.

Self-questioning

Self-questioning encourages readers to become actively engaged in reading and less dependent on external aids by learning either to formulate self-posed or to imitate teacher-posed questions (Frase & Schwartz, 1975). To learn to pose questions, attention must be directed to important content and away from less relevant detail. For example, the important points in a particular story may include a character selecting a plan for achieving a goal and encountering an obstacle to reaching that goal. Examples of questions that would improve organization include: "Who is the main character?" "What does the main character appear to be striving for?" "How does the character deal with this obstacle?" "Did the character reach the goal; if so, what helped most?" (Singer & Donlan, 1982). It is important to remember that students must be taught how to construct good comprehension questions if the technique is to be effective. By learning how to generate questions, appropriate information is selected from the text to organize information in a meaningful way, thereby improving students' understanding and recall of text.

Teaching students to generate questions has improved recall of textual information for secondary school students (Frase & Schwartz, 1975). Secondary school students with average and low verbal ability can be taught to construct good comprehension questions while reading. For example, in a study by Andre and Anderson (1978-1979), students learned how to generate questions by identifying the main idea in each paragraph, then forming questions that asked for new examples of these main ideas and/or concepts.

MacDonald (1986) reported a study where teachers were successful in instructing average readers to actively seek information while reading and to generate good comprehension questions. First, teachers demonstrated the difference between specified and implied information. They explained that specified information in a passage is 'something we know for sure' and implied information is 'something we need to find out' because it requires more information before becoming specified. For example, the word *postpone* implies that the time of some event was changed to a later date, but the specific time is unknown, so further reading is required to specify the term. Then students practiced identifying the types of information needed and the questions required to obtain that information, and played a 20-questions game to practice answering questions. Another game to practice identifying missing or given information as they read involves answering 'things I know for sure' and 'things we need to find out' for isolated words, for sentences, for isolated paragraphs, and for paragraphs in story context. This is done to teach students to ask good comprehension questions as they read a story.

Next, students were taught how to identify main ideas and supporting details, including the most common locations of these within paragraphs. Finally, students were taught which main ideas are most important for understanding and remembering a story; they practiced ranking the main ideas and generating questions about the ones that ranked highest. Instruction occurred during four days; in each training session, a summarization of the previous sessions and an overview of what was to be done in the current session preceded new instruction. Students were then given a demonstration, an explanation, guided practice on what was demonstrated, feedback, and then more extensive practice in pairs. Starting after the second session, students spent 20 minutes of each subsequent session applying what they had learned to reading a novel. Each session ended with a review and rationale for what was covered in that session.

MacDonald (1986) summarized the question generation strategy instruction as:

> (1) identify the main idea in each paragraph; (2) after reading four paragraphs, decide which is the most important idea so far; (3) make up a question about what you need to find out about this main idea; and (4) read further to see if you can answer the question (p. 295).

Although these training sessions improved the quality of questions for students with average reading ability, it did not improve the questioning skills and recall of text material of students with below-average ability in reading. However, Wong and Jones (1982) were successful in teaching a self-questioning technique to eighth- and ninth-grade students with learning disabilities. Instruction increased their ability to identify important textual passages, as well as their ability to construct good comprehension questions. One important difference in the Wong and Jones study was that students received extensive pretraining to ensure that they understood the concept of a main idea. Students were first taught to paraphrase the main idea into a question before underlining the main idea and formulating questions on the remainder of the paragraphs in the passage. They received corrective feedback on their identification of main ideas. Students then received instruction on the application of the self-questioning technique. This preparatory training was important because these students needed to understand the concept of a main idea before starting the self-questioning training.

Training students to ask questions does improve comprehension of textual material. This strategy encourages active involvement in reading and, when combined with instruction in strategy monitoring, increases students' awareness of important textual content as well as their ability to construct good comprehension questions. It seems that students must first learn to identify main ideas in order to benefit from self-questioning training. Students with learning disabilities may need longer training sessions in both main idea identification and written prompts to be as fluent in the use of this strategy as students without learning disabilities.

Semantic Mapping

Semantic maps are visual representations of the meaning or organization of text that illustrate how text concepts are structurally related to each other and how ideas in texts are organized in associative ways (Flood, 1986). Semantic mapping is often recommended for learning expository prose, since students may lack understanding of the structure of text that is not written in a narrative format. Semantic maps highlight the interrelatedness of ideas, and help students to understand the main ideas and gist of text. The visual representation may also aid recall, as it provides a visual cue for recalling the material. Much of the research on semantic mapping involves providing students with prepared structural aids, known as *graphic organizers,* but students can be taught to generate their own graphic representations of the meaning of text. Hereafter, the student-generated graphic organizers will be referred to as semantic maps.

While instruction in semantic mapping is often recommended, it should be noted that effective use of semantic mapping may be difficult to teach; it is best incorporated in a multidimensional approach to cognitive strategy instruction. For example, Bean, Singer, Sorter and Frazee (1986) found that training in semantic mapping improved secondary school students' reading comprehension only when there had been previous training in summarization and question generation. Following such instruction, Bean et al. (1986) taught tenth-grade students to generate semantic maps using the following three-step procedure: 1) selecting a topic sentence that tied together subordinate ideas; 2) drawing a graphic organizer displaying interrelationships among ideas in the text; and 3) creating a generalization or concluding statement based on the information depicted in the graphic organizer. Students contributed ideas and constructed organizers in groups, while teachers gave feedback until students could construct their own organizers. The particulars of the semantic maps were negotiated by the teacher and the students, with the consensus being that a map listing the background details on the left, the main events and people in the middle, and the results on the right would provide a good way of visually depicting the content of history passages. An example of a map generated by a student to depict the Industrial Revolution in Japan is provided in Figure 4-3 (from Bean et al., 1986).

Students with reading disabilities have also benefited from instruction in semantic mapping. Bos and Anders (1990) compared the effectiveness of three interactive vocabulary strategies and definition-based instruction on the reading comprehension of adolescents with learning disabilities. They contended that vocabulary instruction fo-

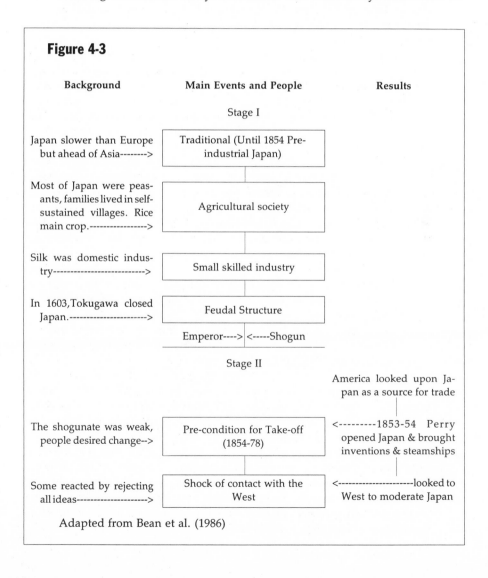

Figure 4-3

Background	Main Events and People	Results

Stage I

Japan slower than Europe but ahead of Asia--------> | Traditional (Until 1854 Pre-industrial Japan) |

Most of Japan were peasants, families lived in self-sustained villages. Rice main crop.----------------> | Agricultural society |

Silk was domestic industry---------------------------> | Small skilled industry |

In 1603,Tokugawa closed Japan.----------------------> | Feudal Structure |

Emperor---->|<-----Shogun

Stage II

America looked upon Japan as a source for trade

The shogunate was weak, people desired change--> | Pre-condition for Take-off (1854-78) | <---------1853-54 Perry opened Japan & brought inventions & steamships

Some reacted by rejecting all ideas--------------------> | Shock of contact with the West | <----------------------looked to West to moderate Japan

Adapted from Bean et al. (1986)

cused on active learning and the promotion of deep processing of meaning would have a "spillover" effect on comprehension; the results of their study support this prediction. The syntactic/semantic analysis instruction group were taught how to use a relationship matrix that lists the important ideas along the top and the related vocabulary along the side. The task for the students was to decide how the vocabulary items were related to the important ideas in the text. The chart can be developed by the teacher and used by the students as a learning strategy. An example of such a chart for the topic of the Fourth Amendment and the right to privacy (from Bos, Anders, Filip, & Jaffe, 1989) is provided in Figure 4-4.

In addition to the use of the relationship matrix, students also completed "cloze" type sentences that were based on the matrix. Students were required to supply a missing word in a sentence, for example, "Joan went to the lake to ___ [*swim, fish*, etc.]." Prior to reading the passages, students predicted the relationships using the matrix and predicted the answers to the cloze sentences. After reading the passage, the students discussed their relationship matrices and were encouraged to describe how the text confirmed/disconfirmed their predictions. This type of interactive vocabulary instruction was compared to vocabulary instruction where students were directly taught the definitions of the vocabulary items, with oral recitation to encourage accurate pronunciation and speed, and memorization of brief definitions. They found that an approach they labelled *semantic/syntactic feature analysis* was better than traditional definition-based instruction on a variety of indices, including understanding of the instructed vocabulary and comprehension of the passage, and several measures of the vocabulary and conceptual units included in the students' written recall of the instructed passage. These learning gains were maintained at a four-week follow-up. Bos and Anders (1990) concluded:

> Learning, especially long-term learning, seems to occur under conditions that provide adequate opportunities for students to (a) activate and instantiate prior knowledge, (b) share that knowledge with each other, (c) make predictions concerning the relationships among concepts, and (d) read to confirm and justify their predictions.

There is support for the recommendation that teaching students to represent the meaning of text visually does appear to improve comprehension and recall of text content. The research in this area should be interpreted with some caution, in that there has been very little work done with secondary school students and very little research conducted with actual teachers in actual classrooms. Perhaps a conservative approach is warranted here. This strategy may be effective when used in combination with other strategies—discussion groups activating prior knowledge (Bos & Anders, 1990) or summarization and question generation (Bean et al., 1986).

Figure 4-4

Important Ideas

+ = positive relationship - = negative relationship 0 = no relationship ? = uncertain Related Vocabulary	Citizens right to privacy versus	Society needs to keep law and order	Police search with a search warrant	Police search without a search warrant	Evidence allowed in court
search and seizure					
unreasonable search and seizure					
probable cause to search					
your property and possessions					
absolute privacy					
you give consent					
hot pursuit					
moving vehicles					
stop-and-frisk					
plain view					
during an arrest					
evidence					
exclusionary rule					

Adapted from Bos et al. (1989).

Summary and Concluding Comments

The aim of this chapter was to describe some of the strategies that are associated with good reading and to provide some instructional hints on how to start teaching strategies that promote active reading. The task of the teacher implementing strategy instruction is to develop a good understanding of the thinking associated with using a strategy, and then to provide opportunities that encourage students to use the strategy independently. The strategies described in this chapter require varying degrees of materials and teacher support. With those strategies that require materials support, such as structural analysis and semantic mapping, the long-term goal is for students to internalize these knowledge structures as a framework for acquiring new information.

All of the strategies described in this chapter share the common goal of encouraging more "active" reading (Singer, 1980). In the words of Pearson and Fielding (1991):

> Students understand and remember ideas better when they have to transform those ideas from one form to another. Apparently it is this transformation process the *author's* ideas become *reader's* ideas, rendering them more memorable. Examined from the teacher's perspective, what this means is that teachers have many options to choose from when they try to engage students more actively in their own comprehension; summarizing, monitoring, engaging relevant knowledge, creating visual representation, and requiring students to ask their own questions all seem to "generate learning." (p. 847)

This ambitious goal cannot be achieved through short-term interventions; meaningful instruction must take place in a variety of domains over the long term. It is our contention, however, that increasing students' use of strategies that are associated with active reading is warranted. The expectation should not be that students can be taught to use these strategies flexibly and independently in just a few sessions of instruction but, rather, that students can become more actively engaged in the reading process through teacher modeling and direct instruction of cognitive strategies.

Recommended Readings

The reader interested in reviews of the literature on secondary school reading, studying, comprehension instruction, and cognitive strategy instruction is referred to the following sources:

Alvermann, D.E., & Moore, D.W. (1991). Secondary school reading. In R. Barr, M.L. Kamil, P. Mosenthal, & P.D.

Pearson (Eds.), *Handbook of reading research* (vol. 2) (pp. 815-860). White Plains, NY: Longman.

Anderson, T.H., & Armbruster, B.B. (1984). Studying. In P.D. Pearson, R. Barr, M.L. Kamil, & P. Mosenthal (Eds.), *Handbook of reading research* (vol. 1) (pp. 657-679).

Pearson, P.D., & Fielding, L. (1991). Comprehension instruction. In R. Barr, M.L. Kamil, P. Mosenthal, & P.D. Pearson (Eds.), *Handbook of reading research*, vol. 2 (pp. 815-860). White Plains, NY: Longman.

Pressley, M., Harris, K.R., & Guthrie, J.T. (Eds.) (1992). *Promoting academic competence and literacy in school*. San Diego, CA: Academic Press.

REFERENCES

Alvermann, D.E., & Moore, D.W. (1991). Secondary school reading. In R. Barr, M.L. Kamil, P. Mosenthal, & P.D. Pearson (Eds.), *Handbook of reading research* (vol. II, pp. 951-983). White Plains, NY: Longman.

Alvermann, D.E., Smith, L.C., & Readance, J.E. (1985). Prior knowledge activation and the comprehension of compatible and incompatible text. *Reading Research Quarterly, 20,* 420-436.

Anderson, T.H., & Armbruster, B.B. (1984). Studying. In P.D. Pearson, R. Barr, M.L. Kamil, & P. Mosenthal (Eds.), *Handbook of reading research* (vol. 1) (pp. 657-679).

Andre, M.E.D.A., & Anderson, T.H. (1978-1979). The development and evaluation of a self-questioning study technique. *Reading Research Quarterly, 14,* 605-623.

Baldwin, R.S., Peleg-Bruckner, Z., & McClintock, A.H. (1985). Effects of topic interest and prior knowledge on reading comprehension. *Reading Research Quarterly, 20,* 497-504.

Bean, T.W., Singer, H., Sorter, J., & Frazee, C. (1986). The effect of metacognitive instruction in outlining and graphic organizer construction on students' comprehension in a tenth-grade world history class. *Journal of Reading Behavior, 18,* 153-169.

Bos, C.S., Anders, P.L., Filip, D., & Jaffe, L.E. (1989). The effects of an interactive instructional strategy for enhancing reading comprehension and content area learning for students with learning disabilities. *Journal of Learning Disabilities, 22,* 384-390.

Bos, C.S., & Anders, P.L. (1990). Effects of interactive vocabulary instruction on the vocabulary learning and reading comprehension of junior-high learning disabled students. *Learning Disability Quarterly, 13,* 31-42.

Bretzing, B.H., & Kulhavy, R.W. (1979). Notetaking and depth of processing. *Contemporary Educational Psychology, 4,* 145-153.

Brown, A.L., & Day, J.D. (1983). Macrorules for summarizing texts: The development of expertise. *Journal of Verbal Learning and Verbal Behavior, 22,* 1-14.

Clark, F.L., Deshler, D.D., Schumaker, J.B., Alley, G.R., & Warner, M.M. (1984). Visual imagery and self-questioning: Strategies to improve comprehension of written material. *Journal of Learning Disabilities, 17,* 145-149.

Deshler, D.D., & Schumaker, J.B. (1988). An instructional model for teaching students how to learn. In J.L. Garden, J.E. Zins, and M.L. Curtis (Eds.), *Alternative educational delivery systems: Enhancing instructional options for all students* (pp. 391-411). Washington, D.C.: NASP.

Duffy, G.G., Roehler, L.R., Sivan, E., Rackcliffe, G., Book, C., Meloth, M.S., Vavrus, L.G., Wesselman, R., Putnam, J., & Bassiri, D. (1987). Effects of explaining the reasoning associated with using reading strategies. *Reading Research Quarterly, 23,* 347-368.

Flood, J. (1986). The text, the student, and the teacher: Learning from exposition in middle schools. *The Reading Teacher, 39,* 784-791.

Frase, L.T., & Schwartz, B.J. (1975). Effect of question production and answering on prose recall. *Journal of Educational Psychology, 67,* 628-635.

Gajria, M., & Salvia, J. (1992). The effects of summarization instruction on text comprehension of students with learning disabilities. *Exceptional Children, 58,* 508-516.

Graesser, A., Golding, J.M., & Long, D.L. (1991). Narrative representation and comprehension. In R. Barr, M.L. Kamil, P. Mosenthal & P.D. Pearson (Eds.), *Handbook of reading research,* Vol. II (pp. 171-205). New York: Longman.

Gurney, D., Gersten, R., Dimino, J., & Carnine, D. (1990). Story grammar: Effective literature instruction for high school students with learning disabilities. *Journal of Learning Disabilities, 23,* 335-348.

Halpern, D.F., Hansen, C., & Riefer, D. (1990). Analogies as an aid to understanding and memory. *Journal of Educational Psychology, 82,* 298-305.

Hare, V., & Borchardt, K.M. (1984). Direct instruction of summarization skills. *Reading Research Quarterly, 21,* 62-78.

Harris, K.R., & Pressley, M. (1991). The nature of cognitive strategy instruction: Interactive strategy construction. *Exceptional Children, 57,* 392-404.

Hayes, D.A., & Tierney, R.J. (1982). Developing readers' knowledge through analogy. *Reading Research Quarterly, 17,* 256-280.

Kintsch, W., & van Dijk, T.A. (1978). Toward a model of text comprehension and production. *Psychological Review, 85,* 363-394.

MacDonald, J.D. (1986). Self-Generated questions and reading recall: Does training help? *Contemporary Educational Psychology, 11,* 290-304.

Malone, L.D., & Mastropieri, M.A. (1992). Reading comprehension instruction: Summarization and self-monitoring training for students with learning disabilities. *Exceptional Children, 58,* 270-279.

Meyer, B.J.F., Brandt, D.M., & Bluth, G.J. (1980). Use of top-level structure in text: Key for reading comprehension of ninth-grade students. *Reading Research Quarterly, 16,* 72-103.

Montague, M., Maddux, C.D., & Dereshiwsky, M.I. (1990). Story grammar and comprehension and production of narrative prose by students with learning disabilities. *Journal of Learning Disabilities, 23,* 190-197.

Olson, M.W., & Gee, T.C. (1988). Understanding narratives: A review of story grammar research. *Childhood Education, 64,* 302-306.

Paivio, A. (1986). *Mental representations: A dual coding approach.* New York: Oxford University Press.

Palincsar, A.S., & Brown, A.L. (1984). Reciprocal teaching of comprehension-fostering and comprehension-monitoring activities. *Cognition and Instruction, 1,* 117-175.

Pearson, P.D., & Fielding, L. (1991). Comprehension instruction. In R. Barr, M.L. Kamil, P. Mosenthal, & P.D. Pearson (Eds.), *Handbook of reading research* (pp. 815-860). White Plains, NY: Longman.

Perfetti, C., & Curtis, M. (1986). Reading. In R.F. Dillon & R.J. Sternberg (Eds.), *Cognition and instruction* (pp. 13-57).

Pressley, M., Goodchild, F., Fleet, J., Zajchowski, R., & Evans, E.D. (1989). The challenges of classroom strategy instruction. *Elementary School Journal, 89,* 301-342.

Pressley, M., Harris, K.R., & Guthrie, J.T. (Eds.) (1992). *Promoting academic competence and literacy in school.* San Diego, CA: Academic Press.

Recht, D.R., & Leslie, L. (1988). Effect of prior knowledge on good and poor readers' memory of text. *Journal of Educational Psychology, 80,* 16-20.

Schmidt, H.G., DeVolder, M.L., DeGrave, W.S., Moust, J.H.C., & Patel, V.L. (1989). Explanatory models in the processing of science text: The role of prior knowledge activation through small-group discussion. *Journal of Educational Psychology, 81,* 610-619.

Short, E.J., & Ryan, E.B. (1984). Metacognitive differences between skilled and less skilled readers: Remediating deficits through story grammar and attributional training. *Journal of Educational Psychology, 76,* 225-235.

Singer, H. (1980). Active comprehension: From answering to asking questions. In C.M. McCullough (Ed.), *Inchworm, inchworm: Persistent problems in reading education* (pp. 222-232). Newark, DE: International Reading Association.

Singer, H., & Donlan, D. (1982). Active comprehension problem-solving schema with question generation for comprehension of complex short stories. *Reading Research Quarterly, 17,* 166-186.

Slater, W.H., Graves, M.F., & Piche, G.L. (1985). Effects of structural organizers on ninth-grade students' comprehension and recall of four patterns of expository text. *Reading Research Quarterly, 20,* 189-202.

Weaver, III, C.A., & Kintsch, W. (1991). Expository text. In R. Barr, M.L. Kamil, P. Mosenthal & P.D. Pearson (Eds.), *Handbook of Reading Research Volume II* (pp. 230-245). New York: Longman.

Woloshyn, V.E., Paivio, A., & Pressley, M. (1994). Use of elaborative interrogation to help students acquire information consistent with prior knowledge and information inconsistent with prior knowledge. *Journal of Educational Psychology, 86,* 79-89.

Wong, B.Y.L., & Jones, W. (1982). Increasing metacomprehension in learning disabled and normally achieving students through self-questioning training. *Learning Disability Quarterly, 5,* 228-240.

CHAPTER 5

Strategy Instruction for Improving Writing

Pamela Beard El-Dinary • **Georgetown University**
Rachel Brown • **SUNY-Buffalo**
Peggy Van Meter • **University of Maryland**

In the past, many American students graduated from secondary school without being able to express their ideas clearly in writing. Most secondary school assignments required little writing, even of paragraphs (Applebee, 1984). When writing was required, it was usually restricted to a page or less with the first-and-final draft being written in class. Furthermore, the primary purpose of most secondary school writing tasks was to convince the teacher that the student had learned specific content. Students rarely wrote to entertain, inform, or convince an audience. Teachers were often more concerned about the correctness of information than about how effectively students communicated through writing. In sum, traditional writing instruction emphasized grammar, mechanics, and rules over the meaning of text, equating mastery of editing skills with effective writing (Scardamalia & Bereiter, 1986; Weaver, 1990).

Contemporary views of writing instruction stress that students need to write frequently and for a variety of purposes. For example, advocates of whole language support the following goals: 1) teaching reading and writing as integrated processes; 2) blending skills instruction into meaningful communicative activities; 3) fostering student involvement, with students learning from both their peers and teacher; 4) having students learn to read and write by involving them in authentic reading and writing activities; and 5) focusing on the quality of students' thinking processes rather than the mastery of specific rules for writing (Weaver, 1990).

THE RECURSIVE PROCESSES OF WRITING

Most writing models are based on observations of both good and poor writers (e.g., Flower, 1979; Hayes & Flower, 1980; Scardamalia & Bereiter, 1983; Scardamalia, Bereiter, & Steinbach, 1984). One of the earliest models (Rohman, 1965) suggested that writing consisted of three basic processes: *planning* (also called prewriting, or organizing); *drafting* (also called translating, or producing); and *revising* (also called reviewing, or rewriting). Current models still focus on these three fundamental processes, emphasizing that they are *recursive processes* (Flower & Hayes, 1980; Hayes & Flower, 1980; Humes, 1983; Scardamalia et al., 1984). In other words, expert writers move fluidly among planning, drafting, and revising processes. They continue to plan after they have started a draft, they revise parts of a draft before the full draft is completed, they write another draft after revisions show that parts are off-base, and so on (see Gaskins & Elliot, 1991; Harris & Graham, 1992).

In contrast to expert writers, novices tend to follow more linear and nonreflective approaches to writing. For example, they often include everything they know about a selected topic (Bereiter & Scardamalia, 1983; Scardamalia et al., 1984; Flower, 1979) and often fail to rethink their initial decisions, making few if any substantive revisions (Nold, 1981; Scardamalia & Bereiter, 1983). In the following section, other differences between expert and novice writers during the planning, drafting, and revising processes are highlighted.

Planning

Besides following a more rigid approach to writing, novices tend to spend much less time planning than experts (Bereiter & Scardamalia, 1987; Flower, Stein, Ackerman, Kantz, McCormick, & Peck, 1990; MacArthur & Graham, 1987). Novices also experience more difficulties with specific aspects of planning, like forming an appropriate topic (Morocco & Neuman, 1986). Once they determine a topic, novice writers often stop planning and simply start stating everything they know about the subject (Bereiter & Scardamalia, 1983, 1987; Scardamalia et al., 1984). Bereiter and Scardamalia call this a *knowledge-telling* approach. Consider the following 12-year-old's description of his/her approach to writing:

> I have a whole bunch of ideas and write down until my supply of ideas is exhausted. Then I might try to think of more ideas up to the point when you can't get any more ideas that are worth putting down on paper and then I would end it.
> (Bereiter & Scardamalia, 1987, p. 9)

Furthermore, although poor writers rely on knowledge-telling, they often fail to systematically search their memories for what they know about the topic (Graham, 1990; Pressley with McCormick, 1995; Thomas, Englert, & Gregg, 1987; Scardamalia & Bereiter, 1986).

Expert writers perform several critical functions when they plan

(Hayes & Flower, 1980; Scardamalia et al., 1984). Specifically, experts *set goals*, deciding their purpose for writing and identifying the audience for whom they will write. They *generate information* to provide content for the paper, thinking about what they already know about the topic. They also make choices about how to *organize* the information. For example, "constructive planners" in Flower et al.'s (1990) college study thought not only about the content, but also about the goals of the paper, criteria for evaluating it, potential challenges in designing it, and alternative approaches to the task.

Drafting

Planning provides a framework for ideas in a written piece. Drafting builds on that framework by transforming the ideas into sentences and paragraphs (Pressley with McCormick, 1995). Expert writers keep their plans in mind when they construct drafts; they monitor not only whether the draft is meeting the plan, but whether the plan is helping develop a decent draft.

When drafting, good writers can produce text that expresses what they mean, whereas poor writers often have difficulty doing so (Pressley with McCormick, 1995). To express meaning clearly, writers need to consider the readers' knowledge (Nystrand, 1986) and anticipate and answer questions readers might have (McCutchen & Perfetti, 1983; Scardamalia & Bereiter, 1986). Thus, communicating ideas to an audience is the expert writer's overarching goal.

In contrast, secondary school students often focus more on mechanics, rules, and formulas than on the text's communicative function (Scardamalia & Bereiter, 1986). They tend to strictly follow formulas for producing specific kinds of writing (Durst, 1984). For example, students may write all essays in five paragraphs: the first paragraph states the thesis, the next three paragraphs provide supporting points, and the final paragraph offers a conclusion (see Foley, 1989; Nunnally, 1991). While having a set of such formulas can help students produce various types of writing (e.g., laboratory reports, essays, and research papers), they sometimes apply each formula rigidly, failing to adapt them or consider alternative approaches (Applebee, 1984; Durst, 1984; Foley, 1989; Marshall, 1984b; Nunnally, 1991; Rose, 1980). Thus, novice writers are less flexible and strategic when drafting than are experts, who rely on a variety of strategies to develop drafts.

Revising

Like planning and drafting, expert writers' revising is much different from that of novices (see Fitzgerald, 1992, for a summary of effective revising). Novices focus on grammar, mechanics, and construction of individual sentences, whereas experts focus on the organization of text as a whole (Berkenkotter & Murray, 1983; Hayes, Flower, Schriver, Stratman, & Carey, 1987). While effective writers do pay attention to grammar, spelling, and stylistic "rules" (Hayes et al., 1987; Hull, 1987), they realize that merely changing mechanics is not sufficient for effective revision (MacArthur & Graham, 1987; MacArthur, Graham, & Schwartz, 1991).

Good writers also keep their goals in mind as they revise. For example, they focus on meeting the readers' needs (Berkenkotter & Murray, 1983; Hayes et al., 1987), and they evaluate whether the text expresses their intended writing style (e.g., Graves, Slater, Roen, Redd-Boyd, Duin, Furniss, & Hazeltine, 1988). In contrast, weaker writers may not even be aware of criteria that would enhance their writing (McCormick, Busching, & Potter, 1992; Nold, 1981; Scardamalia & Bereiter, 1983). Novices often fail to see errors or inconsistencies in their own writing, or when they do, are unable to solve them (e.g., Fitzgerald & Markham, 1987).

In general, secondary school students are much better at revising than elementary school students. Some secondary school students understand that revising is a necessary part of writing, and they often focus their first revisions on providing a clear meaning, worrying later about mechanics (Butler-Nalin, 1984). Nevertheless, many secondary school students do not revise at all, or they do so ineffectively (Applebee, 1984; Durst, 1984; Marshall, 1984a, 1984b).

Helping Novice Writers Become Experts

The emphasis of current programs is on writing as a holistic process. Therefore, only programs that address all aspects of the writing process are included in this chapter. For each program, we provide some background information including the philosophy underlying the program. We then introduce the strategies associated with each program. Finally, when presenting these strategies, we identify whether they focus on planning, drafting, revising or a combination of these.

A GENERAL MODEL FOR TEACHING WRITING STRATEGIES

Each writing strategy program we describe in this chapter entails instruction that could apply to teaching strategies for any content area (see Englert et al., 1991; Graham & Harris, 1989; Schumaker, Deshler, Alley, Warner, Clark, & Nolan, 1982). Before discussing each program, we present a general writing instructional model based on a synthesis of all the programs contained in this chapter. These steps are presented in Table 5-1.

Table 5-1
Writing Instructional Model

1. Assess and Make Commitments

2. Develop Prerequisite Skills

3. Describe the Strategy

4. Model the Strategy

5. Have Students Explain and Memorize Strategy Steps

6. Guide Practice with Feedback and Controlled Tasks

7. Have Students Practice

8. Post-test and Practice Generalizing

9. Coordination of Strategies

Adopted from Englert et al., 1991; Graham & Harris, 1989; Schumaker et al., 1982.

Assess and Make Commitments

Assess students' current writing habits, having them examine their strengths and weaknesses. Before teaching a strategy, test for target skills using activities both at the students' ability level and at grade level (see Schumaker, Deshler et al., 1982). Work with students to set goals. Make a commitment to work together to learn a strategy and discuss the value of learning that strategy.

Develop Prerequisite Skills

Students need to learn to identify components of text that relate to the strategy being taught. For example, before being taught the TREE strategy for opinion essays (Note Topic sentence, Note Reasons, Examine reasons, Note Ending; Harris & Graham, 1992), students need to learn about topic sentences.

Describe the Strategy

Explicitly teach the strategy to students, including information about how, why, when, and where to use the strategy. Present the steps of the strategy, along with any mnemonic device, or "remembering system," for memorizing the steps (e.g., SPACE—Setting, Purpose, Action, Conclusion, Emotions; Harris & Graham, 1992). Emphasize that the strategy is a tool to help students keep track of their thinking. Have students compare the strategy steps with their current approach to writing, and have them compare the quality of writing produced as a result of each procedure (Harris & Graham, 1992; Schumaker, Deshler, Alley et al., 1982).

Model the Strategy

Show students how to use the strategy by thinking aloud while writing. Tell the student what is going on in your mind as you write. Focus on explicitly showing students how you are applying the strategy. Teachers can also model other important thinking processes, such as viewing writing as a problem-solving activity, monitoring and positive thinking (e.g., "I can do this"; Schumaker & Deshler, 1992; Graham & Harris, 1989).

Have Students Explain and Perhaps Memorize Strategy Steps

Students must be able to verbally explain the strategy steps before they can practice using the strategy. Their explanations need to reflect that they understand what they are doing and why they are doing it. Therefore, students need to elaborate beyond rote memorization. They need to talk with awareness about the strategy and its steps.

Guide Practice with Feedback and Controlled Tasks

Guide students' attempts when they initially use a strategy. Guided practice can begin with the teacher and students applying the strategy together. Later, the students can apply the strategy independently, with the teacher providing specific feedback to individual students (Kline et al., 1992). Ask students what they are thinking and doing as they use the strategy. Respond to students by pointing out ways that they are applying the strategy and how it is helping them. Provide hints when students forget the next step in the strategy. Make these hints less explicit and less frequent as students gain competence in controlling their own writing.

Have Students Practice

Have students practice with materials at or above instructional level (tasks that are too easy will not require strategies, so students are more likely to see the value of strategies when they are challenged). After students master the strategy with guidance, have them practice with more complex tasks. Expose students to a variety of realistic writing tasks so that they can learn to modify strategies according to task demands. Continue to provide feedback and guide the student as necessary. Encourage students to seek opportunities to use the strategy.

Post-test and Practice Generalizing

Teachers need to regularly check whether students have mastered the targeted writing strategy. Involve students in evaluating their own performance and the effectiveness of the strategy. Celebrate students' successes and work with them to plan applying the strategy to other situations by making them aware of situations in which they could use the strategy and by helping them modify the strategy. Check periodically whether students are using the strategy in a variety of contexts.

Coordination of Strategies

Teach strategies individually. Later instruction should focus on how to use strategies in a coordinated and flexible fashion. Not all strategies are necessarily taught to all students. Rather, teachers select, modify, and combine strategies to meet the task and students' needs. The key to multiple strategy instruction is to provide students with a repertoire of powerful tools and to *explicitly* teach the students how, when, and why to use them.

UNIVERSITY OF KANSAS STRATEGIES INTERVENTION MODEL AND LEARNING STRATEGIES CURRICULUM [1]

Donald Deshler, Jean Schumaker, and their colleagues at the University of Kansas Center for Research on Learning have developed what is probably the best-validated strategy intervention program available for older students (Deshler & Schumaker, 1986; Kline, Deshler, & Schumaker, 1992; Schmidt, Deshler, Schumaker, & Alley, 1988; Schumaker & Deshler, 1992). The Strategies Intervention Model has been successfully used with learning disabled secondary school students (Deshler & Schumaker, 1988), minority students (Bulgren, McKnight, Deshler, & Schumaker, 1989; Moccia, McKnight, Deshler, & Schumaker, 1990), and college students (Denton, Seybert, & Franklin, 1988; Hock, Deshler, & Schumaker, 1991).

The Kansas group designed the Learning Strategies Curriculum (Deshler & Schumaker, 1986) for teaching a range of strategies for studying, reading, and writing. For writing, the curriculum includes strategies for sentence writing (Schumaker & Sheldon, 1985), paragraph writing (Schumaker & Lyerla, 1993), error monitoring (Schumaker, Nolan, & Deshler, 1985), and theme writing (Schumaker, in preparation). The steps for each strategy are listed in Table 5-2. Each strategy

---

[1] For teachers interested in more detailed information about the Strategies Intervention Model, explicit lessons are provided as part of a workshop series, which is available by contacting Janet Roth, Training Facilitator, phone (913) 864-4780, University of Kansas Center for Research on Learning, 3061 Dole Center, Lawrence, Kansas 66045.

Table 5-2
Writing Strategies in the University of Kansas Learning Strategies Curriculum

Sentence Writing Mnemonic device: PENS	Paragraph Writing Mnemonic device: SCRIBE	Error Monitoring Mnemonic device: WRITER	Theme Writing Mnemonic device: TOWER
1. Pick a formula to write your sentence.	1. Set up a diagram.	1. Write on every other line of paper using PENS (see first column.)	1. Think of ideas
2. Explore words to fit the formula [and express your idea].	2. Create the title.	2. Read for meaning	2. Order ideas
	3. Reveal the topic [write topic sentence].		3. Write ideas—connected paragraphs
		3. Interrogate yourself using **COPS:** Check your:	• Introductory paragraph
3. Note the words [write them].	4. Iron out the details [write detail sentences].	• Capitalization	• Detail paragraphs
4. Search for the verb(s) and subject(s) [to make sure your sentence is complete].	5. Bind it together with a clincher.	• Overall appearance	• Concluding paragraph
	6. Edit your work [ensure topic, details, clincher are same tense/point of view, diverse structures.]	• Punctuation	4. Error Monitor: Organization, sentence structure, minor errors **(COPS)**
		• Spelling	
		4. Take the paper to someone for help.	5. Recopy [for neatness, format]
		5. Execute a final copy.	
		6. Reread your paper	

is considered a prerequisite for the next (Schumaker, in preparation). We summarize instruction in each strategy, discussing the strategies in the order they are presented to students.

Drafting Strategies

The Sentence Writing and Paragraph Writing Strategies focus on structural aspects of drafting—how to put together complete sentences and organized paragraphs. These strategies are important because students often have difficulty consciously controlling syntax (Scardamalia & Bereiter, 1986). For example, even when students can identify sentences with good form and can explain why they are proper, students often are unable to produce these sentences. Students' difficulties using appropriate sentence structure may be due to the limited capacity of working memory (Scardamalia & Bereiter, 1986). That is, students may become "mentally overloaded" when they try to remember sentence structures while also trying to keep in mind the content of their ideas. Thus, strategies that make a variety of sentence structures accessible may improve students' ability to write complete sentences.

Instruction in both the Sentence Writing and Paragraph Writing Strategies focus on explicitly teaching students about text structures, whether it be ways of structuring sentences or paragraphs. Most researchers believe that formal text structures, such as cause/effect and comparison/contrast, represent the structure of knowledge that writers use to produce text and that readers use to comprehend text (Scardamalia & Bereiter, 1986). That is, expert writers already have these patterns in mind.

During *Sentence Writing Strategy* instruction (Schumaker & Sheldon, 1985), students learn to *choose* from a set of formulas that guide them in writing a variety of sentence types, such as subject-verb [SV]. Sentence structures are usually presented in the following sequence: simple, compound, complex, compound-complex. For each sentence type, the teacher first describes the sentence and then models writing by thinking aloud and demonstrating the strategy steps. After students have memorized the formulas for the target sentence structure, they practice writing sentences and checking whether the sentences fit the formulas (the mnemonic device PENS guides them through this process). In early practice lessons, students identify parts of a sentence and the associated formula. Later they need to use the formula to generate sentences. Instruction moves from generating random sentences to crafting a paragraph that includes a variety of sentences. The teacher then cues students to practice the strategy in their regular writing assignments. The developers suggest that teachers spend 30 minutes a day for nine to 10 weeks on the Sentence Writing Strategy (Schumaker & Sheldon, 1985). Alternatively, teachers may want to focus on one sentence structure at a time, spreading instruction across the school year. Because students tend to apply formulas rigidly when left to their own devices, teachers need to emphasize the reasoning behind learning the formulas and the importance of knowing when to apply each formula.

Having mastered the basic tools of sentence structure, the emphasis on writing to express ideas is introduced in the *Paragraph Writing Strategy* (Schumaker & Lyerla, 1993). The Paragraph Writing Strategy focuses on insuring that students' expository paragraphs contain sentences that fit three major roles—topic, detail, and "clincher" (Schmidt et al., 1988). Students first learn how to write sentences that fit each role, then they learn how to apply these basic sentence types to four kinds of paragraph structures.

First, students learn to develop a topic sentence that clearly states the main idea of a paragraph. Second, students are taught to develop detail sentences that support, elaborate, or define elements of the main idea. They are also taught how to organize these details, thus structuring the body of the paragraph. Third, students learn how to develop a clincher sentence that concludes and summarizes the paragraph. Instruction includes explanations about the role of each sentence type, including requirements that each sentence should fulfill (Schumaker & Lyerla, 1993). This is followed by introducing different types of sentences that can fill each role (e.g., general, cluing, and specific topic sentences). Finally, students are reminded about how to apply the Sentence Writing Strategy (PENS).

After learning to develop each of these basic components of a paragraph, students learn to use them to construct whole paragraphs. The mnemonic device SCRIBE guides students in constructing a paragraph by having them create a diagram. A paragraph diagram sheet is provided to students. The paragraph diagram includes slots for notes about the selected topic, details, tense, point of view, and the order of details. It also has lines on which students can arrange the order of details, as well as transitions.

Students learn to apply the SCRIBE steps to four major kinds of paragraphs: sequential (including narrative), descriptive, expository, and compare/contrast. Students are provided examples of each of these paragraph types. For each example, the teacher and students talk about what kinds of topic, detail, and clincher sentences are appropriate. The teacher then guides the class in developing a paragraph. The program developers suggest that paragraph instruction be carried over a semester or even over the whole school year. Again, teachers must focus on flexible use of the Paragraph Writing Strategy so that students do not apply it as a rigid formula. Teachers should also emphasize the recursive use of the various strategies. For example, the writer's intentions for the contents of the topic sentence may guide selection of a sentence type, with a more complex main idea requiring a more complex sentence format.

Revising Strategies

The Learning Strategies Curriculum also includes an *Error Monitoring Strategy (WRITER)* that focuses on identifying and correcting a set of common mechanical errors (Schumaker, Deshler et al., 1982). Cohen and Scardamalia (1983) found that students could learn to make high quality revisions if they were instructed to read text, mark problems, and then diagnose and solve problems. After writing on every other line to leave space for corrections students go back to read their writing for meaning. Students look for clarity, consistency, and cohesion in their writing. Later, by questioning themselves, students check for capitalization, overall appearance, punctuation, and spelling (COPS). (When learning COPS, students practice finding inserted errors in teacher-prepared passages and eventually in their own writing. The teacher provides students with feedback about their successes and failures at correcting errors.) After making corrections in the blank spaces above sentences, students take their draft to someone to read and ask for feedback. Students then make a second copy. The last step is to reread this copy, as a final check before handing in their work.

Teachers presenting the Error Monitoring Strategy make it clear to students that revising should involve examining overall clarity as well as attending to mechanics. Students are taught to expand their initial understanding of editing and revising as part of instruction on the Theme Writing Strategy.

Planning/Drafting/Revising Strategy

The Theme Writing Strategy guides students through the sequential process of generating and ordering ideas, connecting paragraphs, correcting errors, and recopying to produce a final draft (see Schmidt et al., 1988). In other words, this strategy guides students through the entire writing process. The Theme Writing Strategy also integrates the previous strategies taught for sentence writing, paragraph writing, and error monitoring.

Through the mnemonic device TOWER, students learn how to use an idea diagram to keep track and order of ideas. After generating subtopics and related details, students number subtopics and details to indicate the order in which they will write them. The analogy of a blueprint is used to provide a rationale for using the idea diagram. Having a sketched version of the theme is believed to reduce the cognitive demands on students when constructing their draft.

Students practice constructing idea diagrams in successive steps. First, they learn to construct an idea diagram for ideas that have already been developed. Then, students gradually begin constructing diagrams in which they generate some of the ideas. Eventually, students practice using the strategy to generate an original essay. Students use the TOWER strategy first with short passages (e.g., paragraphs, essays, and reports). Students then apply the same strategy to write longer papers. The suggested time frame for instruction in TOWER is one quarter to one full semester.

Coordination Among the Strategies

In the Strategies Intervention Model, instruction builds from one strategy to the next. For example, as students learn to write paragraphs, they are required to include the variety of sentence types they know. Coordination of the strategies is built into the structured lessons so that students will maintain strategies they have already learned. Once students have learned all four strategies, they are expected to use them in coordination—first organizing the theme, then combining the Sentence Writing and Paragraph Writing Strategies to develop a draft, and finally applying the Error Monitoring Strategy when editing their draft.

The strategies in the Learning Strategies Curriculum were designed to be highly structured to meet the needs of learning disabled students. Because of the high degree of structure, teachers need to avoid focusing on the strategies as rigid formulas. These structured strategies may also be more appropriate for lower achievers than for higher achievers, who tend to benefit from flexible tasks that encourage creativity. The small group instruction and individualized feedback that characterize the original model of instruction may also not be feasible in large secondary school classes. In larger classes, strategies can be described and modeled to the whole class, supported with whole-class guided practice. Homework worksheets can provide students with individual practice and help the teacher identify students who have not mastered the strategy.

SELF-REGULATED STRATEGY DEVELOPMENT[2]

Harris and Graham's Self-Regulated Strategy Development approach focuses on teacher/student collaboration in setting and reaching goals (see Harris & Graham, 1992; Sawyer, Graham, & Harris, 1992). The purpose of instruction is for students to regulate their own writing processes and strategy use through goal-setting, self-monitoring, self-instructions to be persistent and confident, and self-reinforcement for success. A distinguishing feature of Self-Regulated Strategy Development is the explicit teaching of *self-statements* (also called *self-instructions*). Self-statements are intended to guide the learner through the writing process. Self-statements are presented to students as statements good writers say to themselves to keep them motivated and on task. Students are taught self-statements to help them do the following (Graham & Harris, 1989; Harris & Graham, 1992):

a) Define the problem (e.g., "What is it I have to do?")
b) Develop a plan (e.g., "What strategies will I use?")
c) Use composition and regulatory strategies (e.g., "Let my mind be free; think of new, fun ideas." "What ideas do I see in this picture?")
d) Monitor performance (e.g., "Am I using all my strategies so far?")
e) Cope with problems, anxiety, and negative attitudes (e.g., "Take my time; good parts will come to me.")
f) Praise their own performance (e.g., "Good! I like these parts!")

At first students say the statements and strategy steps out loud when working. Through repeated practice, students internalize the self-statements. Students are encouraged to develop and practice their own

[2] For more detailed information about Self-Regulated Strategy Development, contact Dr. Karen Harris or Dr. Steve Graham, Department of Special Education, University of Maryland, College Park, MD 20742.

preferred self-statements.

Strategy instruction takes the form of mini-lessons that are part of Writers' Workshops. During these workshops, students respond to each other's writing and sometimes write together (see Atwell, 1987; Calkins, 1986; Harris & Graham, 1992). The instruction generally spans five to six instructional hours over six to eight weeks. After instruction, students are able to apply the strategies to similar writing tasks (see Pressley with McCormick, 1995). The following sections describe several of the individual strategies that Graham and Harris have developed as part of their Self Regulated Strategy Development program.

Planning/Drafting/Revising Strategies

Most of the strategies developed by Harris and Graham and colleagues (Danoff et al., 1993) are intended to encompass planning, drafting, and revising into a fluid, recursive writing process (see Table 5-3). Early steps in each strategy are intended to guide students' planning, whereas subsequent steps help students in drafting and revising. The following paragraphs describe the rationale behind each strategy.

PLANS

One way that expert writers plan purposefully is by translating their high-level goals into sub-goals (Flower & Hayes, 1981). For example, a goal might be to "Make this part interesting"; the sub-goal might be "So I'll start with a list of jobs the reader might consider, related to the skill I'm discussing." The PLANS mnemonic device guides students in both setting goals and developing ideas for meeting them.

The second step of the PLANS strategy is a self-reminder to "Write and say more." When writing, learners need to spend a great deal of effort into thinking about what to say (Scardamalia & Bereiter, 1986). Experienced writers tend to generate much more content than they intend to use. In contrast, novice writers often have problems finding enough to say (Scardamalia & Bereiter, 1986). Research has shown that nearly any prompt that encourages students to thinking about content can help them produce content (Scardamalia & Bereiter, 1986).

The third step in the PLANS strategy involves checking whether the writing goals were achieved. Just as students often fail to detect mechanical errors in their writing, they may also fail to see inconsistencies or ambiguities in their writing. Such ineffective monitoring is not surprising in light of the metacognitive deficiencies that students often experience when reading, including being unaware that they have failed to understand text (Brown, 1980). The PLANS strategy teaches students that they need to explicitly check whether they have met their writing goals.

Table 5-3
Self-Regulated Strategies for Planning/Drafting/Revising

PLANS (Harris & Graham, 1992, p. 54)

1. Do PLANS

Pick goals

List ways to meet goals

And make

Notes

Sequence notes

2. Write and say more [A prompt that simply encourages production of more text]

3. Test goals [Check whether the text meets goals that were set initially]

WWW, What=2, How=2 (Danoff et al., 1993, pp. 303-304)

1. Think of a story you would like to share with others.

2. Let your mind be free.

3. Write down the story part reminder: WWW, What=2, How=2

Who is the main character? Who else is in the story?

When does the story take place?

Where does the story take place?

What does the main character want to do?

What happens when the main character tries to do it?

How does the story end?

How does the main character feel?

4. Write down story part ideas for each part.

5. Write your story. Use good parts and make sense.

Report writing strategy (Graham & Harris, in press)

1. Select a topic.

2. Think about what you already know and what you want to know about the topic.

3. Identify your main points and web your details.

4. Read to check the accuracy of your webbed ideas and seek new information to add to your web.

5. Use the web to generate the report.

6. Check that you used the web as intended.

Generating & framing writing content (Harris & Graham, 1992, p. 49)

1. Think— Who will read this? Why am I writing this?

2. Plan what to say, using one of the following prompts:

TREE (opinion essays): Note the *Topic* sentence

Note *Reasons*

Examine reasons

Note *Ending*

SPACE (stories): Note the *Setting*

Note the *Purpose*

Note the *Action*

Note the *Conclusion*

Note *Emotions*

3. Write and say more.

TAP and Count (Harris & Graham, 1992, pp. 74-77)

T= task (What do I have to do?)

A=audience (Who do I have to write for?)

P= purpose (Why do I have to write?)

Count for topic sentence:

1 = How did it begin?

2 = What happened in the middle?

3 = How did it end?

(Strategy developed to help students on a functional writing test)

Report writing strategy

The demand for report writing increases dramatically as students proceed through the elementary and secondary school grades. Facility in report writing includes prewriting tasks such as identifying a topic, searching through a variety of resources (e.g., encyclopedias, expository texts, hypermedia), gathering pertinent facts, and organizing information. For many students, particularly those with learning disabilities, the many demands of planning, drafting, and revising a report may seem daunting (Graham & Harris, in press). Thus, Graham, Harris and their colleagues have devised a strategy to guide students' through this complex process (Graham & Harris, in press).

This strategy (see Table 5-3) takes students through various steps of report writing. Students pick a topic, think about the knowledge they already possess about the topic, and consider what they would like to learn about their topic. Using their prior knowledge, students organize their main points and details graphically, using a web. They then seek new information. Students use that information to modify their webs, verifying the accuracy of their facts, elaborating details, and deleting irrelevant information. Next, students use the web to guide their report writing, monitoring their performance as they proceed. Finally, students check their drafts to ensure that they have included all the webbed information.

WWW, What=2, How=2

Most researchers believe that formal text structures, such as story grammars (characters, setting, problem, solution), represent the knowledge that writers use to produce text and that readers use to comprehend text (Scardamalia & Bereiter, 1986). Consistent with this view, WWW, What=2, How=2 focuses on teaching students about these story parts.

Generating and framing writing content

The strategy for generating and framing writing content begins by focusing students' attention on their writing purpose. In addition, the strategy focuses the writer's attention on the audience. This strategy also includes framing content within either an expository or narrative text structure. Like the PLANS strategy, this strategy includes a prompt to write more. This prompt helps students focus on their background knowledge about the topic and use that knowledge to support their writing purposes.

TAP and Count

Like the generating and framing writing content strategy, TAP and Count focuses attention on the writer's purpose and audience. The strategy also helps students remember that their writing should have a clear beginning, middle, and that these sections should flow together.

Revising Strategies

In addition to strategies that encompass the process as a whole, Harris and Graham (1992) have also developed specific strategies for revising. Two of these strategies are presented in Table 5-4. Students are most likely to generate new knowledge when they rethink the content and goals of their writing (Scardamalia & Bereiter, 1986). Therefore, both of the revising strategies that Harris and Graham have developed for revising focus on thinking about the content and making sense. Specifically, the *SCAN* strategy was developed as a self-check for opinion essays. The *peer revising* strategy applies across genres and focuses on both providing and using feedback.

Examples of Teaching These Strategies[3]

To illustrate more concretely the instructional process advocated by Harris and Graham, we have included descriptions of how to teach two of the strategies contained in Table 5-2, WWW, What=2, How=2 and PLANS.

The first step in teaching the story writing strategy is to teach students the mnemonic device WWW, What =2, How=2. This mnemonic can be used to define, identify and generate common story parts (see Table 5-2). The mnemonic device and its explanation are presented on a chart, and the class talks about what each part means. Using existing stories, students identify these key story parts, talking about how various authors developed the parts differently. As a class, students use pictures to help them generate ideas for each story part. Students then meet with the teacher to review one of their previously written stories. Students identify which of the story parts they included or omitted in their stories.

Another chart is then used to introduce the specific strategy steps. Using the strategy and mnemonic charts as guides, the teacher thinks aloud while following the steps to write a story. The teacher also models self-statements, like "I can do this. Let my mind be free to think of new ideas."

Students then memorize the strategy steps, including the mnemonic device. They also generate their own self-statements, which they would use to motivate themselves during writing. At first, the teacher writes collaboratively with students, providing support when the

---

[3] Copies of strategy lesson plans, including sample scripts for modelling the strategies, are available from Steve Graham or Karen Harris, Department of Special Education, University of Maryland, College Park, MD 20742.

Table 5-4

Self-Regulated Strategies for Revising

SCAN (Harris & Graham, 1992, p. 62; for opinion essays)

Peer-revising—includes steps for revising and proofreading (Harris & Graham, 1992, p. 67)
1) Read the first draft of your essay
2) Find the sentence that tells what you believe
3) Add 2 more reasons why you believe it
4) SCAN each sentence and ask
   Does it make Sense?
   Is it Connected to my belief?
   Can I Add more?
   Note errors.
5) Make my changes

Revise:
Listen [as the author reads the paper aloud] and read along.
Tell what the paper is about and what you liked best.
Read and make notes — Is everything clear? Can any details be added?
Discuss suggestions with the author.

Proofread:
Check your paper and correct errors.
Exchange papers.
Check for errors—sentences/capitals/punctuation/spelling.
Discuss corrections.

students need help or cannot remember the next step. Students are encouraged to use the charts and list of self-statements when needed, and to practice their self-statements out loud if they need extra motivation. Eventually, students write without using the charts or relying on prompts from the teacher. As part of independent work, students consult with each other to determine whether any story parts are missing and, if so, how and where they could be included. When students have completed a final draft, they meet individually with the teacher to assess their story.

Instruction for the PLANS strategy occurs in a similar manner. First, the mnemonic device PLANS is presented to students with a discussion of what is meant by each step of the strategy. Existing essays may be used to identify how other authors selected goals, met these goals, noted important points through the essay and sequenced this information. As a class, students may discuss how they would follow the PLANS strategy to write an essay. Students may meet individually with the teacher to review a previous essay. The remaining steps of the strategy are introduced, with the teacher modelling the strategy and motivational self-statements. Students would then memorize the strategy steps and generate their own motivational self-statements. They would be provided opportunities to use these strategies with the teacher's guidance gradually being reduced. Students could meet in groups to discuss how they used the strategy to develop their draft and how their drafts could be improved.

COGNITIVE STRATEGIES INSTRUCTION IN WRITING

Cognitive Strategies Instruction in Writing, developed by Englert, Raphael, and their colleagues (1988), teaches students that it takes time and effort to write effectively. Students write daily, not finishing a piece in one day, but taking time to develop the topic, think through the writing, and collaborate with peers. Verbal modelling of writing processes is an integral part of the program, with both the teacher and the students talking about their thoughts while writing. To date, this program has been effectively used with fourth- and fifth-grade learning disabled students and upper-elementary school students (Englert, Raphael, Anderson et al., 1991).

Cognitive Strategies Instruction in Writing teaches strategic writing through a set of *think-sheets*. Information contained in think-sheets for each of the steps in Englert et al.'s POWER process is included in Table 5-5. The think-sheets help students plan, organize, monitor and evaluate their writing and learn the questions they ultimately need to ask themselves to become expert writers. Consistent with the rest of this chapter, we specify which strategies correspond to planning, drafting, and revising processes.

Planning Strategies

Before writing, students complete the *Planning* think-sheet. The planning think sheet encourages the cognitive processes of goal-setting, attention to audience, activating background knowledge and making connections among ideas. The last part of the planning think-sheet requires students to select a text structure for organizing their ideas (e.g., comparison/contrast, problem/solution, explanation, other). Based on the selected text structure, students then complete an *Organizing* think-sheet. The organizing think sheet explicitly states elements of the text structure that need to be included. For example, Table 5-5 shows questions that guide the development of papers explaining how to perform a task (Englert et al., 1991).

Drafting Strategies

Cognitive Strategies Instruction's *Writing* think-sheet is a blank, lined sheet on which students construct a draft of their paper (Raphael,

Table 5-5
Think-sheets for Cognitive Strategies Instruction in Writing

Planning	**Who** will read this? **Why** am I writing this? **What** do I know about it? **How** can I group my ideas/facts? (Englert et al., 1991, p. 346)
Organizing	(Example for writing an explanation of how to do something) What am I explaining? What materials are needed? What is an appropriate setting for the activity? What are the steps to complete the task? (Englert et al., 1991, p. 347)
Writing	[blank, lined sheet to construct draft of paper] (Raphael et al., 1988)
Editing	**Read to Check Information** What is this paper about (main point)? What part is best? Put * next to the part I like best. Tell why I like it. What parts are unclear? Put ? next to unclear parts. Explain why that part is unclear. Is the paper interesting? Why or why not? **Question Yourself to Check Organization** [For comparison/contrast] Did I: (for each: YES Sort of NO) Tell what I am comparing and contrasting? Tell what I am comparing/contrasting them on? Tell how the things are alike? Tell how the things are different? Use good comparison key words? **Plan for Editing Conference** What do I want to change? (If I marked it or answered "Sort of" or "No," will I add more, take it out, change order?) What questions will I ask my editor? (Raphael et al., 1988, p. 26)
Revising	**Suggestions from My Editor** List all suggestions my editor has given me. **Decide on Suggestions to Use** Put * next to suggestions I will use in revising my paper. **Making My Paper More Interesting** List ideas for making the paper more interesting for my reader. **Return to My First Draft** Make all changes on my draft that I think will improve the paper. (Raphael et al., 1988, p. 29)

Englert, & Kirschner, 1988). While writing a draft, students are encouraged to refer to their plans and to translate them into text by fleshing out ideas and adding key words, creating engaging introductions and conclusions that use questions, dialogue, and personal examples, and deciding how to clue readers about text structure (Englert et al., 1991).

Revising Strategies

Cognitive Strategies students use peer conferences to obtain feedback that will guide them in revising. In preparation for the peer conference, the author and a peer respond to parallel "*Editing* think-sheets." (See Table 5-5 for an example of an author's editing think-sheet for comparison/contrast papers; Raphael et al., 1988. Different editing think-sheets are used for other types of writing, such as providing instructions.) After the conference, students complete the *Revising* think-sheet to form their final copy (Raphael et al., 1988).

TRANSACTIONAL STRATEGIES INSTRUCTION[4]

The term Transactional Strategies Instruction is based on the many transactions that occur among students, teachers, and written text. What happens during lessons is co-determined by the students and teacher rather than predetermined by the teacher before class (Bell, 1968; Bjorklund, 1989; Sameroff, 1975). Thus, transactional instruction takes advantage of "teachable moments." Students are expected to learn about writing through transactions with their teachers and peers. Strategies are explained, modeled, and practiced in the context of realistic writing tasks. Teachers encourage independent use of strategies by praising students for their thought processes and putting less emphasis on the outcomes or products of writing. Through discussions about strategies, teachers help students to become aware of factors that affect their thinking and to take control of their own thinking and writing processes. Transactional Strategies Instruction is long-term— students are expected to build and refine a flexible repertoire of strategies over several years. After continued exposure to effective writing thought processes, students are expected to engage in such processes on their own (Pressley et al., 1992; Vygotsky, 1978).

Transactional Strategies Instruction emphasizes self-regulation of writing. While students are taught a repertoire of effective writing strategies, they are required to select their own strategies and evaluate these choices. Transactional Strategies Instruction emphasizes the

[4] For more detailed information about Benchmark writing instruction, contact Dr. Irene Gaskins, Director, Benchmark School, 2107 North Province Road, Media, PA 19063.

importance of students' attitudes, motivation, and beliefs about themselves as learners and writers. For example, teachers explicitly talk about the need for students to become independent learners. Teachers also tell students that they can succeed as long as they apply effort through good strategies. Transactional Strategies Instruction also emphasizes students' using their knowledge about the world in conjunction with their strategies for learning and writing. Students are taught that they already know a lot of information and that they can use what they know to become good writers. In the words of Gaskins and Elliot (1991):

> We see writing as problem-solving activity that is purposeful, takes place over time—rather than in discrete lessons—and is socially constructed (the result of asking for and receiving feedback from peers and teachers). (p. 57)

Table 5-6
Benchmark School's Writing Strategies
(Transactional Strategies Instruction)

1. Access knowledge
   a) Brainstorm ideas for possible topics.
   b) Identify the audience.
   c) Call to mind plans, patterns, and other guides for writing (e.g., known story grammars or text structures).

2. Plan
   a) Gather necessary information by recalling relevant information and/or doing research.
   b) Organize by categorizing, outlining, generating new ideas based on relationships, and picturing how the information will be integrated.
   c) Set procedural and substantive goals such as determining the pattern of organization to be used and determining main points to be made.

3. Draft
   a) Focus initially on capturing ideas in rough form.
   b) Keep the audience in mind.

4. Review
   a) Evaluate and re-work during writing and at the conclusion of each draft.
   b) Solicit feedback from others which encourages refinement of thinking processes.
   c) Revise based on self-evaluation or the reactions of others by organizing, clarifying, and elaborating.

From Gaskins & Elliot (1991), p. 57.

Strategies for Planning/Drafting/Revising

Like Graham and Harris, Gaskins and Elliot (1991) presented their writing strategies as a holistic program that works through the processes of planning, drafting, and revising. However, strategies are organized differently than those of Graham and Harris. Graham and Harris organize their strategies around writing tasks. Each strategy includes steps that encompass a particular type of text, so that students move back and forth among the steps within one strategy. In contrast, Gaskins and Elliot's strategies are organized around four steps to writing (access knowledge, plan, draft, and review), with each strategy embedded in one of these steps. An outline of the processes and strategies presented by Gaskins and Elliot (1991) is presented in Table 5-6. The strategies support several cognitive processes including: activating background knowledge about content, audience, text and structures; organizing content and making connections among information; goal-setting; monitoring; and seeking feedback.

In addition to learning specific cognitive writing strategies for the four steps to writing (i.e., accessing knowledge, planning, drafting, and reviewing), students are taught appropriate metacognitive strategies to guide their performance. These metacognitive strategies include consideration of task demands, personal factors, and environmental concerns (Gaskins & Elliot, 1991). For example, students are taught to monitor their progress and overall performance based on the goals they set and to take corrective measures as required (i.e., task demands). They also are encouraged to think about how much they value a task and how their feelings might influence task completion (i.e., personal factors). Finally, students are asked to consider optimal contexts and conditions for completing their work (i.e., environmental factors).

During peer conferences, editors apply the same kinds of strategies that they use when writing. For example, an editor might ask, "Is it clear who this paper was written for, why it was written, and how much the author knows about the topic? Are the ideas clearly organized?" Editors not only make recommendations about content, but also suggest additional strategies that address any weaknesses.

How the Strategies Are Taught

Consistent with the general model of instruction, Transactional Strategies Instruction begins with explanation, modelling, and guided practice of individual strategies. Transactional strategies instruction also places explicit emphasis on students' coordinating strategies and evaluating the strategies they choose.

Students are taught to coordinate several individual strategies as they work through the processes of writing. For example, when editing, a student may decide that parts of a draft are unclear. One option would be to use an organizing strategy to improve the structure of the information. Another option would be to think about the audience and what might be clearest to them.

Instruction emphasizes that students need to be able to choose appropriate strategies for themselves. After a few strategies have been introduced and practiced, teachers encourage students to choose their own strategies. Teachers follow up by having students evaluate how well the selected strategy worked and reminding students that they can choose another strategy if the first choice was not helpful.

CONCLUSION

We believe that the programs described here outline several strategies that may be helpful in secondary school classrooms. However, until the programs described here have been validated with regular secondary school populations, we do not recommend that teachers simply apply them in their classrooms. Instead, we recommend that teachers carefully select strategies according to their students' needs and monitor students' successes after implementing a strategic program.

General Guidelines for Structuring Writing Classrooms

Although strategy instruction can be a critical component in helping students become effective, independent writers, strategy instruction does not exist in a vacuum. Rather, strategy instruction is best implemented as a part of the regular curriculum, with some curricula and instructional approaches being more supportive of strategy instruction than others. In this section we list a set of general guidelines for structuring writing classrooms. These ideas are largely based on Writer's Workshop approaches to instruction (Atwell, 1987; Calkins, 1986; see also Schwartz & MacArthur, 1990).

Time to write. Schedule time for writing daily. Give students extended writing time so they can develop the topic and think through the writing. They should not be expected to finish a piece in one day.

Ownership of writing. Students should write for realistic purposes that are meaningful to them. This includes not only selecting topics, but also deciding which suggested revisions from teacher and peers they will follow. (See Schwartz & MacArthur, 1990.) Encourage students to write about familiar topics. Encourage writing for enjoyment and for self-expression to increase motivation for writing (Britton, 1982).

Writing for a variety of purposes. Atwell (1987; see pp. 263-269 for more examples) also encourages diverse forms of writing, including:

- Bulletin board for class or school (poems, jokes, advertise-ments, announcements, riddles....)
- Correspondence—pen pal letters, greeting cards, letters to the editor, letters of inquiry, complaints, fan letters, mes-sages in bottles, time capsule lists
- Class magazine, school newspaper or yearbook, local newspaper
- Writing contests, trade magazines that publish student writing, popular teen magazines
- Petitions to principal, school board, city council, etc.

Share writing. Publication should not just be reserved as an award for writing that teachers or students judge as good. Let students write some pieces that will not be graded, and involve them in evaluating whether their work is ready to share.

Collaboration and feedback. Students need frequent opportunities to discuss their writing with peers (e.g., through group sharing, confer-ences, and peer editing), as well as with their teacher. Hold individual conferences with students to discuss their writing. Conferences provide a good opportunity to coach students through the writing process, encouraging them to effectively apply strategies they have learned. Take caution not to take over goal-setting, memory search, and other processes that students need to learn to carry out on their own.

Grammatical and linguistic instruction connected to writing (mini-lessons). Focus on mechanical, grammatical, and linguistic aspects of writing in response to particular student needs, rather than in isolation. For example, if it is important that students distinguish between standard written English and spoken dialects, talk to them about various pieces they are writing and what type of dialect might be most appropriate and effective. Instruction will be more meaningful if students see direct connections to improving their own writing. Several writing programs suggest presenting grammar and mechanics as part of mini-lessons presented by the teacher or by students (see Atwell, 1987).

Process. Encourage students to view writing as a process:

- Express to students that writing is challenging; present writing as a problem to be solved.
- Express to students that writing includes a set of processes —planning, drafting, and revising—that are used interac-tively.
- Give students opportunities to revise and resubmit papers. Better still, evaluate drafts before assigning a grade for the final paper.
- Model effective writing; point out to students times when

you need to write, both personally and professionally.
- Talk about your own processes and challenges in writing, and encourage students to do so.
- Frame common skills and teaching techniques as strategies (Duffy & Roehler, 1987). For example, instead of just giving students a list of prompts to guide them through a task, teach students to use the prompts on their own. Instead of just giving worksheets on which students combine sentences, teach students to identify sentences in their own writing that could be combined effectively.

Connections between reading and writing. One of the best ways to help students understand the importance of good writing is to help them see the connections between reading and writing. For example:

- Talk explicitly with students about the relationship between reading and writing—between the reader's needs and the writer's responsibilities. In both writing and reading, talk about the concepts of authorship, publishing, and so on.
- Encourage students to write in response to what they read.
- Evaluate the writing of texts read in class. Discussions about genres, dialect, grammar structure, etc., can take place in reference to both reading and writing.
- Integrate both reading and writing with other content areas. Consider coordinating writing assignments across one or more departments. (For suggestions about how to do this, see Applebee, 1977; Brown, Campione, & Day, 1981; and Lehr, 1980.)

Physical space for writing. Schwartz and MacArthur (1990) argue that the physical space of the classroom should support mobility and flexibility for writing. Private areas should be available for individual conferences and small group instruction, whereas students working together should be free to talk out loud.

Clear routines. Students need routines for writing time so they know what is expected and can develop strategies to meet those expectations (Schwartz & MacArthur (1990). Atwell (1987) and Calkins (1986) recommend dividing class time into four components: Class status (finding out where each student is in writing various pieces); mini-lesson (five to 10 minute lessons by teacher or student that give specific information about writing—a good place to incorporate explicit strategy explanations, as well as skill instruction); workshop proper (about 2/3 of the time is spent writing and conferencing); and closure (sharing writing with the class and getting feedback). Calkins (1986) suggests that these components can be thought of as modules that can be scheduled flexibly, depending on the class's needs.

Final Comment

We believe it is important that teachers begin integrating strategy instruction into process-oriented writing instruction. Strategy instruction supports students' understanding of writing as a flexible process for communicating ideas and feelings. In the future, we expect more research to be carried out with respect to writing instruction in secondary school. In the meantime, we hope this chapter will provide a starting point for implementing strategy instruction to help secondary school students become effective and reflective writers.

Recommended Readings

For information on writer's workshop & process writing:

Atwell, N. (1987). *In the middle: Writing, reading, and learning with adolescents*. Portsmouth, NH: Heinemann.

Calkins, L.M. (1986). *The art of teaching writing*. Portsmouth NH: Heinemann.

For a review of research on writing instruction:

Scardamalia & Bereiter (1986). Research on written composition. In M. C. Wittrock (Ed.), *Handbook of research on teaching* (3rd ed., pp. 778-803). New York: Macmillan.

For information about the instructional programs presented here:

Englert, C.S., Raphael, T.E., Anderson, L.M., Anthony, H.M., & Stevens, D.D. (1991). Making strategies and self-talk visible: Writing instruction in regular and special education classrooms. *American Educational Research Journal, 28*, 337-372.

Gaskins, I.W., & Elliot, T.T. (1991). *Implementing cognitive strategy instruction across the school: The Benchmark manual for teachers*. Cambridge, MA: Brookline Books.

Harris, K.R., & Graham, S. (1992). *Helping young writers master the craft: Strategy instruction and self-regulation in the writing process*. Cambridge, MA: Brookline Books.

Schmidt, J.L., Deshler, D.D., Schumaker, J.B., & Alley, G.R. (1988). Effects of generalization instruction on the written language performance of adolescents with learning disabilities in the mainstream classroom. *Journal of Reading, Writing, and Learning Disabilities International, 4*(4), 291-309.

REFERENCES

Applebee, A. N. (1977). ERIC/RCS Report: Writing across the curriculum: The London projects. *English Journal, 66*(9), 81-85.

Applebee, A. N. (1984). *Contexts for learning to write*. Norwood NJ: Ablex.

Atwell, N. (1987). *In the middle: Writing, reading, and learning with adolescents*. Portsmouth, NH: Heinemann.

Bell, R.Q. (1968). A reinterpretation of the direction of effects in studies of socialization. *Psychological Review, 75*, 81-95.

Bereiter, C., & Scardamalia, M. (1982). From conversation to composition: The role of instruction in a developmental process. In R. Glaser (Ed.). *Advances in instructional psychology* (Vol. 2, pp. 1-64). Hillsdale, NJ: Lawrence Erlbaum.

Bereiter, C., & Scardamalia, M. (1983). Does learning to write have to be so difficult? In A. Freedman, I. Pringle, & J. Yalden (Eds.), *Learning to write: First language, second language*. London: Longman's International.

Bereiter, C., & Scardamalia, M. (1987). *The psychology of written communication*. Hillsdale, NJ: Erlbaum & Associates.

Berkenkotter, C., & Murray, D. (1983). Decisions and revisions: The planning strategies of a publishing writer and responses of a laboratory rat—-or being protocol. *College Composition and Communication, 34*, 156-172.

Bjorklund, D.F. (1989). *Children's thinking: Developmental function and individual differences*. Monterey, CA: Brooks/Cole.

Britton, J. (1982). Spectator role and the beginnings of writing. In M. Nystrand (Ed.), *What writers know: The language, process, and structure of written discourse* (pp. 149-169). New York: Academic Press.

Brown, A. L. (1980). Metacognitive development and reading. In R. J. Spiro, B. C. Bruce, & W. F. Brewer (Eds.), *Theoretical issues in reading comprehension* (pp. 453-481). Hillsdale, NJ: Erlbaum.

Brown, A.L., Campione, J.C., & Day, J.D. (1981). Learning to learn: On training students to learn from texts. *Educational Researcher, 10*, 14-21.

Bulgren, J. A., McKnight, P., Deshler, D. D., & Schumaker, J. B. (1989). *The 1989 INROADS program report*. Lawrence KS: University of Kansas, Institute for Research in Learning Disabilities.

Butler-Nalin, K. (1984). Revising patterns in students' writing. In A. N. Applebee (Ed.), *Contexts for learning to write: Studies of secondary school instruction* (pp. 121-133). Norwood NJ: Ablex.

Calkins, L. M. (1986). *The art of teaching writing*. Portsmouth NH: Heinemann.

Cohen, E., & Scardamalia. M. (1983). *The effects of instructional intervention in the revision of essays by grade six children*. Paper presented at the annual meeting of the American Educational Research Association, Montreal.

Danoff, B., Harris, K. R., & Graham, S. (1993). Incorporating strategy instruction within the writing process in the regular classroom: Effects on the writing of students with and without learning disabilities. *Journal of Reading Behavior, 25* (3), 295-322.

Denton, P. H., Seybert, J. A., & Franklin, E. L. (1988). Ideas in practice: A content-based learning strategies program. *Journal of Developmental Education, 11*(3), 20-24.

Deshler, D. D., & Schumaker, J. B. (1986). Learning strategies: An instructional alternative for low-achieving students. *Exceptional Children, 52*(6), 583-590.

Deshler, D. D., & Schumaker, J. B. (1988). An instructional model for teaching students how to learn. In J. L. Graden, J. E. Zins, & M. J. Curtis (Eds.), *Alternative educational delivery systems: Enhancing instructional options for all students* (pp. 391-411). Washington: National Association of School Psychologists.

Duffy, G. G., & Roehler, L.R. (1987). Teaching reading skills as strategies. *The Reading Teacher*, 414-418.

Durst, R. K. (1984). The development of analytic writing. In A. N. Applebee (Ed.), *Contexts for learning to write: Studies of secondary school instruction* (pp. 79-102). Norwood NJ: Ablex.

Englert, C. S., Raphael, T. E., Anderson, L. M., Anthony, H. M., Fear, K., & Greg, S. (1988). A case for writing intervention: Strategies for writing informational text. *Learning Disabilities Focus, 3*(2) 98-113.

Englert, C. S., Raphael, T. E., Anderson, L. M., Anthony, H. M., & Stevens, D. D. (1991). Making strategies and self-talk visible: Writing instruction in regular and special education classrooms. *American Educational Research Journal, 28*, 337-372.

Fitzgerald, J. (1992). Variant views about good thinking during composing: Focus on revision. In M. Pressley, K. R. Harris, J. T. Guthrie (Eds.), *Promoting academic competence and literacy in school* (pp. 337-358). San

Diego CA: Academic Press.

Fitzgerald, J., & Markham, L. (1987). Teaching children about revision in writing. *Cognition and Instruction, 4*, 3-24.

Flower, L. (1979). Writer-based prose: A cognitive basis for problems in writing. *College English, 41*, 19-37.

Flower, L., & Hayes, J. (1981). The pregnant pause: An inquiry into the nature of planning. *Research in the Teaching of English, 15*, 229-244.

Flower, L., Stein, V., Ackerman, J., Kantz, M. J., McCormick, K., & Peck, W. C. (1990). *Reading to write: Exploring a cognitive and social process.* New York: Oxford University Press.

Foley, M. (1989). Unteaching the five-paragraph essay. *Teaching English in the Two-Year College, 16*(4), 231-35.

Gaskins, I. W., & Elliot, T. T. (1991). *Implementing cognitive strategy instruction across the school: The Benchmark manual for teachers.* Cambridge MA: Brookline Books.

Graham, S. (1990). The role of production factors in learning disabled students' compositions. *Journal of Educational Psychology, 82*, 781-791.

Graham, S., & Harris, K. R. (1989). Components analysis of cognitive strategy instruction: Effects on learning disabled students' compositions and self-efficacy. *Journal of Educational Psychology, 81*(3), 353-361.

Graham, S., & Harris, K. R. (in press). Addressing problems in attention, memory and executive functioning: An example from self-regulated strategy development. In G. R. Lyon (Ed.), *Attention, Memory, and Executive Function.* Baltimore, MD: Brookes Publishing.

Graves, M., Slater, W.H., Redd-Boyd, T., Duin, A.H., Furniss, D.W., & Hazeltine, P. (1988). Some characteristics of memorable expository writing: Effects of revisions by writers with different backgrounds. *Research in the Teaching of English, 22*, 242-265.

Harris, K. R., & Graham, S. (1992). *Helping young writers master the craft: Strategy instruction and self-regulation in the writing process.* Boston, MA: Brookline Books.

Hayes, J. R., & Flower, L. S. (1980). Writing as problem solving. *Visible Language, 14*, 388-399.

Hayes, J. R., Flower, L., Schriver, K., Stratman, J., & Carey, L. (1987). Cognitive processes in revision. In S. Rosenberg (Ed.), *Advances in applied psycholinguistics: Reading, writing, and language processing.* Cambridge England: Cambridge University Press.

Hock, M., Deshler, D. D., & Schumaker, J. B.

(1991). *Annual report on the GOALS program.* Lawrence KS: University of Kansas, Institute for Research in Learning Disabilities.

Hull, G. A. (1987). The editing process in writing: A performance study of more skilled and less skilled writers. *Research in the Teaching of English, 21*, 8-29.

Humes, A. (1983). Putting writing research into practice. *Elementary School Journal, 81*, 3-17.

Kline, F. M., Deshler, D. D., & Schumaker, J. B. (1992). Implementing learning strategy instruction in class settings: A research perspective. In M. Pressley, K. R. Harris, & J. T. Guthrie (Eds.), *Promoting academic competence and literacy in school* (pp. 361-406). San Diego: Academic Press.

Lehr, F. (1980). ERIC/RCS Report: Writing as learning in the content areas. *English Journal, 69*(8), 23-25.

MacArthur, C., & Graham, S. (1987). Learning disabled students' composing with three methods: Handwriting, dictation, and word processing. *Journal of Special Education, 21*, 22-42.

MacArthur, C., Graham, S., & Schwartz, S. (1991). Knowledge of revision and revising behavior among learning disabled students. *Learning Disability Quarterly, 14*, 61-73.

Marshall, J. D. (1984a). Process and product: Case studies of writing in two content areas. In A. N. Applebee (Ed.), *Contexts for learning to write: Studies of secondary school instruction* (pp. 149-168). Norwood NJ: Ablex.

Marshall, J. D. (1984b). Schooling and the composing process. In A. N. Applebee (Ed.), *Contexts for learning to write: Studies of secondary school instruction* (pp. 103-119). Norwood NJ: Ablex.

McCormick, C. B., Busching, B. A., & Potter, E. F. (1992). Children's knowledge about writing: The development and use of evaluative criteria. In M. Pressley, K. R. Harris, & J. T. Guthrie (Eds.), *Promoting academic competence and literacy in school* (pp. 311-336). San Diego CA: Academic Press.

McCutchen, D., & Perfetti, C. A. (1983). Local coherence: Helping young writers manage a complex task. *Elementary School Journal, 84*, 71-75.

Moccia, R. E., McKnight, P., Deshler, D. D., & Schumaker, J. B. (1990). *The 1990 INROADS Program Report.* Lawrence KS: University of Kansas, Institute for Research on Learning Disabilities.

Morocco, C. C., & Neuman, S. B. (1986). Word processors and the acquisition of writing strategies. *Journal of Learning Disabilities, 19*(4), 243-247.

Nold, E. W. (1981). Revising. In C. H. Frederiksen & J. F. Dominic (Eds.), *Writing: The nature, development, and teaching of written communication* (pp. 67-79). Hillsdale, NJ: Erlbaum.

Nystrand, M. (1986). *The structure of written communication: Studies in reciprocity between writers and readers.* New York: Academic Press.

Nunnally, T. E. (1991). Breaking the five-para-graph-theme barrier. *English Journal, 80*(1), 67-71.

Paris, P. (1980). *Discourse schemata as knowledge and as regulators of text production.* Unpub-lished master's thesis. York University, Downsview, Canada.

Pearson, P. D. (1985). Changing the face of reading comprehension instruction. *Read-ing Teacher, 38,* 724-738.

Pressley, M., El-Dinary, P. B., Gaskins, I., Schuder, T., Bergman, J. L., Almasi, J., & Brown, R. (1992). Beyond direct explana-tion: Transactional instruction of reading comprehension strategies. *Elementary School Journal, 92*(5), 513-555.

Pressley, M. with McCormick, C. (1995). *Ad-vanced educational psychology for educators, researchers, and policy makers.* New York: Harper Collins.

Raphael, T. E., Englert, C. S., & Kirschner, B. W., (1988). Acquisition of expository writ-ing skills (Tech. Rep. No. 421) Institute for Research on Teaching: Michigan State University.

Rohman, D. G. (1965). Pre-writing: The stage of discovery in the writing process. *College Composition and Communication, 16,* 106-112.

Rose, M. (1980). Rigid rules, inflexible plans, and the stifling of language: A cognitivist analysis of writer's block. *College Composi-tion and Communication, 31*(4), 389-400.

Sameroff, A.J. (1975). Early influences on devel-opment: Fact or fancy? *Merrill-Palmer Quar-terly, 21,* 267-294.

Sawyer, R., Graham, S., & Harris, K. R. (1992). Direct teaching, strategy instruction, and strategy instruction with explicit self-regu-lation: Effects on learning disabled stu-dents' composition skills and self-efficacy. *Journal of Educational Psychology, 84,* 340-352.

Scardamalia, M., & Bereiter, C. (1983). The development of evaluative, diagnostic, and remedial capabilities in children's compos-ing. In M. Martlew (Ed.), *The psychology of written language: A developmental approach.* London: John Wiley.

Scardamalia, M., & Bereiter, C. (1986). Research on written composition. In M. C. Wittrock (Ed.), *Handbook of research on teaching* (3rd ed., pp. 778-803). New York: Macmillan.

Scardamalia, M., Bereiter, C., & Steinbach, R. (1984). Teachability of reflective processes in written composition. *Cognitive Science, 8,* 173-190.

Schmidt, J. L., Deshler, D. D., Schumaker, J. B., & Alley, G. R. (1988). Effects of generaliza-tion instruction on the written language performance of adolescents with learning disabilities in the mainstream classroom. Journal of Reading, Writing, and Learning Disabilities International, 4(4), 291-309.

Schumaker, J. B. (in preparation). *TOWER: A theme writing strategy.*

Schumaker, J. B., & Deshler, D. D. (1992). Validation of learning strategy interven-tions for students with learning disabili-ties: Results of a programmatic research effort. In B. Y. L. Wong (Ed.), *Contemporary intervention research in learning disabilities: An international perspective* (pp. 22-46). New York: Springer-Verlag.

Schumaker, J. B., Deshler, D. D., Alley, G. R., Warner, M. M., Clark, F. L., & Nolan, S. (1982). Error monitoring: A learning strat-egy for improving adolescent academic performance. In W.M. Cruickshank and J.W. Lerner (Eds.), *Coming of Age: Vol. 3, The Best of ACLD.* Syracuse, NY: Syracuse University Press.

Schumaker, J. B., & Lyerla, K. (1993). *The para-graph writing strategy: Instructor's manual.* Lawrence KS: University of Kansas, Cen-ter for Research on Learning.

Schumaker, J. B., Nolan, S. M., & Deshler, D. D. (1985). *The error monitoring strategy: Instructor's manual.* Lawrence, KS: Univer-sity of Kansas.

Schumaker, J. B., & Sheldon, J. (1985). *The sentence writing strategy: Instructor's manual.* Lawrence KS: University of Kansas.

Schwartz, S. S., & MacArthur, C. M. (1990). Creating a community of writers: The com-puters and writing instruction project. *Pre-venting School Failure, 34*(4), 9-13.

Thomas, C. C., Englert, C. S., & Gregg, S. (1987). An analysis of errors and strategies in the expository writing of learning dis-abled students. *Remedial and Special Educa-tion, 8,* 21-30.

Vygotsky, L. S. (1978). *Mind in society: The development of higher psychological processes.* M. Cole, V. John-Steiner, S. Scribner, & E. Souberman (Eds.). Cambridge, MA: Har-vard University Press.

Weaver, C. (1990). *Understanding whole language: From principles to practice.* Portsmouth NH: Heinemann.

CHAPTER 6

General Problem Solving Strategies

Alice Corkill Dempster • University of Nevada, Las Vegas

Mr. Ramsey, the social studies teacher, wants his students to learn about the difficulties faced by early explorers: he wants them to learn about map reading and early navigation; he wants them to experience the fears and frustrations of New World explorers. He wants them to learn about it through some method other than by lecturing to his students or having his students read from a textbook.

Jane is in Mr. Ramsey's social studies class and has been given an assignment. A computer-assisted instruction program has been made available to the students for their unit about New World Exploration. The students have been assigned the task of sailing to and from the New World (with the assistance of the computer) in an attempt to acquire gold. The students will make navigation decisions and the computer will provide feedback about the results of those decisions. Good navigation decisions result in more progress to and from the New World and a chance for gold, while poor decisions result in setbacks and maybe even a wrecked vessel.

Both Mr. Ramsey and Jane have a problem—how can I achieve all of these goals? How can Jane and Mr. Ramsey solve their problems? Both Jane and Mr. Ramsey need to use their general problem solving skills.

Why is it important for secondary students—and teachers—to acquire general problem solving skills? The simplest explanation is that we face problems continually in our everyday lives. Anytime you are doing one thing, would rather be doing another, and don't quite know how to move from where you are to where you would like to be, you have a problem. The problem is: how can you move from point A (where you are now) to point B (where you want or need to be)? We spend a good deal of our time solving problems of all shapes and sizes, from deciding what to have for dinner to determining the best method of teaching something to our students. Given this broad definition of problem solving, we can see that our secondary students, as they move from subject to subject, are continually encountering problems to solve.

Frequently when we think about problem solving we think "math," but problem solving is much broader than this one area. If the student has to write a term paper, he or she has a problem; if the student has a test to take, he or she has a problem; if the student is given a homework assignment, he or she has a problem; and the list could go on and on.

This chapter focuses on strategies that can be used for any problem solving situation, but particularly for nonmathematical, academic problems (for mathematical problem solving strategies, see Chapter 7 of this volume). As secondary school teachers, and indeed as teachers at any level, we are concerned that students are able to take what they learn in school, in our classes in particular, and use those skills in their everyday lives. For example, an English teacher may have a student who writes beautiful and complicated short stories but can't write a cover letter for a job inquiry. A foreign language teacher may have a student who scores very high on written exams but, when he or she visits a country that uses the foreign language, can ask for directions but can't understand the response. A civics teacher may have a student who understands "just cause" in terms of why a police officer may search a person who is seen running from a building where the burglar alarm is sounding, but cannot understand how "just cause" applies to an administrator or parent searching the student's locker. In all academic areas, students should encounter many opportunities to acquire these skills through problem solving.

Let us reconsider the problems that Mr. Ramsey and Jane have to face. Mr. Ramsey's problem is that he is in one situation—his students don't know anything about early exploration—and he wants to be in another situation—he wants his students to know about early exploration, and not from listening to him lecture, and not by reading about it from the textbook. Mr. Ramsey's problem is moving from students who don't know to students who do know. Jane's problem is this: her current situation is that she is in Spain and she has no gold; she would rather be in a situation where she is in Spain and has gold that she acquired from the New World. What can Mr. Ramsey and Jane do? In order to answer this question, let us first take a look at how we can "set up" or *represent* both problems.

Whether we search back 10, 25, or 50 years, we will find practically the same set of suggestions concerning problem solving. The differences lie mostly in the vocabulary and/or degree of elaboration of the suggestions (for example, the IDEAL Problem Solver, Bransford & Stein, 1984; or the CoRT problem solving system, de Bono, 1973). Although these models have different procedures, the basic premise underlying successful problem solving does not change. The first thing we must do is understand the problem. Polya (1945) states, "It is foolish to answer a question that you do not understand" (p. 6). More recently it has been suggested that what problem solvers do, and need to do, is to construct a "problem representation" (see Bransford & Stein, 1984; Hayes, 1978).

A problem representation has four parts: the initial state, the goal state, the operators, and the restrictions on the operators. In order to solve a problem, the problem solver must understand these four aspects. The *initial state* is the situation a person is in when they begin their problem solving journey—"where I am now." Mr. Ramsey has students who don't know much about early exploration. Jane is one of those students, but her initial state is different; she imagines herself as a potential early explorer who is in Spain and has no gold. Even though Mr. Ramsey and Jane are involved the same project, they do not have the same problem. As a result they do not have the same initial state.

The *goal state* is the situation the person would like, or needs, to be in. Mr. Ramsey wants his students to have a better understanding of many aspects of early exploration. Jane, on the other hand, just wants to be in Spain with gold that she has acquired from the New World. Once again, even though Mr. Ramsey and Jane are involved in the same project, they have different goal states, which means their problems are different.

The *operators* are different actions the problem solver can take in trying to solve the problem. The operators, however, carry restrictions. *Restrictions on the operators* are limitations or obstructions. They can be thought of as the weaknesses of a particular potential solution (operator), or they may be limitations imposed by the problem or the solver. Consider Mr. Ramsey: he wants his students to learn about early exploration, *but* he does not want to lecture or assign reading material. What he does not want to do are his restrictions. He could have created a lecture; he could have assigned reading material, but he wants the students to learn this material in some other way.

Figure 6-1 shows how we might represent a problem graphically. In this representation assume that there are 5 potential solutions (operators) to the problem. Each of the arrows representing an operator will move the problem solver to the goal state from the initial state. A problem can have any number of operators; it depends on how many the problem solver creates. Understanding the initial state, the goal state, and any preexisting restrictions will help the problem solver understand the problem better.

We already know what Mr. Ramsey selected as the best operator to move him from his initial state to his goal state: he found a computer-assisted instruction program which will tell students the consequences of their sailing decisions. The operator that the problem solver chooses to use to solve the problem is called the *solution path*. Generally the operator with the lowest number of, or least severe, restrictions on it will be selected as the solution path. Mr. Ramsey hopes that his solution path will allow the students to learn all kinds of things about early exploration and it avoids potential restrictions: he is not lecturing and the students are not reading their textbooks.

The problem solver must take great care in identifying the initial and goal states. How they are defined will have an impact on what kind of operators will be considered. Another student in Mr. Ramsey's class, Mack, has interpreted the problem differently. He figures that getting

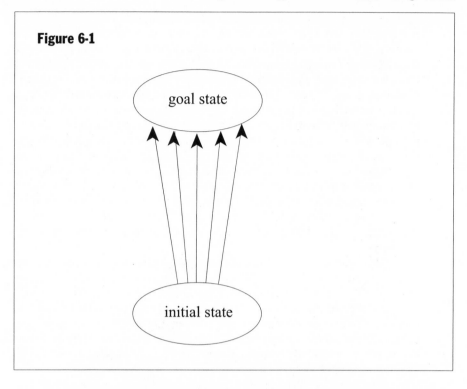

Figure 6-1

to and from the New World with gold is not as important as getting to the New World as quickly as possible. That is, if he gets there first, there will be more gold for him and less for others that follow. His initial state is that he imagines himself in Spain; his goal state is to be in the New World and to get there quickly. How he has defined his problem will affect his sailing decisions (operators).

In identifying the initial and goal states, problem solvers should be encouraged to look at their problem from many perspectives. Dixon (1984) found that when helping people solve problems (in a counseling setting) if they could visualize the problem from several perspectives, then they would have a wider variety of actions that might be considered when looking for potential solutions (operators). How can we encourage careful attention to the definition of the initial and goal states? One fruitful approach has been the use of cooperative groups. Research that compares the effectiveness of groups (of 3 to 5 students) to individuals has found, over and over again, that, under most circumstances, groups are more productive in solving problems than individuals (Johnson & Johnson, 1989).

Solving Problems Using Cooperative Groups

What exactly is it about cooperative groups that results in greater success? Some suggest that working in groups minimizes anxiety and competition (Parker, 1984). Some suggest that cooperative groups encourage students to talk about a problem, take a position, and defend that position (Gilbert-Macmillan, 1983). Cooperative groups are thought to encourage use of higher reasoning strategies (Johnson, Johnson, Holubec, & Roy, 1984). Most importantly, cooperative group problem solving is thought to give students the opportunity to focus on the problem solving processes (e.g., defining the problem, creating potential solutions, testing and checking solutions) rather than the solution (Gilbert-Macmillan, 1983).

Many students, when faced with a problem, tend to focus on the answer rather than the process (Duren & Cherrington, 1992). The focus of the students is probably determined by the teacher. If the teacher focuses on the solution, so do the students, but when the teacher shifts his or her focus to the process, so will the students. Helping students with general problem solving skills requires that we encourage them to shift their focus from the product to the process. The "correctness" of the solution should be de-emphasized, perhaps even left out completely, while success in process tasks should be stressed.

How should a cooperative group function? Simply having students work together in small groups will not necessarily increase individual achievement, instead it appears that students should engage in something called "group processing" (Johnson, Johnson, Stanne, & Garibaldi, 1990). In group processing, students work in groups, but they spend time at regular intervals determining which actions, either group or individual, have been helpful and unhelpful, and they decide which to continue or change.

For the best use of cooperative groups, group members should be assigned tasks. Johnson et al. (1990) suggest that each student be assigned responsibility for monitoring one of three important social skills for group work, as monitoring is an important component of metacognition. In cooperative groups, monitoring is not left up to the individual, but rather to the group as a whole. The monitoring tasks include (1) summarizing the contributions of group members during the discussion, (2) encouraging active participation on the part of all group members, and (3) making sure all members are in agreement about a decision that is being made. At regular intervals, the groups should be interrupted for a teacher-led session which focuses on whether the group social skills are being used and how well they are being used. After each teacher-led session, the groups should be encouraged to discuss how frequently individual group members are using the group social skills.

Johnson et al. (1990) used this approach in research where students were attempting to solve a social studies type problem. It is the same problem we have used in our example of Mr. Ramsey and his social studies class, where students were to sail an ancient ship to the New World and back on a gold-seeking mission. They had to read maps, learn about navigation, and make decisions about what actions to take.

A computer was used to record their decisions and to supply feedback concerning their progress. Groups where students were assigned specific monitoring tasks, and where teacher- and student-led processing (the discussions about how group members were performing) occurred, were more successful in sailing to and from the New World, and they also accumulated more gold. The students in these groups also participated in the group discussion more than in groups where students were not assigned monitoring tasks.

Beyond greater success (in terms of solving the problem) and more group discussion, there are other advantages to using cooperative groups in problem solving. Reconsider our two students who are involved in solving this problem: Jane and Mack. Each student is likely to define the problem differently, since each acts independently. Jane's definition is likely to lead her to learn what Mr. Ramsey wants the students to learn, while Mack's definition may lead to hasty decisions and an early shipwreck. When Jane and Mack along with a couple of other students are put into a cooperative group, Jane may be able to help Mack see that getting to the New World quickly is not how the problem should be defined. With groups, everyone has the opportunity to contribute to the problem's representation. As a result, they may examine the problem from more perspectives than a person solving a problem alone would have considered, which may produce more careful selection of an initial state, goal state, and operators.

The students may also acquire a better understanding of the restrictions. Laughlin and McGlynn (1986) found exactly this in their problem solving research. Students, either alone or in a group of four, tried to figure out an arbitrary rule that would divide a normal deck of 52 playing cards into two groups: example and nonexample. For instance, if the rule was "face card," the jack of hearts would be an example while the four of hearts would not. Many characteristics for dividing a deck of cards exist, like color, suit, number, and so forth. The arbitrary rule could be simple, "diamonds," or complex, "odd spades alternate with even hearts." In this study, the experimenter would show the group or individual an example of the rule. Then either the group, as a whole, or the individual would create a hypothesis about the rule. After creating and recording the hypothesis, the group or individual would select a card to play based on this hypothesis and receive feedback from the experimenter as to whether it was an example or nonexample of the rule. The subjects were attempting to figure out a rule using what is called induction. Laughlin and McGlynn (1986) found that when subjects exchanged ideas in terms of hypotheses and evidence—either the group working together or an individual who was given information from the group—problem solving success increased.

Cooperative groups work together to understand the parameters of the problem. Even though group work may result in great benefit to students, frequently students are required to work independently. What if using groups is inappropriate or impossible? Using groups early in a semester may help students learn many problem solving strategies which they could then use when working independently. Watching how others approach problems, experiencing success (or lack thereof) in problem solving, being exposed to a variety of problems, and learning the processes can only benefit students.

When students are working alone, they should be encouraged to concentrate on and identify the most important components of the problem. Irrelevant information in the problem may cause difficulties in solving the problem (Marr & Sternberg, 1986). Consider the following example of a verbal analogy problem, which is frequently used in the assessment of general mental ability and requires the student to understand the parameters of a problem including what is relevant and what is irrelevant: Elephant is to small as _____ is to _____; a) large: little; b) hippopotamus: mouse; c) lion: timid; d) turtle: slow. Do you know the correct answer? It isn't "a"! The correct answer is "c." Many students incorrectly identify "a" as the answer. Their reasoning seems sound: they would probably suggest that an elephant is large and *small* is another way to say *little*, so "a" is a correct answer. Using this line of reasoning, letter "b" could also be correct. In fact, although the relationship "an elephant is large" holds true, *small* is 'a characteristic not usually associated with elephants'. Therefore we need to find an animal that is listed with a characteristic that is not usually associated with it—lion: timid. The irrelevant information is the size component (Whimby, 1985).

Research with gifted students, in fact, suggests that the ability to focus on relevant information and exclude irrelevant information is crucial. For example, non-gifted students were more likely to focus as much attention on relevant and irrelevant information when solving verbal analogies, while gifted students were more likely to dismiss irrelevant information and focus on relevant information (Marr & Sternberg, 1986). Furthermore, problems with irrelevant information are more difficult to solve than those without.

Although there are no clear research-based strategies for how to best (a) encourage students to focus on relevant information or (b) determine what constitutes relevant or irrelevant information, making students aware that sometimes there is information in the setup of the problem that is not necessary for solving the problem and that may impede problem solving may help them to discount irrelevant information. The point is that understanding the problem is essential for solving it. If I do not understand the problem, I won't be able to solve it. If I am working alone, I want to make sure that I carefully attend to the problem in terms of what is important (relevant information), what is misleading (irrelevant information), and what the problem is actually asking me to do.

Setting up a problem representation, whether working alone or in a group, helps the problem solver to better understand the problem, especially the initial state, the goal state, and any global restrictions. This is the first important goal in problem solving. The second goal is to devise a plan for solving the problem (Polya, 1945). Devising a plan involves examination of the information supplied in the problem, as well as employing a series of questions to help select a potentially successful set of operations that will lead to a satisfactory solution. The operations are what were earlier called "operators." Operators are potential solutions to a problem. *Operations* are acts, steps, or transactions that will move the problem solver from the initial state to the goal state.

During this phase of problem solving, many operators (potential solutions) will be considered, then rejected because the costs (or restrictions) are too great. It is important for the problem solver to create and evaluate as many operators as possible; more choices for solutions may result in greater satisfaction with the solution finally selected. Using cooperative groups would help in the creation and evaluation of operators; more problem solvers attempting to solve a problem should result in more potential solutions (operators). In addition, more problem solvers with a variety of perspectives and different types of prior knowledge should result in better evaluation of each operator. That is, with more problem solvers evaluating each operator, the restrictions should be clearer.

Solving Problems Via Analogy

One way to begin creating or forming operators is to ask yourself a question or two. Polya (1945) suggests: 1) "Do you know a related problem?" and 2) "Can you restate the problem?" By the time the problem solver is attempting to formulate operators, the problem should be understood in terms of an initial state and a goal state. In effect, if the problem can be restated, it already should have been by this point. The problem solver may have also already tried to consider a similar problem, but if he or she hasn't, now is a good time. What the problem solver needs to do is search his or her memory for a problem that is analogous to the current problem.

Solving a problem via analogy suggests that the problem solver will find a similar problem in memory (a particular schema), take the solution to that problem, and modify it for use with the current problem; this is also referred to as "transfer." The structure, including the solution, of the problem in memory which matches (or comes closest to matching) the problem to be solved is "transferred" to another, perhaps new, schema. After transfer, the solution to the problem is altered or modified so that it will potentially solve the new problem. A simple example would be using a previously written letter to help write a new and similar letter. Let's say a student asks for a letter of recommendation for a job. You have written letters of recommendation before and happen to have a copy of one on a diskette. Instead of starting from scratch, you might take the previously written letter and modify it for the new letter. In effect, the first letter is like the original schema from which a solution, the new letter, will be taken.

Let's consider another example of solving problems via analogy. When I was in college I rode my bicycle almost everywhere I went. One day something went wrong with my bicycle. My brother has always seemed very mechanically inclined to me, so I thought he might be able to help. I called him, and he was able to fix my bicycle. Several years later when I was visiting my parents, my car broke down. Whom do you think I called for help? Of course I called my brother. The first problem was mechanical and so was the second one. The same solution was attempted for the second problem because it worked in solving the first one. In effect, the solution from problem one was transferred to problem two. This, however, was a very simple example. Frequently, solving problems via analogy is not quite so straightforward.

Holyoak and his colleagues (e.g., Gick & Holyoak, 1980; 1983; Holyoak & Koh, 1987) have conducted a series of studies dealing with analogical problem solving. In particular, Gick and Holyoak (1980) used the following problem as a source for a solution that might be used later.

A small country was ruled from a strong fortress by a dictator. The fortress was situated in the middle of the country, surrounded by farms and villages. Many roads lead to the fortress through the countryside. A rebel general has vowed to capture the fortress. The general knows that an attack by his entire army would capture the fortress. So he gathers his army at the head of one of the roads, ready to launch a full-scale direct attack. However, the general then learns that the dictator has planted mines on each of the roads. The mines have been set so that small groups of people could pass over them safely, since the dictator needed to move his troops and workers to and from the fortress. However, a large force would detonate the mines. Not only would this blow up the road, but it would also destroy many neighboring villages. It therefore seemed impossible to capture the fortress.

The general, however, devised a simple plan. He divided his army into small groups and dispatched each group to the head of a different road. When all was ready he gave the signal and each group marched down a different road. Each group continued down its road to the fortress so that the entire army arrived together at the fortress at the same time. In this way, the general captured the fortress and overthrew the dictator.

In their study, Gick and Holyoak asked subjects to carefully read and write a summary of the problem. In this problem, there are two main components in the solution: (1) use of multiple, smaller forces (the small groups marching down the road to the fortress) and (2) simultaneous convergence (the entire army arrives at the fortress at the same time). Subjects, after reading and summarizing this problem, were then given another problem—this one—to solve.

A patient has been complaining about stomach problems for a considerable period of time. A number of tests are run and it is discovered that the patient has a malignant tumor in his stomach. Suppose you are the specialist called in to treat this patient. You know that it is impossible to operate on the patient, but unless the tumor is destroyed the patient will die. There is, however, a kind of ray that can be used to destroy the tumor. If the ray reaches the tumor at a sufficiently high intensity, the tumor will be destroyed. Unfortunately, at this intensity the healthy tissue that the ray passes through on the way to the tumor will also be destroyed. At lower intensities the ray is harmless to healthy tissue, but it will not affect the tumor either. A full-intensity dosage of the ray appeared impossible. What type of procedure might you use to destroy the tumor with the ray and at the same time avoid damaging the healthy tissue surrounding it?

This problem is analogous to the previous problem and can be solved in a similar fashion. Can you figure out the solution? The use of multiple, smaller forces (multiple weaker rays) that simultaneously converge on the target (the tumor) is also the solution to this problem. If weaker rays are angled such that they all intersect at the site of the tumor, the intensity will be sufficient to destroy the tumor at the intersection but will not destroy the healthy tissue through which they pass. This is very similar to sending small troops (weak rays) down multiple roads (angled rays) that converge on the fortress (intersect at the site of the tumor).

In this example, you had an advantage over the subjects in the Gick and Holyoak study: you had been given a hint to use what was learned from the first problem. Seeing the connection between the problems is essential for transfer. Gick and Holyoak (1983) discovered that subjects who had identified both components of the solution to the general problem had a better chance at solving the surgeon problem. In effect, if a subject had identified the most important components of the first problem and its solution, they had a better chance of transferring that solution to the second problem. Gick and Holyoak found in their studies that a hint or cue was especially important in solving problems via analogy. More simply, solving problems via analogy is a strategy that is not often spontaneously used without direct instruction or a cue or suggestion to try and find a related problem (Holyoak, 1985). Encouraging students to try and think of similar problems and their solutions may help in solving problems.

This strategy is appropriate for either group or independent problem solving. The advantage of using cooperative groups at this point in the problem solving process, however, is that with more problem solvers engaged in solving the problem, there is a greater likelihood that a similar problem from memory will be accessed. Nevertheless, all problem solvers, whether working alone or in groups, should be encouraged to search their memories for similar problems that might assist in solving current problems.

Solving Problems Using Imagery

Another strategy that is often useful in problem solving is visualizing the problem. Drawing a picture or imagining the problem helps us see connections between the components of a problem (Polya, 1945). Visualizing information is a powerful aid to comprehension of written material (Bransford & Johnson, 1972), and also to encoding: taking information in from the environment in order to place it in memory (Paivio, 1986). Visualization helps us to represent the problem more clearly.

Using mental imagery in group settings (Schwab & D'Zamko, 1988) may also result in greater problem solving success. In using group mental imagery, participants are instructed to do two things. First, they should individually create a mental image that meets a need. This need could be solving the problem in question. Individuals could create representations of the problem—picture it, and maybe a solution, in their heads. Second, group members should share their images and look for a common theme among the images. The identified theme may help group members determine what action will meet the need. In effect, the theme represents the majority opinion of the group. Think back to Jane and Mack. They each defined the problem differently. If they are in the same group and other group members converge on one definition over the other, then they have a common theme upon which they may work. No one person holds ultimate sway over the theme identified; all members contribute to its creation.

In some situations, drawing a picture is an unusually effective visualization strategy, whether working alone or in cooperative groups. If the image is at least roughly sketched, then all members of the group may get a better idea of one person's representation. Creating charts, graphs, matrices, or other written or drawn aids may also assist in solving the problem. Many logic problems, for example, are most easily solved when a chart or matrix is created to help the solver keep track of the information provided by the problem and the deductions made by the problem solver. Consider the following problem taken from Levine (1988):

> Four men own the following musical instruments: Matt; oboe and bassoon; Hank, trumpet and flute; Jack, flute and clarinet; Bill, trumpet and oboe. If the bassoon is cheaper than the oboe, the trumpet is more expensive than the flute, the oboe is cheaper than the flute, and the bassoon is more expensive than the clarinet, who owns the most expensive instruments?

At first glance, the problem might seem overwhelming. Rearranging the information and recording it on a grid is a useful strategy for solving this problem (see Figure 6-2). In order to solve this problem, first the solver should figure out how expensive the various instruments are in relation to one another. By listing all of the instruments together in their various cost relationships, we see the ordering of instruments from most to least expensive. The final list, from most to least expensive, is this: trumpet, flute, oboe, bassoon, clarinet. In this list you can see that all of the cost descriptions from the problem have been accurately represented. The bassoon is cheaper than the oboe, the trumpet is more expensive than the flute, the oboe is cheaper than the flute, and the bassoon is more expensive than the clarinet. Now all we need to do is determine who owns the most expensive instruments, and a grid will help with this. Even the most casual inspection of the grid plainly demonstrates that Hank owns the most expensive instruments. This was a relatively simple problem. Problems with more components require more elaborate grid systems. Even so, creating a grid and filling it out may assist in keeping track of all the information (for more about visualization see Levine, 1988).

Solving Problems Via Means-Ends Analysis

Sometimes the problem may be too complex (i.e., consisting of a series of subproblems) to solve easily or in one or two simple moves. The logic problem we considered (the men and their musical instruments) was fairly simple, but the problem faced by Mr. Ramsey's students is not so simple. What Mr. Ramsey's students have to do is solve a series of problems that they will encounter on their trip to and from the New

Figure 6-2
Grid visualization

Instrument Ownership

		Matt	Hank	Jack	Bill
most expensive	Trumpet		X		X
	Flute		X	X	
	Oboe	X			X
	Bassoon	X			
least expensive	Clarinet			X	

World. Mr. Ramsey's students should use what is called a *means-ends analysis* (Newell & Simon, 1972). Because the problem facing Jane and her classmates requires them to make a number of decisions regarding their journey to the New World, we can imagine that rather than having one problem to solve, Jane and the rest have several problems to solve. Each sailing decision made by the group will result in something different. They may make progress toward the New World; they may face difficulties. Breaking the problem into smaller pieces would be helpful. Jane's group should create *reduction goals*: small problems that need to be solved so that the larger problem may be solved. Each time Jane and her group make a sailing decision, they are attempting to solve a reduction goal. As each reduction goal is reached, the problem solvers (hopefully) move closer to a satisfactory solution to the larger problem.

Figure 6-3 may help us better understand means-ends analysis. In Figure 6-3 we see that our problem solvers start at the initial state and have created 3 operators that will move them to reduction goal 1. From reduction goal 1 to reduction goal 2, our problem solvers have created 2 operators. From reduction goal 2 to reduction goal 3, there are 4 operators, and so on. As the problem solver moves through each reduction goal, he or she moves closer to the goal state. Notice that different numbers of operators have been created for each reduction goal, as the number of operators created depends on the individual problem solver. Only one of each set of operators will be the solution path for the reduction goal. In this instance, our problem solver would have 5 solution paths, one for each reduction goal.

Let's take a closer look. Jane and her group first have to decide when to set sail; the time of day they select will have implications for their progress. Imagine that Jane's group decides to set sail at dawn. They will face a different set of parameters for their next problem (reduction goal) than will a group who decided to leave at noon or dusk. Each decision will change the "where they are" part of the problem and require that reduction goals be created. Each reduction goal has its own "initial state" and sets of operators with restrictions will be considered in choosing a solution path for the reduction goal. This series of reduction goals will continue until Jane and her group either achieve the overall goal—being in Spain with gold that was acquired in the New World—or wreck their vessel.

Let's look at another example. Earlier I suggested that writing a term paper was a problem. If I were solving this problem, I'd suggest that the initial state is that I have no term paper to hand in. My goal state would be to have a term paper to hand in that will receive a satisfactory grade (I define satisfactory for myself—that is, some students may consider a "C" to be satisfactory, while others will only be satisfied with an "A"). Sitting down at my keyboard and starting to write may move me in the direction of the goal state, but writing a term paper is a complex problem. I will probably be more successful if I identify a series of reduction goals. For example, my first reduction goal may be to select a topic. I may have a variety of ways to do this. I might (a) go to the

Figure 6-3

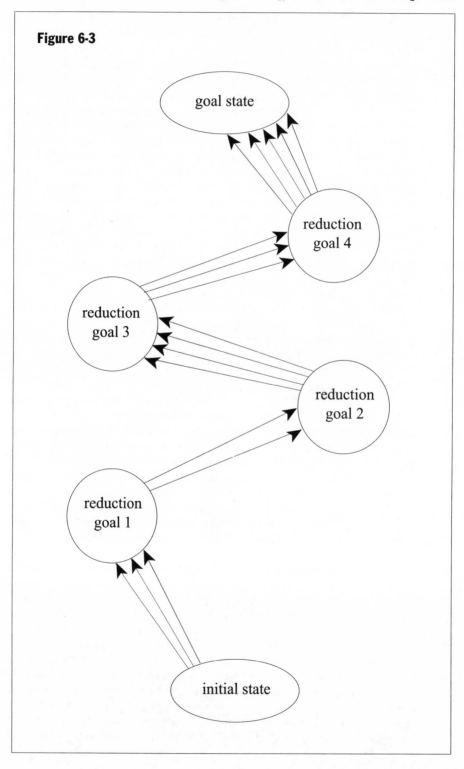

library and do some reading, (b) ask my teacher for ideas, or (c) ask my classmates for ideas. These three ideas are all operators for reduction goal 1. My second reduction goal might be to make an outline. The third reduction goal might be to write the first paragraph. The fourth reduction goal might be to write a rough draft. I continue creating and solving reduction goals until the final goal state is reached. I have used means-ends analysis to solve my problem. In fact, the series of steps I have outlined is very similar to how my 12th-grade English teacher taught me to write a term paper. Breaking a complex problem into smaller units is likely to make the overall problem easier to solve.

During the second phase, a plan was devised—operators were considered and restrictions were identified. Now comes the easy part: carrying out the plan is the third phase. The chosen operator—which is now the solution path—is used. If the problem resulted in selection of a fairly straightforward solution path, our problem solvers should move on to the final phase, checking the solution. If the selected operator resulted in multiple steps or involved a series of reduction goals, each step of the plan should be carefully checked as it is implemented (Polya, 1945).

The final step is to "look back" (Polya, 1945, p. 5), to evaluate not only the solution (i.e., did we get the right answer?) but also the plan itself. Polya insists that problem solvers, even the very good ones, miss this final, important phase. How the solution is checked, whether simple or complex, is a critical component of the problem solving process and one that is often ignored. By reexamining the solution and the process, the problem solvers could strengthen their knowledge in the problem area and enhance their problem solving abilities.

Checking our work or "looking back" might be enough if we have correctly solved the problem, but what should be done when the solution we have is not the correct one? This is where teachers could best help their students by using elaborated corrective feedback.

Using Elaborated Corrective Feedback in Problem Solving

Elaborated corrective feedback, sometimes called *adaptive feedback*, is a technique that is often associated with research on computer-assisted instruction. Nevertheless, corrective feedback is not a new idea to most teachers. Students need to be told whether their answers are right or wrong, and when the answers are wrong, correct answers need to be supplied. Corrective feedback (a) keeps students from repeatedly practicing incorrect responses, (b) more efficiently uses the teacher's time—he or she may focus on diagnosing and remedying difficulties, and (c) monitors student progress so that, for example, students are not asked to progress to a more difficult unit before they have mastered the prerequisites (Lysakowski & Walberg, 1982).

Here is an example of *simple corrective feedback* (taken from Siegel and Misselt, 1984). A student is learning abbreviations for the 103 chemical elements in the periodic table. When asked what chemical has the abbreviation "Cu," the student responds "cobalt," which is incorrect. This student has made a simple memory error. The student is told that his or her answer is incorrect and is given the correct answer: "Cobalt is Co; Cu is copper."

Elaborated corrective feedback is somewhat different. Instead of only telling the student that he or she is wrong and supplying the right answer, elaborated corrective feedback provides students with a series of rules or prompts that will help them come up with the correct answer on their own (Collins, Carnine, & Gersten, 1987). Elaborated corrective feedback asks the student to attempt to figure out why his or her response is incorrect on his or her own.

We elaborate information in order to process the material in a way such that it may be related to something we already know (Reigeluth, 1983). Students recall information that is elaborated better than nonelaborated information (Stein, Littlefield, Bransford, & Persampieri, 1984). Further, if they create the elaboration themselves, then recall is even greater (Willoughby, Waller, Wood, & MacKinnon, 1993). Having solved some problems and being able to recall information about them, including the problem solution that was used and its effectiveness, is important for future problem solving—remember, one of the earlier suggestions was to ask yourself if you knew a related problem (problem solving via analogy).

In computer-assisted instruction models, the prompts, questions, or cues provided to the problem solver depend upon the incorrect answer that was given. Let's reconsider the "Cu" problem. If one does not wish to give the student the correct answer, telling them they are incorrect and how they are incorrect may have to suffice. Elaborated corrective feedback for this example may have to be as simple as "Co is cobalt." This response should prompt the student to reconsider his or her answer.

Under other circumstances, more direct prompts may be possible. For example, reconsider the musical instruments problem we solved earlier. Suppose a student suggests that Bill has the most expensive instruments (he has the trumpet and the oboe). This student has made a reasoning error. The prompt or question that might work best here would be something about the oboe and the flute. The student understands that his or her answer is incorrect and is given a clue as to how to "re-solve" the problem—sending him or her back to the problem to reconsider whether the oboe or the flute was more expensive. Another student may suggest that Jack, who had the flute and clarinet, has the most expensive instruments. This student might be prompted to look back in order to determine which instrument was the most expensive and if anyone had that instrument. The type of prompts given to the students with incorrect solutions depends on their solution—the feedback is *elaborated* while also telling the student that their current solution is incorrect.

Let us look at another example. Students in foreign languages make many grammatical errors. Consider the English sentence, "I give my brother two books." The sentence, "I give two books to my brother," although different in terms of syntax (word order) from the first sentence, is identical in meaning. Both sentences are grammatically correct. There is a subject, "I;" a verb, "give;" a direct object, "two books;" and an indirect object, "my brother" (or "to my brother" in the case of sentence number 2). Let's imagine that we are students who are attempting to translate the above sentence(s) into German. Translating is our problem. We are in one situation: we have an English sentence. We'd like to be in a different situation: we want the English sentence reproduced in correct German. Our problem is that we have to decide how to get there—we must translate.

This is a complex memory problem. The Cu-is-copper problem requires the learner to access one element from memory. This transla-tion problem requires access to a large number of components that will contribute to the final product. For example, we must know (a) the appropriate German terms for all elements in the English sentence, (b) how to conjugate the verb "to give" in German, (c) the gender of "book" (masculine, feminine, or neuter), (d) the proper endings for possessive pronouns, (e) how to make "book" plural, (f) that in German all nouns are capitalized (not just proper nouns, as in English), and (g) which is the direct object and which is the indirect object.

Let us assume we know all of the things that have just been listed. On top of all of this, we must know the proper syntax. "*Ich gebe meinem Bruder zwei Bücher*" would be the correct translation. This sentence has all of the same components as the English sentence. There is a subject, "*Ich;*" a verb, "*gebe;*" a direct object, "*zwei Bücher;*" and an indirect object, "*meinem Bruder.*" Notice that the syntax of the German sentence is identical to the syntax of the first English sentence. If we had repro-duced the syntax from the second English sentence in our German sentence, "*Ich gebe zwei Bücher meinem Bruder,*" it would be incorrect grammatically. In German, when the direct and indirect objects are nouns (as opposed to pronouns, i.e., "it" or "him"), the indirect object must precede the direct object. Therefore "*meinem Bruder,*" the indirect object, must come before "*zwei Bücher,*" the direct object. This German word order is especially problematic because if the sentence in question had used pronouns instead of nouns, "I give it to him," when translated into German, the direct object must come before the indirect object, "*Ich gebe ihn ihm.*" The similarities between the indirect (*ihm*) and direct (*ihn*) objects in the sentence with pronouns adds to the difficulty.

With this example, all students should be encouraged to "look back" at their solution (the translation) in order to reconsider the syntax. Elaborated corrective feedback for an incorrect response might suggest that the student review the order of indirect and direct objects with special attention to either nouns or pronouns. Based on the list of what we needed to know in order to correctly translate, we see a whole host of other potential incorrect components. Using elaborated corrective feedback would require that we, as teachers, discover the error(s) and then guide the student to find the error(s) on his or her own.

In elaborated corrective feedback, students who get the answer *right* are *not* prompted to "look back." All students, however, whether right or wrong in the problem solution, should be encouraged to evaluate the problem solving process. Why would "looking back" with the assistance of elaborated corrective feedback be helpful as a final step in the problem solving process? Part of our goal in having students solve problems should be for them to focus on problem solving processes . In looking back at the steps taken to solve the problem, the student will reexamine the processes and evaluate the success or failure of those processes. When a problem has been correctly solved and the student looks back, the student is, hopefully, building a repertoire of potential solutions for future situations (solving problems via analogy) or adding new strategies to their collection. When a problem has been incorrectly solved and the student looks back, the student may have the opportunity to find and correct the process mistake on his or her own, which should result in better understanding and memory of the problem and its solution.

Let's think once again about the students in Mr. Ramsey's class. Each group made a number of decisions that could result in problem solving difficulties. They finish the exercise when they either wreck the vessel or get back to Spain with (or without) gold. Jane's group had a shipwreck early on and is now "looking back" at their decisions. The question they should be asking themselves is "Why did we wreck?" Answering this question will help them understand the impact of their decisions.

Let's imagine that Jane's group decided to set sail at midday and then continued with the problem solving exercise. They encountered a storm during their first afternoon at sea which pushed them back towards their launch site, and they had to adjust as a result. Perhaps Jane's group realizes that if they had left earlier they would have missed the storm that pushed them back. Jane and her group have learned something about weather patterns (that storms are more likely after noon than in the morning) and how that would have an impact on early navigation and exploration.

Summary

In order for students to become successful problem solvers, teachers should use some or all of the suggestions in this chapter. Although most of the research cited in this chapter was conducted using university undergraduates as subjects, similar results should be obtained when used with secondary students. First, problem solvers need to understand the problem. Using cooperative groups with assigned monitoring tasks (group processing) should help in identifying the components of the problem. Whether working in groups or alone, when students are creating a plan for solving the problem, they could: 1) use previously solved problems as examples (problem solving via analogy), 2) use visualization, 3) draw a picture or create a chart or graph, or 4) break the problem into smaller pieces and solve the smaller pieces one at a time (means-ends analysis). Finally, problem solvers should be encouraged to "look back" and evaluate their problem solving effort when their solution was correct and especially when their solution was incorrect. If the teacher can provide elaborated corrective feedback when students have incorrectly solved a problem, that would help them understand the problem and their efforts to solve it.

What are students learning by solving problems? They are learning information that we want them to remember, in terms of academic subjects, but they are also learning how to solve problems. What we want is for our students to be able to access an assortment of strategies and/or memories of previously solved problems that might provide assistance under future problem solving situations. In that vein, students should be given ample opportunity to solve problems and evaluate their solutions.

Additional Readings

Levine, M. (1988). *Effective problem solving*. Englewood Cliffs, NJ: Prentice Hall.

REFERENCES

Bransford, J.D., & Johnson, M.K. (1972). Contextual prerequisites for understanding: Some investigations of comprehension and recall. *Journal of Verbal Learning and* VERBAL BEHAVIOR, *11*, 717-726.

Bransford, J.D., & Stein, B.S. (1984). *The ideal problem solver*. San Francisco: Freeman.

Collins, M., Carnine, D., & Gersten, R. (1987). Elaborated corrective feedback and the acquisition of reasoning skills: A study of computer-assisted instruction. *Exceptional Children, 54*, 254-262.

de Bono, E. (1973). *CoRT thinking materials*. London: Direct Education Services.

Dixon, D.N. (1984). *Counseling: A problem solving approach*. New York: Wiley.

Duren, P.E., & Cherrington, A. (1992). The effects of cooperative group work versus independent practice on the learning of some problem-solving strategies. *School Science and Mathematics, 92*, 80-83.

Gick, M.L., & Holyoak, K.J. (1980). Analogical

problem solving. *Cognitive Psychology, 12*, 306-355.

Gick, M.L., & Holyoak, K.J. (1983). Schema induction and analogical transfer. *Cognitive Psychology, 15*, 1-38.

Gilbert-Macmillan, K.M. (1983). Mathematical problem solving in cooperative small groups and whole class instruction (Doctoral dissertation, Stanford University), *Dissertation Abstracts International*, 2700, 4409A.

Hayes, J.R. (1978). *Cognitive psychology: Thinking and creating*. Homewood, IL: Dorsey.

Holyoak, K.J. (1985). The pragmatics of analogical transfer. In G.H. Bower (Ed.), *The psychology of learning and motivation, 9*, 59-87. New York: Academic Press.

Holyoak, K.J., & Koh, K. (1987). Surface and structural similarity in analogical transfer. *Memory and Cognition, 15*, 332-340.

Johnson, D.W., & Johnson, R.T. (1989). *Cooperation and competition: A meta-analysis of the research.* Hillsdale, NJ: Lawrence Erlbaum.

Johnson, D.W., Johnson, R.T., Holubec, E.J., & Roy, P. (1984). *Circles of learning: Cooperation in the classroom.* Alexandria, VA: Association for Supervision and Curriculum Development.

Johnson, D.W., Johnson, R.T., Stanne, M.B., & Garibaldi, A. (1990). Impact of group processing on achievement in cooperative groups. *The Journal of Social Psychology, 130,* 507-516.

Laughlin, P.R., & McGlynn, R.P. (1986). Collective induction: Mutual group and individual influence by exchange of hypotheses and evidence. *Journal of Experimental Social Psychology, 22,* 567-589.

Levine, M. (1988). *Effective problem solving.* Englewood Cliffs, NJ: Prentice Hall.

Lysakowski, R.S., & Walberg, H.J. (1982). Instructional effects of cues, participation, and corrective feedback: A quantitative synthesis. *American Educational Research Journal, 19,* 559-578.

Marr, D.B., & Sternberg, R.J. (1986). Analogical reasoning with novel concepts: Differential attention of intellectually gifted and nongifted children to relevant and irrelevant novel stimuli. *Cognitive Development, 1,* 53-72.

Newell, A., & Simon, H.A. (1972). *Human problem solving.* Englewood Cliffs, NJ: Prentice Hall.

Paivio, A. (1986). *Mental representations: A dual coding approach.* New York: Oxford University Press.

Parker, R. (1984). Small group cooperative learning in the classroom. *OSSC Bulletin, 27*(7).

Polya, G. (1945). *How to solve it.* Princeton, NJ: Princeton University Press.

Reigeluth, C.M. (ed.) (1983). *Instructional design theories and models: An overview of their current status.* Hillsdale, NJ: Lawrence Erlbaum.

Schwab, L.S., & D'Zamko, M.E. (1988). Group imaging for action: Creative thinking and problem solving. *Journal of Creative Behavior, 22,* 101-111.

Siegel, M.A., & Misselt, A.L. (1984). Adaptive feedback and review paradigm for computer-based drills. *Journal of Educational Psychology, 76,* 310-317.

Stein, B.S., Littlefield, J., Bransford, J.D., & Persampieri, M. (1984). Elaboration and knowledge acquisition. *Memory and Cognition, 12,* 522-529.

Whimby, A. (1985). Focusing on trainable g. *The Behavioral and Brain Sciences, 8,* 245-246.

Willoughby, T.E., Waller, T.G., Wood, E. & MacKinnon, G.E. (1993). The effect of prior knowledge on an immediate and delayed associative learning task following elaborative interrogation. *Contemporary Educational Psychology, 18,* 36-46.

CHAPTER 7

Strategies in Learning and Teaching Algebra

Hsiao d'Ailly • University of Waterloo

In the modern society, information, technology, and data manipulation in all fields is expanding and advancing at an incredible rate. Thus, the possession of adequate mathematical skills has become essential for students, not only to advance their careers, but even to function as intelligent citizens. However, in recent years the quality of mathematics education in North America has been under criticism. International testing has shown that north American students are lagging behind their European or Asian peers in mathematics skills (Lapointe, Mead, & Askew, 1992). A strong sense has emerged that something needs to be done to improve the quality of education in general, and of mathematics education in particular.

One way to improve the current situation is to find different strategies that may help the teaching and learning of mathematics. The primary purpose of this chapter is to review research studies that are relevant to the teaching and learning of mathematics and to describe some of the techniques that have been proven effective in helping students to learn. To give some focus to the different teaching and learning techniques, our discussion will concentrate on algebra problem solving. Readers who are particularly interested in the teaching and learning of geometry should refer to Polya (1957, 1981).

Models of Problem Solving

In recent years, consensus has emerged among mathematics educators that the focus of algebra teaching should be shifted from purely algebraic manipulation skills toward more conceptual understanding and problem-solving skills. Several models have been proposed to capture the processes involved in mathematics problem solving. Polya's (1957) stage model and Mayer's (1987) component model for problem solving are two good examples (See Table 7-1).

Polya (1957) listed four stages one has to go through in solving a

Table 7-1

Polya's stage model and Mayer's component model on problem solving

Polya's Model (Stages)	Mayer's Model (Components)
Understanding the problem	Problem Translation
Devising a plan	Problem Integration
Carrying out the plan	Solution Planning & Monitoring
Looking back	Plan Execution

problem, whereas Mayer (1987) described process components involved in solving a problem. Mayer's model divided Polya's "understanding the problem" stage into two separate process components, *problem translation* and *problem integration*. On the other hand, the "devising a plan" and "looking back" stages in Polya's model were integrated into one component, *solution planning and monitoring*, in Mayer's model. Otherwise, the models are similar in their capture of the processes involved in solving a problem.

According to Mayer (1987), each process component consists of specific skills and knowledge. For example, in the process of comprehending and *translating* a problem, students need linguistic and factual knowledge that relates to the problem so that they can restate the problem givens and the problem goal. In the process of problem *integration*, schematic knowledge is required to help students recognize the problem types and identify relevant and irrelevant information so that they can determine information needed for the solution and represent the relevant information in an integrated fashion. Table 7-2 illustrates the various components involved in solving a particular problem and the types of knowledge required for each process component in problem solving.

In the following sections, we will discuss problem solving processes using Mayer's model as a guideline. The skills and knowledge involved in each process will be described and the particular difficulties that students encountered will be identified. We will then describe some instructional studies that address these issues.

Table 7-2
Process components and knowledge required
in Mathematical Problem Solving

Sample Problem

"Floor tiles are sold in squares 30 cm on each side. How much would it cost to tile a rectangular room 7.2 meters long and 5.4 meters wide if the tiles cost $.72 each?"

Problem Solving Components	Type of Knowledge	Examples from Tile Problem
Problem translation	Linguistic knowledge	The room is a rectangle with 7.2 meter width and 5.4 meter length
	Factual knowledge	One meter equals 100 centimeters
Problem integration	Schematic knowledge	Area = length X width
Solution Planning & Monitoring	Strategic knowledge	Find the room's area in meters by multiplying 7.2 X 5.4.
		Then find the area of each tile in meters by multiplying 0.3 X 0.3.
		Then find the number of tiles needed by dividing the area of the room by the area of each tile.
		Then find the total cost by multiplying the number of tiles needed by $.72
Solution Execution	Procedural knowledge	7.2 X 5.4 = 38.88
		0.3 X 0.3 = 0.09
		38.88/0.9 = 432
		432 X 0.72=$311.04

Adopted from Mayer (1987), p. 347, table 13-1

PROCESS COMPONENTS INVOLVED IN SOLVING ALGEBRA WORD PROBLEMS

Problem Translation

The first step in solving a word problem is to understand the problem, and to know what information was given and which question was asked. Some of the difficulties students may have in solving a word problem can simply be attributed to their failure to comprehend the problem adequately.

Restating Problem Givens and Problem Goal

Students' comprehension of a problem can be assessed through their ability to identify the values for the given variables and the unknown. Reed and Ettinger (1987) provided college students a table to fill in while solving algebra problems. They found that students had great difficulty in filling in correct values for each variable. For example, given a problem and a table like the following (with blanks to be filled), only 38% of the college students correctly entered 50 grams of raisins into the table, although this value was directly stated in the problem. Moreover, only 52% of the subjects identified the quantity of dates as an unknown variable (the goal).

Raisins are 8% protein and dates are 4% protein. How many grams of dates should be added to 50 grams of raisins to produce a mixture that is 5% protein?

	Quantity of Food (in Grams)	% of Protein	Quantity of Protein (in Grams)
Raisins	50	8%	$50 * 8\%$
Dates	x	4%	$x * 4\%$
Mixture	$50 + x$	5%	$(50 + x) * 5\%$

If students cannot understand the problem well enough to identify the givens and the unknowns, there is very little chance for them to continue and successfully solve the problem. It is important, therefore, for teachers to make sure that the verbal statement of the problem is well understood. As suggested by Polya (1957), teachers can check students' understanding by asking them to repeat the statement and to point out the principal parts of the problem (the unknown, the data, and the condition). In other words, teachers should encourage students to restate the problem and identify the givens or the problem goal in their own words. Only when an appropriate understanding of the problem has been reached should students proceed to the planning stage of problem solving.

Translating Relational Statements

Another obstacle students encounter in solving a word problem is comprehending and translating relational statements, where a quantitative relation between variables is specified (e.g., *John has 5 more marbles than Tom*). Mayer (1982) found that when asked to recall story problems, students tended to make more errors with relational propositions (e.g., the length is 2 times the width) than with assignment propositions (e.g., the time to fill one pipe is 6 hours). In his study, almost none of the assignment statements were converted into relations, whereas 21% of the relations were converted into assignments. Students' particular difficulty in remembering relational propositions suggests that relational propositions are more difficult to represent internally than other types of propositions.

Indeed, problems containing relational statements, such as "Mary is twice as old as Betty was 2 years ago," were found to be most difficult for students (Loftus & Suppes, 1972). MacGregor and Stacey (1993) gave students in grades 8, 9 and 10 the following multiple choice question:

> I have x and you have y. I have $6 more than you. Which of the following equations must be true?
>
> $x=6y$ $6x=y$ $x=6+y$ $6+x=y$ $x=6-y$

Only 36% of the 1048 students answered this question correctly ($x=6+y$).

As MacGregor and Stacey (1993) pointed out, one of the greatest challenges for beginners in algebra is linking a mathematical situation to its formal description. Teachers must recognize this source of difficulty students encounter in translating a relational statement. Students need to be aware of the fact that some relationships between variables must be paraphrased, reorganized, or reinterpreted before they can be expressed mathematically. Training in the translation from the situation as described in a relational statement into mathematical codes (equations) would appear to deserve special attention.

Instructional Study: Using Diagrams to Represent Relational Statements

Lewis (1989) has reported success in training students to represent relational statements using diagrams. All 96 university students participating in this study made reversal errors in translating relational statements in a screening test. Students were divided into three groups: diagram, structural, and control. The diagram group received training in both translation and integration of information in compare-problem statements. The statement group was given translation training only. The control group received neither translation nor integration training but was exposed to the same problems as the other two groups.

The translation training involved defining and giving examples for the three types of statements used in word problems: statements (e.g., Joe runs 6 miles a week), relations (e.g., Ken runs 3 times as many miles a week as Joe does) and questions (e.g., How many miles does Ken run in 4 weeks?). The integration training consisted of reviewing the statement types and outlining and practicing the diagramming method. As illustrated in Table 7-3, students were taught to use diagrams to integrate the information in assignment and relational statements. Students were provided with nine practice word problems. The training sessions were done in groups with 2 to 15 students in each session.

During the post-test, the statements group was instructed to identify problem statements before solving them, and the diagram group was directed to identify problem statements and then to diagram the problems. No special instructions were given to control-group subjects.

The results showed that the diagram training was effective in improving students' representations of the problem. The diagram group made significantly fewer reversal errors than both the statement and control groups. The statement group, however, did not differ significantly from the control group. This improvement for the diagram group was found to extend to transfer problems with more complex problem situations and to more general types of problems.

Based on these findings, researchers concluded that representation training aimed at remedying students' erroneous comprehension processes for relational statements can be successful, and that the improvement can be transferred to more complex or different problems. There is, however, one drawback in this intervention. The rule used for converting the diagrammed situation into arithmetic operation, "addition and multiplication means increase, and subtraction or division means a decrease," is certainly true for whole-number operations. The rule, however, cannot be applied when the multiplication or division involves fractions (Fischbein, Deri, Nello, & Marino, 1985). The sample problem illustrated in Table 7-3 is in fact a division problem involving a whole number (420) divided by a fraction (1/5). This procedure was translated into a multiplication problem based on the misconception that multiplication makes the result bigger. The translation from the text to the diagram and then to the equation, as illustrated in Table 7-3, seems to be manageable when the fraction in the problem has 1 as the numerator. However, in another situation where the numerator for the fraction is not 1 (e.g., 2/3), the rule taught with the diagramming method will no longer apply. Therefore, the diagramming procedure as described is better used in relational statements where the addition or subtraction operators are called for but not multiplication or division, particularly in cases where multiplication or division with a fraction is involved.

Table 7-3
Diagramming procedure used in Lewis's (1989) study

Sample Problem

Megan has saved $420.00 for her vacation. She has saved 1/5 as much as James has saved. James has been saving for his vacation for 6 months, how much has he saved each month?

Diagramming Steps

1. Draw a number line and place the variable and value from the assignment statement at the middle of the line.

2. Tentatively place the unknown variable (James' savings) on one side of the middle.

3. Compare your representation with the information in the relation statement, checking to see if your representation agrees with the meaning of the relation statement. If it does, then you can continue. If not, then try again with the other side.

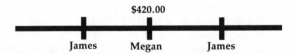

4. Translate your representation into an arithmetic operation. If the unknown variable is to the right of the center, then the operation is an increase, such as addition or multiplication. If the unknown variable is to the left of the center, then the operation is a decrease, such as subtraction or division.

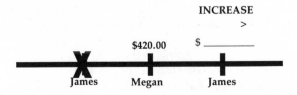

Adopted from Lewis (1989), p. 523.

Problem Integration

After reading a problem, and identifying the givens and the goal, students need to put these fragments of information into an integrated representation. According to Nathan, Kintsch and Young (1992), there are two levels of representation that can be constructed from a problem. One is a *situation model*, a qualitative representation (e.g., picture images, diagrams) of the actual situation described in the text; the other is a *formal representation*, a quantitative representation (e.g., equations, network of the equations) of the given problem.

Nathan et al. (1992) stressed the importance of the construction of a situational model of a problem. They regarded the situational model of a problem, such as a picture or a diagram, as an important intermediate state between the textual understanding of a problem and the formal conceptual structure of a problem. This process of integrating information in a problem and representing the information in a situational model not only facilitates the problem-solving processes but also encourages meaningful learning. Paige and Simon (1966) provided a good example to illustrate this point. A student is given a question like the following:

> A board was sawed into two pieces. One piece was two-thirds as long as the whole board and was exceeded in length by the second piece by 4 feet. How long was the board before it was cut?

Students who use direct translation from text to equation, thus bypassing the situational model, will likely construct an equation of this sort: $(2/3x) + (2/3x+4) = x$. On the other hand, students who construct a situational model from the problem statement will be likely to point out that the problem represents a physically impossible situation.

This kind of model-based reasoning, according to Hall, Kibler, Wenger, and Truxaw (1989), serves four roles in problem solving processes: (1) as preparatory comprehension, (2) as a solution method, (3) as evidence gathering for a candidate solution, and (4) as a recovery method for errors generated earlier in the solution attempt. The construction of a physical representation, a situational model, for the problem has been shown to be positively related to students' ability to derive the correct solution for a problem.

Instructional Study: Constructing a Situational Representation for the Problem

Recognizing the importance of a situational model in problem solving, Nathan et al. (1992) designed and tested an interactive computer tutor, *ANIMATE*, to help students construct a formal problem network for word problems. The problem network was then used to run a simple animation of the problem situation. There were three major components to this tutor: (1) a representation simulating physical conditions (a situational model), (2) a representation providing a manipulable formal problem schema (a formal model), and (3) feedback on these representations.

ANIMATE tutored problems in the amount-per-time rate family of word problems (Mayer, 1981). These problems employed the $D = RxT$ equation including "overtake," "collision," and "distance apart" problems. The following is an example word problem that can be worked out on the tutor program:

> A huge ant is terrorizing San Francisco. It travels east toward Detroit, which is 2400 miles away, at 400 miles per hour. The army learns of this one hour later and sends a helicopter west from Detroit at 600 miles per hour to intercept the ant. If the ant left at 2 p.m., at what time will the helicopter and the ant collide (ignoring any time changes)?

Figure 7-1 is an illustration of these representations on *ANIMATE*. For the situational representation, students specified the object (e.g., the ant), the starting location, and the travel direction. For the formal representation, students worked on the equations, including distance, rate, and time variables in the network. The animation had a clock that showed the elapsed (animation) time, a calibrated ruler at the top of the screen, and distance gauges. It served as the externalization of a student's situation model and provided students with valuable situation-based feedback for assessing the correctness of the problem representations.

Fifty-six undergraduate students participated in this study, where students were randomly assigned to one of the four experimental conditions: (1) network only, (2) stopping condition, (3) animate, and (4) control. For the network-only group, students went through the tutor, where only the manipulation of the formal-model schema was provided. For the stopping-condition group, students were given the opportunity to construct both the situational model and the formal model through the tutor program, without being allowed to run the animation. The animate group had all three components in the *ANIMATE* tutor. The control group was provided with a review of traditional algebra.

With a 30-minute tutorial, students showed a marked difference in their paper-and-pencil post-test performance. The animation group outperformed the other three groups on their post-test. Data from the error analysis showed that the animation group was better able to generate the necessary inferences for a solution compared to the other groups. The results suggested that all three components of the *ANIMATE* program, the construction of situational and formal models and the feedback, are essential in cultivating good problem solving skills.

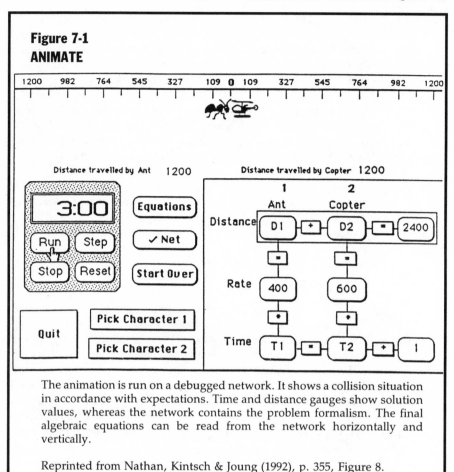

Figure 7-1
ANIMATE

The animation is run on a debugged network. It shows a collision situation in accordance with expectations. Time and distance gauges show solution values, whereas the network contains the problem formalism. The final algebraic equations can be read from the network horizontally and vertically.

Reprinted from Nathan, Kintsch & Joung (1992), p. 355, Figure 8.

Schematic Knowledge and Successful Problem Solving

A *schema* is a mental construct that permits problem solvers to categorize problems according to their solution modes. One of the important components in the problem integration process is to recognize the question type (e.g., the amount-per-time rate type of problems) and to retrieve a schema (e.g., Distance = Speed x Time) that is relevant to the problem. If an appropriate schema is available, students can ignore irrelevant information and extract relevant information to solve the problem.

Reed (1987) argued that the ability to identify the problem type requires an appreciation of the structure of the problem. Thus, structure recognition is considered crucial to successful problem solving. Silver (1979) designed a card-sorting task to examine the dimensions of problem similarity that students perceive in mathematical word problems. Ninety-five eighth-grade students participated in this study. Students sorted 24 verbal problems that varied in their mathematical structure or contextual details. For example, for the following three problems, problem (a) and problem (b) are related in their mathematical structure, whereas problem (a) and problem (c) are related in their contextual details.

a) The students in an 11th-grade class can form committees of exactly 8 students with none left over. This same class can form committees of exactly 6 students with none left over. What is the smallest number of students that could be in the class?

b) Nickolai and Natashe are trained circus bears who perform their act while riding bicycles around a circus ring. Natashe can complete the circle in 4 minutes, but it takes Nickolai 6 minutes to make the entire trip. They start at the same point, and their act is over when they again reach the starting point at the same time. How long does their act last?

c) There are 8 boys and 16 girls at an 11th-grade committee meeting. Every few minutes, one boy and one girl leave together. How many boy-girl pairs must leave so that there are exactly three times as many girls as boys left at the meeting?

(Adopted from Silver, 1979, p. 199)

The card-sorting task was performed on two occasions, once before and once after attempting to solve the problems. The results showed that there was a marked increase in the amount of mathematical structure evident in students' post-solution sorts as compared with pre-solution sorts, suggesting that students did engage in structural analysis of the problem during problem solving.

In another related study, Silver (1981) also showed a strong positive relationship between problem-solving success and judgment of appropriate mathematical relatedness. Good problem solvers tended to group related problems on the basis of common mathematical structure, whereas poor problem solvers tended to group them on the basis of common contextual details.

Low and Over (1990) reported a positive relation between students' general mathematical ability and their ability to classify whether algebraic word problems contained sufficient, missing, or irrelevant information. As Low and Over (1990) suggested, since a person can denote missing information or identify irrelevant information only through correct understanding of the problem structure, success at text editing would be a good demonstration of students' schematic knowledge of a problem. They found that students' ability at text editing for the algebraic word problems was strongly associated with their ability to solve these problems. Students sometimes succeeded at editing and later failed at problem solution, but there was *not a single case* of successful solution after failure at text editing. Furthermore, text-editing ability seemed to be related to students' general mathematics ability.

In short, schematic knowledge about a problem, as tested by the researchers, includes the ability to recognize the structure similarity between problems, to denote missing information in a problem and to identify missing information in a problem. These skills appeared to be essential in successful problem solving.

Difficulties in Recognizing Structural Similarity Among Problems

Although the ability to see the structural similarity among questions and to draw upon appropriate schema is a key factor in the success of problem solving, developing skills in structure recognition has proven to be most difficult for students. Students appear to be influenced by the story context detail of a problem, which inhibits their ability to see the structural similarity between two structurally identical but contextually different problems. For example, Reed (1987) asked university students to rate the potential usefulness of solutions for pairs of problems. The problems were either equivalent, similar, isomorphic, or unrelated as shown in the following.

Target example problem
A small pipe can fill an oil tank in 12 hours and a large one can fill it in 8 hours. How long will it take to fill the tank if both pipes are used at the same time?

Equivalent Problem (same story, same procedure)
A small hose can fill a swimming pool in 6 hours and a large one can fill it in 3 hours. How long will it take to fill the pool if both hoses are used at the same time?

Similar problem (same story, different procedure)
A small pipe can fill a water tank in 20 hours and a large pipe can fill it in 15 hours. Water is used at a rate that would empty a full tank in 40 hours. How long will it take to fill the tank when both pipes are used at the same time, assuming that water is being used as the tank is filled?

Isomorphic problem (different story, same procedure)
Tom can drive to Bill's house in 4 hours and Bill can drive to Tom's house in 3 hours. How long will it take them to meet if they both leave their houses at the same time and drive toward each other?

Unrelated problem (different problem, different procedure)

An airplane can fly from city A to city B at an average speed of 250 m.p.h. in 3 hours less time than it takes to return from city B to city A at 200 m.p.h. How many hours did it take to return?

(Adopted from Reed, 1987, p. 125)

As Reed (1987) reported, university students were influenced only by story content, not by structure, in their rating. Students did not rate isomorphic problems as significantly more useful than unrelated problems. In general, they rated problems with the same story context (equivalent and similar problems) as significantly more useful than problems with a different story context (isomorphic and unrelated problems).

Reed, Dempster, and Ettinger (1985) have also demonstrated how difficult it is for students to see the similarity either between two equivalent problems, or similar problems. In their study, students were asked to solve a practice problem. After the pretest, the solution for the practice problem was given to the students. Students were then asked to solve a test problem that was either an equivalent or similar form of the practice problem. The equivalent problems could be solved in exactly the same way as the practice problem, whereas the similar problems required a slight modification of the procedures used to solve the practice problem. The following is an example of these problems:

Practice Problem
A car traveling at a speed of 30 m.p.h. left a certain place at 10:00 a.m. At 11:30 a.m., another car departed from the same place at 40 m.p.h. and traveled the same route. In how many hours will the second car overtake the first car?
Solution: $30t = 40(t-1.5)$

Equivalent problem
A car is traveling south at the rate of 30 m.p.h. Two hours later, a second car leaves to overtake the first car, using the same route and going 45 m.p.h. In how many hours will the second car overtake the first car?
Solution: $30t = 45(t-2)$

Similar problem
A pickup truck leaves 3 hours after a large delivery truck, but overtakes it by traveling 15 m.p.h. faster. If it takes the pickup truck 7 hours to reach the delivery truck, find the rate of each vehicle.
Solution: $r(3+7) = (r+15)7$
(Adopted from Reed, Dempster, & Ettinger, 1985, p. 109)

The results of this study showed that students could not produce more correct solutions on equivalent or similar problems after seeing the solution for a target problem. Only when allowed to consult an elaborate model solution for the target problem as they worked on a test problem did students show some positive transfer to equivalent problems. They did not, however, show transfer to other similar problems.

In short, although forming a schema based on the structure of a problem is crucial in enhancing students' ability in problem solving, the research has shown that students have great difficulty in this aspect of learning. Thus, there is a strong need for teachers to intervene and help students construct schematic knowledge and learn to access the appropriate schema in solving a problem.

Instructional Study: Structure Mapping Instruction

To develop and recall an appropriate schema for a problem, students need to learn to recognize the structural similarity or dissimilarity among questions. Weaver and Kintsch (1992) proposed that one good way to maximize the transparency of the mapping between problems is to draw students' attention to the conceptual similarities between problems. Students can be taught to form structure graphs for a problem, and to form equations from these structures.

Weaver and Kintsch (1992) gave a tutorial session to university students before asking them to rate the helpfulness of the solution of one problem to solving another problem. One group of students were given equation-based instruction, where the tutor immediately wrote down equations from the problem and explained how the text was used to build up the equation. The other group of students received structure-based instruction, which included an explanation of the notion of schemata and a demonstration of how such schemata could be combined to form structure graphs and how equations could be generated from these structures. Table 7-4 is an example of the instruction given to the two groups on the same problem.

After a 25-minute training session, subjects were given the rating task. Compared to the equation-based instruction, the structure-based instruction helped students to discriminate better between problems with the same and different conceptual structure.

In another experiment, students were not only introduced to the concepts of structure mapping among problems but also given time for practice. During the first session, students were introduced to the concepts, and a number of examples were worked through. The focus was on the conceptual structure for the structure-based instructional group, and on the equation for the equation-based instructional group. During the second session, three more problems were worked through, and all questions were answered. Students were then presented with four new problems plus four worked-out example problems. They were told that they might find the worked-out example problems helpful.

The results showed that brief tutorials in structure-based mapping produced higher levels of performance than did similar tutorials in the equation-based group. Structure-based instruction improved problem-solving performance on all types of problems, regardless of the match between the worked-out example (the base) and the to-be-solved problem (the target).

This study has shown promising results in teaching students how to recognize structural similarity among questions. The success of the intervention depends greatly on making the structure transparent and on using the equation network to represent the problem structure. Apparently, the equation network not only helps students differentiate the structure between questions but also improves their problem-solving ability.

Solution Planning and Monitoring

Devising and monitoring a solution plan is a crucial component in mathematical problem solving. Artzt and Armour-Thomas (1992) provided a profile of the processes involved in solution planning and monitoring during problem solving. They videotaped 27 seventh-grade students in six small groups solving a mathematical problem. Students in the groups were of heterogeneous ability in mathematics. They were asked to solve the following problem:

> A banker must make change of one dollar using 50 coins. She must use at least one quarter, one dime, one nickel, and one penny. How many of each type of coin must she use to do this?

Students' interactions during group discussion were coded and analyzed. Eight different types of activities were identified: read,

---

Table 7-4
The equation-based and structure-based instructions used in Weaver & Kintsch's (1992) study

Problem: A Girl Scout Troop sells the same number of peanut butter and chocolate chip cookies. Peanut Butter cookies come 30 to the box, while Chocolate Chip cookies come 10 to the box. The troop sold 100 more boxes of Chocolate Chip than Peanut Butter. How many peanut butter cookies were sold?

Instruction to the equation-based group:

The number of cookies sold equals the number of cookies in a box multiplied by the total number of boxes sold:

(continued on next pages)

Table 7-4 continued.

Cookies per box x Total number of boxes = Number of cookies sold

The problem says that they sold the same number of cookies, but that they sold 100 more boxes of chocolate chip cookies. We need to add 100 boxes to the peanut butter cookies total to make them even.

Therefore: $(x/10) = (x/30) + 100$

Solving for x: $3x = x + 3000$
                    $2x = 3000$
                    $x = 1500$

Instruction to the structure-based group:

In order to solve this problem, we need to know that the formula used here is:

# of cookies sold = # of cookies per box x total # of boxes sold

The "relational" component in this formula is the "cookies per box," so that goes in the middle of our graph. The first step is to draw the basic graphs for the cookies and fill in the numbers that we are given.

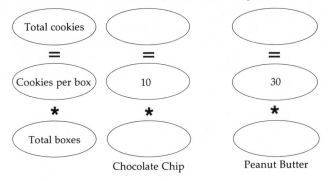

Next, we need to identify the one variable we want to know. In this case it is the number of cookies sold, which is the same for both types of cookies: we'll call it "x". Put that in the graph.

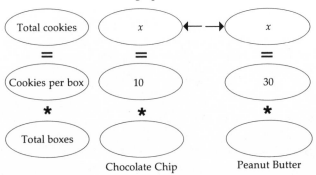

Table 7-4 continued.

Now we want to fill in the relationships between the two types of cookies; we already know that the number of cookies sold is the same. We also know that there were 100 more boxes of chocolate chip cookies sold than boxes of peanut butter cookies, so we need our graph to show that too.

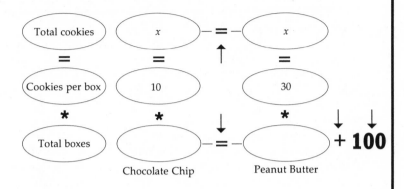

Now, we can use the relationship we have to fill in the rest of the circles.

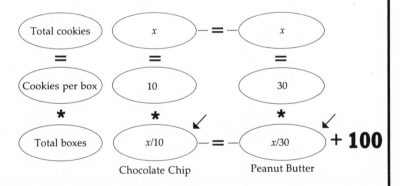

Finally, we can find the two things that we set equal—in this case the total number of cookies sold—and there's the equation we need to solve the problem: $(x/10) = (x/30) + 100$

Solving for x:

$$3x = x + 3000$$
$$2x = 3000$$
$$x = 1500$$

(Materials provided by Weaver through personal communication) understand, analyze, explore, plan, implement, verify, watch and listen. These activities were further categorized as either *cognitive* or *metacognitive*. Verbal or nonverbal actions that indicated actual processing for information were classified as cognitive. On the other hand, statements made about the problem or the problem-solving process, that indicated choosing what to do or monitoring what was being done, were identified as metacognitive. Artzt and Armour-Thomas (1992) concluded from their analysis that a continuous interplay of cognitive and metacognitive behaviors is necessary for successful problem solving and for maximum student involvement in the group.

Days, Wheatley, and Kulm (1979) also investigated students' thinking processes in problem solving. Fifty eighth-grade students participated in this study. Students were tested individually, and were asked to think aloud as they solved problems. The authors coded students' thinking processes into one of eight categories: understanding, representation, recall, production, evaluation, comments about solution, executive error, and strategy. The results showed that compared to the less successful problem solvers, the more successful ones showed more frequent engagement in reasoning deductively, using successive proximation, estimating, checking manipulations, checking conditions, checking by retracing steps, and using a deductive algorithmic approach and systematic trial and error. Apparently, good strategy use and good monitoring are crucial for successful problem solving.

Unfortunately, some earlier attempts in teaching students "general" heuristic strategies have been fruitless (e.g., Post and Brennan, 1976; Smith, 1973; Wilson, 1967), leading to the suggestion that the strategies students use in solving problems may be very task-specific. On the other hand, as Pressley (1986) pointed out, developing good strategy use is a formidable educational challenge, one that probably requires many years. Good strategy use requires knowledge of many strategies, practice of those strategies, and acquisition of extensive metacognition. Studies of successful intervention in strategic problem solving are scarce, but fortunately, they do exist. The following are a few examples.

Heuristics Instruction

Schoenfeld (1979) has reported success in teaching general problem solving strategies to college students. The following five problem solving strategies were taught in the study.

1. **Draw a diagram if at all possible.**
   Even if you finally solve the problem by algebraic or other means, a diagram can help give you a "feel" for the problem. It may suggest ideas or plausible answers. You may even solve a problem graphically.

2. **If there is an integer parameter, look for an inductive**

argument.

Is there an n or other parameter in the problem which takes on integer values? If you need to find a formula for $f(n)$, you might try one of these:

a. calculate $f(1)$, $f(2)$, $f(3)$, $f(4)$, $f(5)$; list them in order, and see if there's a pattern. If there is, you might verify it by induction.
b. See what happens as you pass from n objects to $n+1$. If you can tell how to pass from $f(n)$ to $f(n+1)$, you may build up $f(n)$ inductively.

3. Consider arguing by contradiction or contrapositive.

- Contrapositive: Instead of proving the statement "If X is true then Y is true," you can prove the equivalent statement "If Y is false then X must be false."
- Contradiction: Assume, for the sake of argument, that the statement you would like to prove is false. Using this assumption, go on to prove either that one of the given conditions in the problem is false, that something you know to be true is false, or that what you wish to prove is true. If you can do any of these, you have proved what you want.

These techniques are especially useful when you find it difficult to begin a direct argument because you have little to work with. If negating a statement gives you something solid to manipulate, this may be the technique to use.

4. Consider a similar problem with fewer variables.
If the problem has a large number of variables and is too confusing to deal with comfortably, construct and solve a similar problem with fewer variables. You may then be able to (a) adapt the method of solution to the more complex problem, or (b) take the result of the simpler problem and build up from there.

5. Try to establish a subgoal.

- Can you obtain part of the answer, and perhaps go on from there?
- Can you decompose the problem so that a number of easier results can be combined to give the total result you want?

(Adopted from Schoenfeld, 1979, p. 178)

Seven students from upper-division courses in mathematics at the University of California participated in this study: four in the experimental group, and three in the control group. Students were instructed and tested individually. They sat through five instruction sessions spread over a 2-week period, during which they worked on, and were given the solutions to, 20 problems. These problems were chosen from five classes of similar problems. Problems within each class could all be solved using one of the five strategies as listed above. The differences in treatment between these two groups were:

1. *Naming and describing the strategies*. Students in the heuristics group were told at the beginning of their practice sessions that the experiment would try to show how five specific strategies would help them to solve problems. They were then given the strategies.
2. *Highlighting the strategy use*. Students in the experimental group were provided with highlights of the strategy use in the solution for the problems.
3. *Grouping the questions*. Questions were grouped by strategy for the experimental group, whereas the control group had them scrambled.
4. *Reminders for strategy use*. During post-test, subjects from the strategy group were reminded to look over the list of strategies, whereas the control group were asked to look over their work.

The results showed that all four students who received heuristics training outscored the three who did not. The average net gain for the non-heuristics group was 0; for the heuristics group, it was more than 2 (out of 5 problems, a 45% increase). Thus, it is clear that when problem-solving strategies are identified and taught and when students think to use them, the impact on the students' problem-solving performance can be substantial.

Reciprocal Teaching

Reciprocal teaching is a teaching model designed to promote a learning environment within which students can gradually take on greater responsibility for learning (Campione, Brown, Reeve, Ferrara, & Palincsar, 1991). It features guided practice in applying simple concrete strategies to a task. An adult teacher and a group of students take turns leading a discussion. The reciprocal nature of the procedure forces student engagement, and teacher modelling provides examples of expert performance. Reciprocal teaching has shown to be very effective in reading instruction (Campione, Brown & Connell, 1988). The principles underlying the reciprocal-teaching reading/listening program have been extended and tested in teaching mathematics.

In the reciprocal-teaching math program described by Campione, Brown, and Connell (1988), students and an adult teacher took turns being learning leaders and supportive critics responsible for leading a discussion. The discussion was aimed at understanding algebra word problems. This method, according to the authors, forced externalization of strategies and monitoring of progress, and attempted to impose meaning. The learning leaders guided the group in working on three successive chalkboards designed to help students proceed systematically. These procedures generated an external record of the group's problem solving, which could then be monitored, evaluated, and reflected upon.

As shown in Table 7-5, the three boards used in the program were (1) the Planning board, where the group extracted the relevant facts embodied in the word problem; (2) the Representation board, where the students drew diagrams illustrating the problem; and (3) the Doing board, where they translated the drawings into the appropriate equations and computed the answer.

The subjects were above-average students attending a summer school prior to entering seventh grade. Students were selected based on the criterion that they showed considerable ability to solve algorithms correctly, but did not give evidence of understanding the concepts

Table 7-5
The three boards used in Campione et al.'s (1988) study.

Sample Problem
Harry ate a hamburger and drank a glass of milk which totaled 495 calories. The milk contained half as many calories as the sandwich. How many calories were in the sandwich and how many in the milk?

Planning Board	Drawing Board	Doing Board
A hamburger and a glass of milk totaled 495 calories	**495** **H** **M**	$H + M = 495$ $M + M + M = 495$
The milk contained half as many calories as the hamburger H = calories of hamburger M = calories of milk	**495** **M** **M** **M** **H**	$\begin{array}{r} 165 = M \\ 3\overline{)495} \\ \underline{300} \\ 195 \\ \underline{180} \\ 15 \\ \underline{15} \\ 0 \end{array}$

Adapted from Campione, Brown, & Connell (1988), p. 104

underlying those algorithms. Three different types of problems were used in the instruction: single-variable linear equations, two-variable linear equations, and monomial-by-binomial equations.

The results showed an encouraging pattern. As described by the researchers, the students were enthusiastic and willing to spend considerable periods of time working on individual problems, both in class and at home. Moreover, after 20 days of instruction, their performance did improve significantly over that of the control group, which was given equivalent practice and feedback on the main problem types but without discussions.

Brown and Campione (1990), however, have since reported a failure to replicate the positive results in a follow-up study. In the failed experiment, as described by the researchers, students were not preselected, and the group size was bigger. Students were less attentive in the discussion, and the teacher's scaffolding attempts became more intrusive and authoritarian in response to the students' inattention and faulty math. The teacher did not follow the principles of reciprocal teaching carefully. Consequently, the group lost turn-taking and cooperation, which resulted in low engagement and practice on the students' part (Brown & Campione, 1990).

As the researchers pointed out, the earlier positive results of their reciprocal-teaching program were obtained under optimal conditions: the teacher was an expert teacher of mathematics, the students all possessed adequate algebra skills, and the group was small in size (6 students). The heuristics or strategies were never practiced as independent activities, but always in the context of actual on-line problem solving. These conditions appear essential to successful reciprocal teaching.

Solution Execution

Once a student can devise a plan for solving an algebra word problem, the next step is to carry out the plan, and to work with the algebra. In this section, the focus will be on the processes involved in working with algebra.

Knowledge Required

In an algebraic problem, typically only the features of a desired result are described (e.g., finding the value for x). Thus, planning is required before the execution of solution procedures. Unlike working with arithmetic problems, where execution is the main process, working with algebra involves two types of processes: planning and execution (Matz, 1982). Students have to first identify the proper goal and then work toward it.

For example, if the goal is to factor the expression "$x^2 - 2x - 15$", then "$x (x - 2) - 15$" is not an appropriate result. The goal *factor the expression* means to rewrite the entire expression as a product, as "(x + 5)(x - 3)", not simply factor part of it.

As Lewis (1981) specified, there are two kinds of knowledge to be employed in solving an algebraic equation. First, the solver must know a set of correct operations. Second, the solver must know how to select an appropriate operator to use at a given juncture. The latter is particularly difficult, since there are a large number of operators and literally an infinite number of ways they can be correctly applied. For example, if the goal is to find the value for "x" from "$x + 5 = 2$", a procedure like "$2(x + 5) = 2(2)$" is correct but hardly helpful in bringing the student closer to the goal state.

Basic Strategies in Solving Algebra Equations

Bundy (1975) identified three basic strategies involved in solving algebra equations:

1. **Attraction**: moving two instances of the unknown closer to one another;
$$x/2 + 2x/2 = 1 \longrightarrow (x + 2x)/2 = 1$$
2. **Collection**: carrying out a computation that reduces the number of instances of the unknown;
$$(x + 2x)/2 = 1 \longrightarrow 3x/2 = 1$$
3. **Isolation**: getting the unknown alone on one side and getting a numerical value on the other side of the equality.
$$3x/2 = 1 \longrightarrow x = 2/3$$

Planning a problem solution, according to Bundy (1975), involves applying one or more of these strategies in a given order. Students need to learn not only how to use these strategies in solving problems, but also when to use them.

Schema Acquisition and Rule Automation

Cooper and Sweller (1987) distinguished experts from novices in algebra by two major aspects: the quality of their schemata, and the automation of the problem-solving operators. Expert problem solvers faced with an unfamiliar problem are more likely than novices to incorporate the problem into an existing schema, because their existing schema encompasses a greater variety of problems. In addition, because their problem-solving operators are automated, expert problem solvers have more cognitive capacity available to deal with those aspects of the new problem that are unfamiliar.

Instructional Study—Working with Algebra: The Use of Worked Examples

Cooper and Sweller (1987) illustrated in their study the important role of schemata and rule automation in students' ability to solve transfer algebra problems. They pointed out that the means-ends strategy used by novice problem solvers on conventional problems not only imposes a heavy cognitive load, but also directs attention away from those aspects of a problem that are important in learning. Thus, using means-ends strategy to solve a problem may slow down students' schema formation. On the other hand, providing students with worked examples to study would allow students more cognitive resources for schema formation and thus facilitate the development of problem-solving skills. Moreover, students require sufficient practice periods to allow automation of the skills. Both schema formation and automation of skills are essential to the transfer of learning.

Cooper and Sweller (1987) tested their hypothesis through a series of experiments. Twenty-four eighth-grade students were involved in their first experiment. All students were given an initial explanation sheet that contained a set of three worked examples. They were asked to read the sheet and try to understand it. Questions were answered until subjects claimed they understood the example problems. Following the initial introduction, an acquisition phase followed.

Four problem formats were used: $a+b=c$, $a-b=c$, $a+b-g=c$, $a-b+g=c$, in which "a" was required to be made the subject of the equation. Subjects were given eight problems, two from each problem format, and were instructed to work on the problem as rapidly and accurately as possible. Subjects in the control group were simply required to solve the eight problems by using pencil and paper. Subjects in the worked example group, on the other hand, were given the same problems, except that the first problem of each pair had the solution written out. These students were informed that they should study each worked example until they understood it, as the following problem would be similar.

The post-test was composed of three problems. Two of the problems came from the domain of problem types that had been seen during the acquisition phase of the experiment (e.g., $a-k=t$, $a+c-n=s$). The third problem was a test of transfer. It required the same algebraic rule for solution but contained more variables (e.g., $b+c-f=g+a-v$). The results showed that the two groups did not differ on the first two similar questions. For the third question, however, the experimental group spent significantly less time on solution and made significantly fewer mathematical errors.

In Experiment 2, Cooper and Sweller (1987) manipulated the length of acquisition (4 problems vs. 12 problems) in addition to the worked-example condition (worked-example vs. conventional condition). Moreover, students' ability was taken into consideration. In this case, the use of worked examples was found to have little effect on the transfer problem for the low-ability, short-acquisition group. Effects increased markedly, however, as the length of the acquisition period increased, and to a far lesser extent, as the ability of the students increased. In short, the results of the present study showed that having students read worked examples, and providing them with sufficient practice time, were both effective means to promote students' learning of algebra.

Zhu and Simon (1987) also reported more effective teaching by presenting students with carefully chosen sequences of worked-out examples and problems without lectures or other direct instruction. The study reported success in teaching factoring tasks, exponent tasks, and geometry tasks to students using the method of learning from examples and by doing. Students in the experimental condition were found to spend less time completing the learning module, and they performed equally well or better than students who received the conventional teaching method. The method of learning from examples, according to Zhu and Simon (1987), has been tested successfully with a class covering the entire 3-year curriculum in algebra and geometry in a Chinese middle school.

Bugs in algebra

Another line of research on algebra-solving skill is to examine the errors made by students. Matz (1982) examined students' work on high school algebra and identified three major sources of common errors: (a) incorrect choice of an (otherwise correct) extrapolation technique, (b) unmade developmental changes, and (c) processing errors.

One example for incorrect choice of an extrapolation technique, as illustrated by Matz (1982), is the linear decomposition error, typified by: "$(A+B)^2 = A^2 + B^2$" , "$A(BC) = AB + AC$", or "$A/B+C = A/B + A/C$". This type of error can be seen as an over-generalization of the distribution rule, "$A(B+C) = AB + AC$".

Regarding developmental changes, students have to go through some major conceptual adjustments to move from arithmetic to algebra learning. For example, as Matz (1982) described, students who initially fail to realize that a letter represents a number will find operating with a letter totally alien. Accepting this concept also means relaxing arithmetic expectations about well-formed answers, i.e., that an answer is a number.

Matz (1982) also gave many examples of processing errors found in students' work. One of these is the so-called "Lost Common Denominator" bug: for instance, while working on "$5/(2-x) + 5/(2+x) = 4$", instead of correctly producing "$5(2+x) + 5(2-x) = 4(2+x)(2-x)$", students tend to produce the following: "$5(2+x) + 5(2-x) = 4$".

In short, moving away from arithmetic to algebra is a big step for students to take. There are conceptual adjustments to be made, new rules to be learned, and old rules to be differentiated from the new ones. Moreover, working with algebra requires not only procedural knowledge but also controlled planning strategies. In order to reach expertise in algebra, students need to develop sophisticated and well-connected schemata, and possess well-practiced and automated procedures, which will then allow them the cognitive resources to execute higher-order planning and monitoring activities. Moreover, students need to learn not only how to use certain strategies to solve a problem, but also when it is appropriate to use these strategies.

We have so far reviewed instructional studies based on Mayer's component model for problem solving. There have been a few other instructional studies designed to improve students' general problem-solving strategies. These studies emphasized the sequential stages involved in problem solving, based on Polya's (1957) stage model.

Application of Polya's Stage Model

Polya's model of problem solving has been adopted in a few studies to teach students general problem-solving strategies. Bassler, Beers and Richardson (1975) tested two different approaches in problem solving, namely, key-phrase and key-word translation, and a solution-devising step approach (Polya's approach). Fifty-three ninth-grade algebra students were grouped according to ability. Within each ability group, students were randomly assigned to one of the two treatment programs. Students in the step-approach group were directed to complete the solution of word problems by using the six steps as shown in Table 7-6.

Students in the translation approach group were instructed to translate key phrases such as "increased by" to *plus*, and "decreased by" to *minus*. They were taught to translate all phrases of the word problem into mathematical statements using a direct, pure, piecemeal, and complete translation. Each value to be solved in the problem was translated as "variable equals question mark." They were directed to find relations expressing the values to be found and to solve the resulting equation. When a solution was found, the students were

---

Table 7-6
Six Steps for the step-approach group in Bassler, Beers, & Richardson's (1975) study

1. Read the problem carefully

2. Decide what question the problem asks and choose a variable to represent the unknown

3. Consider the other information given in the problem and how it relates to the unknown.

4. Write an equation or equations expressing the given relationships

5. Solve the equation or equations

6. Check the answer

directed to check their answers in the verbal problem.

The results of this study showed that although there was no significant difference in students' ability to derive a correct answer for the problems between the two groups, students in the step-approach were significantly more able to generate correct equations than students from the translation-approach group.

Other Factors Affecting Mathematics Learning

Researchers have found some other factors that may affect the difficulty level of a problem. The following are a few examples.

Concrete vs. Abstract, and Factual vs. Hypothetical Problems

Caldwell and Goldin (1987) compared the relative difficulties of four types of verbal problems: abstract factual, abstract hypothetical, concrete factual, and concrete hypothetical. Table 7-7 gives sample problems from each category of problems.

Students in junior high (grades 7-9) and senior high school (grades 10-12) were asked to solve these four types of problems. The results of this study showed that for both junior and senior high school children, the concrete problems were significantly less difficult than the abstract problems. The factual problems were also significantly less difficult than the hypothetical problems for both levels of students. The magnitude of the difference in the difficulty between concrete and

---

Table 7-7
Four Different Problem Types tested in Caldwell and Goldin's (1987) study.

Problem Type	Sample Problem
Concrete Factual	A farmer has eight more hens than dogs. Since hens have two legs each, and dogs have four legs each, all together the animals have 118 legs. How many dogs does the farmer own?
Concrete Hypothetical	There are four more girls in an English class than boys. If there were six times as many girls and twice as many boys, there would be 136 pupils. How many boys are there?
Abstract Factual	The value of a given number is six more than the value of a second number. The sum of two times the first number and four times the second number is 126. What is the value of the second number?
Abstract Hypothetical	A given number is six more than a second number. If the first number were four times as large and the second two times as large, their sum should be 126. What is the second number?

abstract problems, however, became smaller with increasing grade level. These results provide some useful information for teachers to sequence the difficulty level of their teaching materials.

Meaningfulness to Students of the Problem Context

Ross (1983) gave pre-service teachers three different versions of learning materials on probability. As shown in Table 7-8, the learning materials consisted of a brief definitional statement of the rule accompanied by its mathematical formula, followed by examples for students to solve on their own. Three different contexts were employed in the problems: abstract version, education-related, and medical-related.

The results of their study showed that pre-service teachers benefited from education-related materials but not from medical- related materials, whereas nursing students benefited more from medical-related materials than from education-related materials. Moreover, students showed more favorable attitudes when the context of the problem was adapted to their background experience.

This context effect has been taken further and tested in a few studies where students' personal information was incorporated in the problem via computer programming. For example, Wright and Wright (1985) developed a computer program to personalize a pool of mathematics word problems by incorporating students' personal information in the problem. They found that students performed better on the personalized test items compared to the standard textbook problems. Arnand and Ross (1987) gave fifth- and sixth-grade children one of three versions of a computer-assisted lesson on the division of fractions. In one version, examples were personalized by incorporating information about the student into the problem contexts. In the other two versions, concrete contexts and abstract contexts were used. The following are examples provided by Arnand and Ross (1987) for three versions of the same problem:

> *Abstract version:* There are 3 objects. Each is cut in one-half. In all, how many pieces would there be?
> *Concrete version:* Billy had 3 candy bars. He cut each one of them in half. In all, how many pieces of candy bar did Billy have?
> *Personalized-context version: Joseph*'s teacher, *Mrs. Williams,* surprised him on *December 15* when she presented Joseph with 3 *Hershey Bars.* Joseph cut each one of them in half so that he could share the birthday gift with his friends. In all, how many pieces of Hershey Bars did Joseph have for his friends?

The results of their study showed that the personalized-context group performed better than the other two groups in solving standard problems and transfer problems, and in recognizing rule procedures. In

Table 7-8
Instructional materials on multiplication rule with three different versions used in Ross's (1983) study.

Multiplication Rule: The probability that event A, which has a probability P(A) of occurring on any one trial, will occur n times in n independent trials is as follows:

$$P(A) \times P(A) \times \ldots \times P(A) = P(A) \times n$$

Different Versions	Sample Problems
Abstract context	A random response is made on each of two trials. The probability of outcome Y occurring on any one trial is 1/3. What is the probability that outcome Y will occur on both trials?
Education context	A student makes a completely random guess on each of two multiple choice items containing three alternatives. The probability of randomly guessing the correct answer is thus 1/3. What is the probability of randomly guessing it on both items?
Medical context	Two patients being treated for vision problems each receive a cataract operation. The probability of that operation being successful in any one case is 1/3. What is the probability that the operation will be successful in both cases?

Adapted from Ross (1983), p. 521.

addition, students in the personalized-context group showed more positive attitudes toward the task.

Thus, it is clear that teachers should make mathematics problems as relevant to students as possible. By doing so, students will not only be more motivated and interested in learning, but indeed will also learn better.

Consideration on Students' Cognitive Load

Another factor to consider in mathematics learning is students' limits in cognitive processing capacity. Teachers should be aware of this limit and try to eliminate unnecessary taxing of students' cognitive resources during learning.

For example, Sweller, Chandler, Tierney, and Cooper (1990) suggested that mathematics instructional materials that require learners to mentally integrate disparate sources of mutually referring information (e.g., text and diagrams) impose a heavy cognitive load on students and, thus, interfere with their learning. They suggested that one way to remedy the problem was to integrate the information for the students. To test this hypothesis, they gave ninth-grade students different versions of instruction on coordinate geometry. The material was to teach students how to calculate the slope of a line that intersected another at its midpoint. Students in the conventional group received instruction in a split-source format, where a coordinate geometry diagram and textual information that referred to elements of the diagram were separate. Students in the modified group received the same instruction, but in a format that integrated diagrammatic and textual information. Table 7-9 shows the contrasts in the instruction between the two groups.

The results of this study showed that students in the modified-instruction group not only spent less time studying the instructions, but also performed at a substantially higher level than the conventional group in the post-test.

This study addressed an important issue in teaching and learning. It showed that when students were not overtaxed on their cognitive processing and could apply most of their cognitive resources, learning was enhanced. As Sweller et al. (1990) illustrated, teachers can lighten students' cognitive load in learning simply by illustrating the instructional materials differently.

Concluding Remarks

The instructional studies reviewed in this chapter differed greatly in their focus on strategy instruction. Some studies were designed to teach more general problem-solving strategies, whereas others tested the treatment effect on specific cognitive processes in solving a problem. In general, studies that yielded positive results from general problem-solving strategy instruction required an extended period of intervention. This coincides with Pressley's (1986) notion that developing good general strategy use is a formidable educational challenge and requires an extended period of time. On the other hand, strategy teaching that is directed to specific problem-solving processes using a specific task seems to provide significant positive effects with a relatively short period of intervention.

Two important features shared by these successful strategy interventions are explicit teaching of the strategy and extended practice on the use of that strategy. As Schoenfeld (1979) pointed out, if we expect students to learn to use the strategies, we should label them explicitly and explicate their use in much the same way we would teach any other mathematical technique. Moreover, the fact that students can master a particular problem-solving technique is no guarantee that they will use it. Students must be taught not only *how* to use the strategies but also *when* to use them.

There are other task variables that may affect students' learning, such as the context of the problem and the arrangement of the instructional materials. Students learn better when the learning materials are more relevant and the cognitive demands of the task are not

Table 7-9

Conventional vs. modified instruction on "The Midpoint of an Interval."

Instruction to the conventional group:

The midpoint N of XY, where X is (4,3) and Y is (8,7), is given by

$$N = (\frac{4+8}{2}, \frac{3+7}{2}) = (6,5)$$

The midpoint M of interval AB, where A is (x_1,y_1) and B is (x_2,y_2), is given by

$$M = (\frac{x_1+x_2}{2}, \frac{y_1+y_2}{2})$$

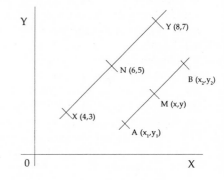

Instruction to the "modified" group:

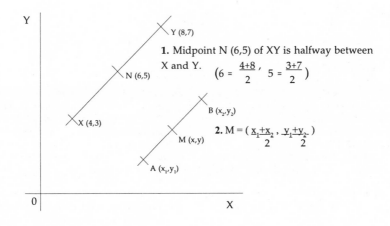

1. Midpoint N (6,5) of XY is halfway between X and Y. $(6 = \frac{4+8}{2}, 5 = \frac{3+7}{2})$

2. $M = (\frac{x_1+x_2}{2}, \frac{y_1+y_2}{2})$

Adapted from Sweller et al. (1990), pp. 190-191

overwhelming. One exciting direction of recent research is to employ media support to engage students in mathematics tasks. For example, the Cognition and Technology Group at Vanderbilt University has developed and tested the effectiveness of presenting mathematical problems using a multimedia approach (The Cognition and Technology Group at Vanderbilt, 1994). A series of videos and corresponding computer software applications were prepared that allowed students to extract critical information and apply it in order to solve the assigned problems. Students using these videos expressed greater interest in completing problems as well as an awareness of the complexity of mathematical problem-solving tasks. Although initial studies were conducted with elementary and university students, the positive gains from this multimedia approach appear likely to benefit secondary school students as well (see The Cognition and Technology Group at Vanderbilt, 1994, for a valuable summary of this approach).

Although few of these studies address the issue of possible interaction between student characteristics and treatment, the effectiveness of strategy instruction does seem to depend very much on students' ability and their prerequisite skills. For example, Brown et al. (1990) were able to illustrate positive learning effects from reciprocal teaching with one group of students who were screened on their ability to solve algorithms correctly, but not with another group of students who were not preselected for ability. In other words, strategy instruction may be beneficial only to those students who possess certain prerequisite skills and are ready to receive it, but not to others. More studies are needed on this particular issue. For now, it is important that teachers keep this factor in mind when implementing strategy instruction.

REFERENCES

Arnand, P.G., & Ross, S. M. (1987). Using computer-assisted instruction to personalize arithmetic materials for elementary school children. *Journal of Educational Psychology, 79,* 72-78.

Artzt, A.F., & Armour-Thomas, E. (1992). Development of a cognitive-metacognitive framework for protocol analysis of mathematical problem solving in small groups. *Cognition and Instruction, 9(2),* 137-175.

Bassler, O.C., Beers, M.I., & Richardson, L.I. (1975). Comparison of two instructional strategies for teaching the solution of verbal problems. *Journal for Research in Mathematics Education, 6,* 171-177.

Bundy, A. (1975). *Analyzing mathematical proofs (or reading between the lines)* (DAI report No. 2). Edinburgh, Scotland: University of Edinburgh, Department of Artificial Intelligence.

Brown, A.L., & Campione, J.C. (1990). Interactive learning environments and the teaching of science and mathematics. In M. Gardner, J.G. Greeno, F. Reif, A.H. Schoenfeld, A.Disessa, & E. Stage (Eds.), *Toward a scientific practice of science education* (pp. 111-139). Hillsdale, NJ: Lawrence Erlbaum Associates.

Caldwell, J.H., & Goldin, G.A. (1987). Variables affecting word problem difficulty in secondary school mathematics. *Journal for*

Research in Mathematics Education, 18(3), 187-196.

Campione, J.C., Brown, A. L., & Connell, M.L. (1988). Metacognition: On the importance of understanding what you are doing. In R.I. Charles & E.A. Silver (Eds), *Research agenda for mathematics education, Vol. 3: The teaching and assessing of mathematical problem solving* (pp. 93-114). Reston, VA: National Council of Teachers of Mathematics, Inc.

Campione, J.C., Brown, A.L., Reeve, R.A., Ferrara, R.A., & Palincsar, A.S. (1991). Interactive learning and on students' mathematics skills individual understanding: The case of reading and mathematics. In Landsmann, L. T. (Ed.) *Culture, schooling, and psychological development, Vol. 4: Human development* (pp. 136-170). NJ: Ablex Publishing Corporation.

Cognition and Technology Group at Vanderbilt (1994). From visual word problems to learning communities: Changing conceptions of cognitive research. In K. McGilly (Ed.), *Classroom lessons: Integrating cognitive theory and classroom practice.* Cambridge, MA: MIT Press.

Cooper, G., & Sweller, J. (1987). Effects of schema acquisition and rule automation on mathematical problem-solving transfer. *Journal of Educational Psychology, 79,* 347-362.

Days, H.C., Wheatley, G.H., & Kulm, G. (1979). Problem structure, cognitive level, and problem-solving performance. *Journal for Research in Mathematics Education, 10,* 135-146.

Fischbein, E., Deri, M., Nello, M.S., & Marino, M.S. (1985). The role of implicit models in solving verbal problems in multiplication and division. *Journal for Research in Mathematics Education, 16(1),* 3-17.

Hall, R., Kibler, D., Wenger, E., & Truxaw, C. (1989). Exploring the episodic structure of algebra story problem solving. *Cognition and Instruction, 6(3),* 223-283.

Lapointe, A., Mead, N.A., & Askew, J.M. (1992). *Learning Mathematics.* Princeton, NJ: International Assessment of Educational Progress, Educational Testing Service.

Lewis, A.B. (1989). Training students to represent arithmetic word problems. *Journal of Educational Psychology, 81(4),* 521-531.

Lewis, C. (1981). Skill in algebra. In J.R. Anderson (Ed.), *Cognitive skills and their acquisition.* Hillsdale, NJ: Lawrence Erlbaum

Associates.

Loftus, E.F., & Suppes, P. (1972). Structural variables that determine problem-solving difficulty in computer assisted instruction. *Journal of Educational Psychology, 63,* 531-542.

Low, R., & Over, R. (1990). Text editing of algebraic word problems. *Australian Journal of Psychology, 42,* 63-73.

MacGregor, M., & Stacey, K. (1993). Cognitive models underlying students' formulation of simple linear equations. *Journal for Research in Mathematics Education, 24(3),* 217-232.

Matz, M. (1982). Towards a process model for high school algebra errors. In D. Sleeman & J.S. Brown (Eds.), *Intelligent tutoring systems* (pp. 25-50). New York: Academic Press.

Mayer, R.E. (1981). Frequency norms and structural analysis of algebra story problems into families, categories and templates. *Instructional Science, 10,* 135-175.

Mayer, R.E. (1982). Memory for algebra story problems. *Journal of Educational Psychology, 74,* 199-216.

Mayer, R.E. (1987). *Educational psychology: A cognitive approach.* Boston: Little, Brown and Co.

Nathan, M.J., Kintsch, W., & Young, E. (1992). A theory of algebra-word-problem comprehension and its implications for the design of learning environments. *Cognition and Instruction, 9(4),* 329-389.

Paige, J.M., & Simon, H.A. (1966). Cognitive processes in solving algebra word problems. In B. Kleinmuntz (Ed.) *Problem solving: Research, method, and theory* (pp. 51-119). New York, London, Sydney: John Wiley & Sons, Inc.

Polya, G. (1957). *How to solve it* (2nd ed.). Garden City, NY: Doubleday Anchor Books.

Polya, G. (1981). *Mathematical discovery: On understanding, learning, and teaching problem solving* (combined edition). New York: John Wiley & Sons.

Post, T.R., & Brennan, M.L. (1976). An experimental study of the effectiveness of a formal versus an informal presentation of a general heuristic process on problem solving in tenth-grade geometry. *Journal for Research in Mathematics Education, 7,* 59-64.

Pressley, M. (1986). The relevance of the good strategy user model to the teaching of mathematics. *Educational psychologist, 21(1*

& 2), 139-161.

Reed, S.K. (1987). A structure-mapping model for word problems. *Journal of Experimental Psychology: Learning, Memory, and Cognition, 13*(1), 124-139.

Reed, S.K., Dempster, A., & Ettinger, M. (1985). Usefulness of analogous solutions for solving algebra word problems. *Journal of Experimental Psychology: Learning, Memory, and Cognition, 11*(1), 106-125.

Reed, S.K., & Ettinger, M. (1987). Usefulness of tables for solving word problems. *Cognition and Instruction, 4(1),* 43-59.

Ross, S.M. (1983). Increasing the meaningfulness of quantitative material by adapting context to student background. *Journal of Educational Psychology, 75,* 519-529.

Schoenfeld, A.H. (1979). Explicit heuristic training as a variable in problem-solving performance. *Journal for Research in Mathematics Education, 10,* 173-187.

Silver, E.A. (1981). Recall of mathematical problem information: solving related problems. *Journal for Research in Mathematics Education, 12,* 54-64.

Silver, E.A. (1979). Student perceptions of relatedness among mathematical verbal problems. *Journal for Research in Mathematics Education, 10,* 195-210.

Smith, J.P. (1973). *The effect of general versus specific heuristics in mathematical problem-solving tasks.* Unpublished doctoral dissertation, Columbia University.

Sweller, J., Chandler, P., Tierney, P. & Cooper, M. (1990). Cognitive load as a factor in the structuring of technical material. *Journal of Experimental Psychology: General, 119*(2), 176-192.

Weaver, C.A., & Kintsch, W. (1992). Enhancing students' comprehension of the conceptual structure of algebra word problems. *Journal of Educational Psychology, 84,* 419-428.

Wilson, J.W. (1967). *Generality of heuristics as an instructional variable.* Unpublished doctoral dissertation, Stanford University.

Wright, J.P. & Wright, C.D. (1985). Personalized verbal problems: An application of the language experience approach. *Journal of Educational Research, 79,* 358-362.

Zhu, X., & Simon, H.A. (1987). Learning mathematics from examples and by doing. *Cognition and Instruction, 4,* 137-166.

CHAPTER 8

Science

Vera Woloshyn • Brock University

Approximately 30 years ago, inspired by the launching of Sputnik, the United States acknowledged that it faced a crisis in science education. There was general concern that students did not possess adequate scientific knowledge or skills—knowledge that is needed to cope in an increasingly technological society (Staver & Small, 1990; Yager & Penick, 1987). In an attempt to resolve this crisis, science curricula were modified to emphasize hands-on activities and process skills that emulated those carried out by real scientists (McIntosh & Zeidler, 1988). However, despite pouring over $1.5 billion into science education, many educators and researchers would agree that students' knowledge and performance in science-related domains remains in a state of crisis.

Simply allocating greater educational funds does little to promote a society that truly understands and appreciates science (Yager & Penick, 1987). One important aspect of reform involves reevaluating how science is presented to students. Science classrooms need to include instructional methods that have been empirically demonstrated to enhance students' acquisition of both scientific knowledge and skills. The primary purpose of this chapter is to review learning techniques (both teacher-directed and student-directed) that promote such scientific understanding. First, however, the current status of science instruction is reviewed so that readers may become more familiar with the present-day science classroom.

THE CURRENT STATUS OF SCIENCE INSTRUCTION

Science is a mainstay of the secondary school curriculum. Yet many students demonstrate inadequate understanding of basic science concepts, even after extensive classroom instruction (e.g., Hackling & Treagust, 1984). Furthermore, many students do not view themselves as future scientists, believing that science is "something to be done by someone other than themselves" (Welch, Klopfer, Aikenhead, & Robinson, 1981). These pessimistic attitudes are translated into lower numbers of young people obtaining college degrees in the sciences, relative to the arts, humanities, or other subjects (National Center for Education Statistics, 1990). Why are more students not motivated to pursue advanced studies and careers in the sciences? While there does not appear to be one answer to this question, it is probable that improving teaching materials and instructional techniques may increase some students' motivation for the sciences.

In a survey of over 12,000 science teachers, between 90% and 95% of the teachers reported relying on texts for curriculum and instruction (Yager, 1983; cited in Lloyd, 1990). Unfortunately, commercial texts often do little to facilitate student learning. Textbooks that are used most often by elementary- and secondary-school students are increasingly content-oriented. For example, in grade three, students are introduced to approximately 300 new terms and concepts per text, with there being over 3000 terms and symbols in a tenth-grade text (Woodward & Noell, 1991). One concern is that the level of learning promoted by the activities and questions included in the text often tend to be superficial. For example, these exercises generally promote retention- and comprehension-level skills rather than higher-order thinking skills such as application, analysis, synthesis and evaluation (Bloom, Englehart, Hill, Furst, & Krathwohl, 1956).

Many commercial texts also fail to elaborate or embellish critical concepts. Lloyd (1990) reviewed three popular high school biology texts. Each textbook was intended for one of three high school populations: (1) non-college bound students with average ability but below-grade level success, (2) average-ability students with low achievement, and (3) students at all levels. Overall, she found that all the textbooks lacked elaboration, with the text designed for the least able student containing the fewest examples and elaborations. This is a particularly disturbing finding, as low-ability students are the least likely to either possess relevant background knowledge or activate that information spontaneously when reading (Schneider & Pressley, 1989).

Textbooks are not the only places where the demands placed on students fail to promote higher-level cognitive processing (Mergendoller, Marchman, Mitman, & Packer, 1988; Sanford, 1987; Tobin, 1987; Welch et al., 1981). Classroom interactions, like textbook learning, can also fail to stimulate higher-level thinking processes. While there is great diversity among classrooms and among teachers, in many cases students are faced with less challenging tasks than are ideal. For example, although students initially may be presented with challenging questions (ones that require application, analysis, synthesis, or evaluation of science concepts), these questions are often simplified to "yes" or "no" responses before students are provided the opportunity to respond. Other times, advanced learning questions are "worked out" for the whole class (e.g., completing a problem-solving exercise on the blackboard), with students perceiving their responsibility to be limited to copying out procedures and memorizing correct answers. Students often fail to understand that worked examples are intended to demonstrate the logic or conceptual underpinnings of a problem, rather than promote simple memorization or repetition (rewriting). When students are asked challenging questions, they are often provided with a variety of "safety-nets" that ensure task success (Sanford, 1987). For example, greater credit may be assigned to the completion of memory and procedural components than to higher-level ones so that a passing grade is not dependent upon successfully completing the more conceptually challenging task.

In addition, instruction is sometimes based on methods that have not been demonstrated to be effective (Yager & Penick, 1987). For instance, Tobin (1987) observed that many teachers (58%) used whole-class activities extensively, relying on lectures, large-group activities, and "around-the-class" text reading where only a small number of select students tended to participate in these activities (Jones, 1990; Tobin, 1987). Individual work assignments accounted for 27% of class time, whereas small-group work accounted for only 15% (Tobin, 1987). Empirical research, on the other hand, suggests that including more small-group activities would increase greater participation and learning (Johnson & Johnson, 1991).

Emphasis on lectures and other traditional modes of instruction may, in part, be reflective of the belief that the primary purpose of science education is to prepare students for the next level of instruction (Yager & Penick, 1987; Welch et al., 1981). While many teachers make positive statements about the merits of inquiry and discovery methods in science, they believe that they are constrained to teaching "facts" or "the basics." In fact, many teachers view science as the mastery of words and terms, a belief that is internalized by many students who believe that science is static and consists of a collection of unrelated facts and ideas (Songer & Linn, 1991).

The concerns raised in this introduction are presented to provide a historical perspective of the science classroom. Fortunately, there is a brighter side to science education. In fact, both educators and researchers have made substantial gains in understanding how to best structure the science classroom (Pressley, 1995). Furthermore, there are numerous instances of exemplary science instruction (e.g., Tobin & Fraser, 1990). In these classrooms, teachers implement many of the learning strategies and teaching approaches that are described in this chapter and throughout this book. Students in these classrooms generally tend to enjoy science and are actively engaged in the scientific process.

In the following section, effective science teaching techniques and learning strategies are reviewed. Because students who are successful lifelong learners possess a repertoire of effective learning strategies and study techniques, and because not every strategy is suitable for all students across all contexts, it is recommended that educators use a variety of the science strategies discussed in this chapter in their classrooms. In addition, because success in science is usually contingent on possessing effective reading, writing and study skills, the science strategies contained in this chapter should be taught in conjunction with other effective learning strategies reviewed in this book. For instance, teachers could instruct students to use a summarization strategy or an imagery strategy (see Chapter 4: Reading Comprehension) in order to increase their comprehension and recall of science texts, or have them participate in group questioning sessions (see Chapter 3: Learning from Direct Teaching) to enhance their conceptual understandings of scientific concepts.

Throughout this chapter, no distinction is made between the three major sciences (biology, chemistry, physics). Instead, teaching techniques and learning strategies that are applicable across all the sciences are reviewed with examples provided from each discipline. Whenever possible, secondary-school literature has been used. However, when information has not been available from this population, material has been drawn from the junior/intermediate or college divisions. Teachers should use the latter information with caution. That is, they should "test out" these techniques with a small number of students and a limited amount of content before implementing the learning strategy or teaching technique in the classroom.

INQUIRY BASED LEARNING

During the 1960s and 1970s, science programs underwent massive restructuring to develop what has been referred to as the "new science curriculum." Although never clearly defined, this curriculum was associated with inquiry methods and process objectives, where learning how to do science was valued over the acquisition of factual information (Ajewole, 1991; Shymansky, Kyle & Alport, 1983). In a meta-analysis of 81 empirical studies involving more than 40,000 kindergarten through 12th-grade students, Shymansky and colleagues (Shymansky et al., 1983; Shymansky, Hedges, & Woodworth, 1990) concluded that the new science curriculum enhanced students' science achievement and process skills, as well as positively affected their attitudes about science, relative to traditional textbook-based programs. This was especially true for high school biology and physics programs. Improvements in students' achievement scores abated some fears that inquiry methods would enhance students' process skills and attitudes at the expense of academic attainment. Central to inquiry methods is the science laboratory.

Science Laboratories

Laboratory activities where students actively design investigations and predict outcomes have been part of science instruction since the 19th century. Ideally, laboratory activities promote deep understanding, creative thinking, and problem-solving (Hofstein & Lunette, 1982). They are the epitome of "learning by doing." There is substantial evidence that having learners carry out laboratory exercises facilitates their learning to the same extent or better than having them participate in didactic instruction where teachers describe or demonstrate laboratory experiences (e.g., Coulter, 1966; Glasson, 1989; Hall & McCurdy, 1990; Russell & Chiappetta, 1981; Saunders & Dickinson, 1979; Yager, Engen, & Snider, 1969). Participating in laboratory activities appears to be especially beneficial for lower-ability students (Bredderman, 1985; Odubunmi & Balogun, 1991; Shymansky & Penick, 1981).

Laboratories can be designed to promote opportunities for experimentation, prediction, and independent interpretation rather than "cookbook exercises" where students follow a prescribed set of procedures (Fuhrman, Lunette, & Novick, 1982; Lederman & O'Malley, 1990). In educator-structured laboratories, the teacher directly instructs students about what to do, when to do it, and how to do it. Students are provided with explicit feedback about their performance (Shymansky & Penick, 1981). In contrast, in student-directed laboratories, learners are not provided with explicit instructions or feedback from the teacher. Instead, the teacher's primary role is that of facilitator, challenging students with thought-provoking questions about their activities. Students who participate in educator-structured laboratories are more dependent on their teachers and peers than are students who participate in student-directed ones. The former tend to view science as a collection of correct answers that are beyond interpretation. Learners exposed to student-directed instruction, on the other hand, believe that science is an evolution of knowledge and explanations and that scientists are creative individuals who use the scientific process to solve problems—attributes which they view themselves as possessing (Shymansky & Penick, 1981).

COOPERATIVE LEARNING

Cooperative learning involves having students work in small heterogeneous groups of four to six individuals (Watson, 1991). However, effective cooperative learning involves more than simply placing students into groups (Kagan, 1990; Nastasi & Clements, 1991). Students must be taught how to work collaboratively and be provided with opportunities to acquire the skills necessary for successful group interactions. Johnson and Johnson (1990a) outline five elements of cooperative learning, including: (1) positive interdependence (individuals' successes are dependent on group success); (2) face-to-face positive interaction (e.g., sharing, understanding, and developing group knowledge); (3) individual accountability; (4) interpersonal and small-group skills (e.g., communication, conflict-resolution, decision-making); and (5) reflection (both of academic and social processes). Often teachers must spend substantial amounts of instructional time providing students with opportunities to practice these skills before groups can successfully address academic content (interested readers are referred to Johnson & Johnson,1990b, 1991, for examples of activities that foster each of the five processes).

Two decades of research on collaborative learning documents that instructing students to use cooperative-learning techniques improves their academic performance, social behavior, and attitudes towards school (Davidson & Shearn, 1990; Gabbert, Johnson, & Johnson, 1986; Sharon, 1990; Watson, 1991). Having students work together encourages them to conceptualize materials in new ways by generating examples and translating new information into familiar terms (Bargh & Schul, 1980). In addition, collaborative efforts expose learners to new and alternative points of view. Verbal interactions can also facilitate the correct use of scientific vocabulary (Champagne, Klopfer & Gunstone, 1982). In sum, by working together, learners can share and discover information that is beyond their existing knowledge.

Cooperative learning procedures can be especially beneficial in the science classroom (e.g., Humphreys, Johnson & Johnson, 1982; Okebukola, 1985; Okebukola & Ogunniyi, 1984; Watson, 1991). Humphreys and his colleagues (1982) assigned 44 grade-nine students to either cooperative learning, competitive, or individualistic instruction. Over a period of six weeks, students completed three two-week units, about heat, sun and light, and nuclear energy.

In the cooperative learning group, students' achievements were positively correlated so that the success of any one student was contingent on group success. These students were instructed to complete assignments together, reach decisions by consensus, and consult each other for clarification of concepts. The teacher praised and rewarded these students as a group. In the competitive learning group, students' achievements were negatively correlated. When one student achieved his or her goal, others failed to reach theirs. These students were instructed to outperform their peers (with test and assignment grades prominently displayed in the classroom), to work independently, and to seek clarification from the teacher only. Praise was given to those students whose grades exceeded their peers. In the individualistic learning group, students' achievements were independent. Like students in the competitive condition, these students were instructed to work independently, consulting only the teacher for assistance. However, the instructor praised each student's performance on the basis of preset criteria.

After each unit, students completed a multiple-choice test. They also completed a cumulative test at the end of the instructional period. On both tests, students assigned to the cooperative learning condition outperformed students assigned to either the individualistic or competitive conditions. Cooperative-learning students also evaluated their classroom experiences more favorably than did their peers. Finally, school attendance was higher for these students than their peers, who, collectively, missed over a week of instruction.

Teachers must remember, however, that in order for high-quality collaboration to occur, each element of the cooperative process must be explicitly taught, modeled, and practiced—a process that requires substantial instructional time. (See Sherman, 1988, and Gayford, 1989, 1992, for examples of the learning decrements that occur when insufficient time or interactive opportunities occur in cooperative learning contexts.) Students must also possess relevant prior knowledge to effectively participate in group discussion (knowledge that is often lacking; Basili & Sanford, 1991). In situations where students lack critical background knowledge, it is the responsibility of the educator to provide this information. Tobin and Fraser (1990) observed that exemplary science teachers constantly monitor students' understanding, clarify their misunderstandings, and prompt relevant extensions of their thinking. These teachers not only provide direct instruction of collaborative learning and scientific thinking but also model these processes.

COMPUTERS AND OTHER RELATED TECHNOLOGY

Computers and other related technology present science teachers with unique opportunities for advanced instruction, often combining elements of science laboratories and cooperative learning procedures. In 1994, it was estimated that there were more than 4,000,000 microcomputers in U.S. schools. However, only one in four high school science teachers regularly used the computer (Simmons, 1991).

Those teachers who used computers believed that their students worked more cooperatively with each other and were more independent learners as a result of their technological experiences. These beliefs are not without support. For instance, Kinzie and her colleagues (Kinzie, Sullivan, & Berdel, 1992) noted strong preferences for computer instruction among ninth-grade students, with affinity for science study increasing from 27% to 71%.

The microcomputer allows students to explore, experiment, and manipulate scientific concepts (Simmons, 1991). In contrast to the laboratory experiment where usually only one trial is carried out (most often by the classroom teacher) and redesign of the experiment is rare, the computer allows for multiple repetitions of experiments and for student redesign. Finally, the computer provides the opportunity for experimentation that otherwise would be either too expensive, too dangerous, or too costly to carry out in the classroom (Simmons, 1991).

For these reasons, there should be optimism about the role of computers in the science classroom. This optimism, however, is mixed with caution, as there have been relatively few studies investigating the effectiveness of computer-based instruction (with many of these studies not employing stringent experimental procedures, or being restricted to very select groups of students). Furthermore, the available findings are mixed, with some studies reporting that computer-based instruction is no more effective than traditional laboratory exercises (e.g., Beichner, 1990; Choi & Gennaro, 1987; Morrell, 1992). Having students complete computer exercises that parallel those in the science laboratories does not guarantee that students will demonstrate sophisticated problem-solving or other scientific skills (Nachmias & Linn, 1987; Slack & Stewart, 1990). For these reasons, computer-based instruction should only be used as a supplement to regular instruction and with the guidance of a teacher. The following is a review of a few computer programs that enjoy some empirical support (for an extended review of such computer software, see Simmons, 1991).

Microcomputer-based Laboratories and Graphing Packages

As part of a five-year project to improve science education, the Microcomputer-Based Lab (otherwise known as MBL) at the Technical Education Research Centers developed software to assist students in experimental data collection and analyses (Mokros & Tinker, 1987). The software is designed to be used in conjunction with an actual experiment. Specifically, the computer is interfaced with probes that measure physical phenomena (e.g., temperature, light, force, sound). As the experiment progresses, students are provided with immediate feedback about the phenomena in the form of an evolving graph. The students are expected to make predictions about the future shape of the graph and to clarify any discrepancies between their predictions and the graph.

For example, the software package *Heat and Temperature* graphs the evaporation of water and alcohol. One temperature probe is placed in water for approximately 20 seconds, the other in alcohol. When the probes are removed, the liquids on the probes evaporate. The computer records provide immediate feedback to the students about the temperatures of the probes (Krajcik, 1991). See Figure 8-1 for an example of such a graph.

Completing microcomputer-based labs improves most students' comprehension of science materials as well as their graphing skills (e.g., Brasell, 1987; Linn & Songer, 1991; Mokros & Tinker, 1987). For instance, Brasell (1987) documented improvement in high school physics students' comprehension of distance and velocity graphs (as measured by a multiple-choice test where students transformed a verbal description of a physical event to a graphic representation), relative to their peers who completed parallel pen-and-paper activities (e.g., producing graphs and making experimental predictions). Most impressive, this improvement occurred over one class period.

Microcomputer Simulations of Microworlds

Interactive microcomputer models provide students with the opportunity to safely and efficiently view scientific models that are difficult to observe firsthand. Often, the scientific models are simplified by omitting superfluous details or by speeding up or slowing down time (Krajcik, 1991).

Krajcik (1991) had 18 ninth-grade biology students use one of two computer software packages as part of their instruction in kinetic molecular theory. One program included a tutorial with interactive visuals (particle animations; *Molecular Velocities*), while the other only included the tutorial dialogue (i.e., no visual accompaniment). Prior to working with the computer packages, only one student in each group expressed beliefs that were consistent with the scientific model of particles in a gaseous phase. Following their computer experiences, six of the nine students who had used the interactive computer program expressed ideas consistent with molecular theory. Only two of the nine students who had used the tutorial package expressed similar views.

Videodisks

Videodisks combine pictures, animation, graphics and computer-based instruction, allowing students to witness reactions that would otherwise be too expensive, hazardous or time-consuming to observe. For instance, with videodisks, students can safely view the noxious reaction between liquid bromine and aluminum foil or the reaction between sodium and water. Unfortunately, research investigating the effectiveness of videodisk technology with secondary-school students, or for that matter with any other level student, is not yet available. Given that videodisk technology provides students with the same benefits as microcomputer laboratories and simulations (e.g., visual representa-

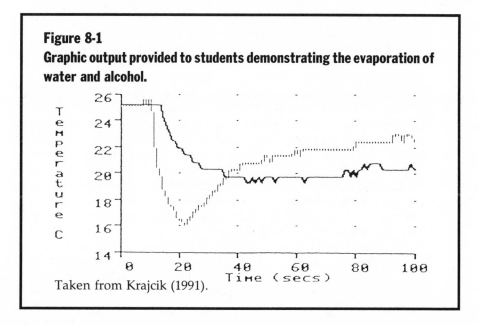

Figure 8-1

Graphic output provided to students demonstrating the evaporation of water and alcohol.

Taken from Krajcik (1991).

tion of phenomena, repetition, and immediate corrective feedback), teachers should be encouraged to cautiously use these programs (i.e., carry out trial runs with selected groups of students).

WORKED EXAMPLES

There is considerable evidence that students' mathematical learning and problem-solving skills can be improved by having them study worked examples versus independently solving problems (Cooper & Sweller, 1987; Sweller & Cooper, 1985; Zhu & Simon, 1987; also see Chapter 7, this volume). Worked examples can also facilitate students' science learning. Essentially, worked examples consist of presenting students with both problem questions and their solutions. Providing students with worked examples allows them to focus attention on problem states and the processes required to solve them (Ward & Sweller, 1990).

Ward and Sweller (1990) carried out a series of studies with tenth- and eleventh-grade students reviewing geometric optics and kinematics. As part of these studies, instructors explained target rules to all the students, provided them with a worked example, had them solve two practice questions, and presented them with solutions to the problem questions. Students were then provided with five pairs of homework questions, with each pair being identical in format. For half the students, the first member of each pair was presented as a worked example and the second as a conventional problem. For the remaining students, all problems were presented in the conventional fashion (i.e., to be solved independently by the student). When subsequently tested for their knowledge and understanding of these problems, students who received worked examples significantly outperformed their peers on both items that shared similar structure to the homework questions and on items that contained different structures (i.e., transfer questions).

Ward and Sweller found that only a certain type of worked example facilitated students' learning. Effective worked examples were ones that did not require students to divide their attention between the problem statement and the problem solution. (When students are required to divide their attention, the solution path is essentially meaningless without referring back to the problem statement). Worked examples that contain excessive explanatory information also impede learning, especially if this information requires students to divide their attention. Table 8-1 lists examples of effective worked examples and ones that require students to divide their attention.

Worked examples are a readily usable instructional technique that can facilitate students' science learning. However, the method of presenting these problems is critical, with the most effective problems being those that integrate all relevant information into a single unit.

Table 8-1
Worked examples that require students to divide their attention versus ones that do not.

Worked Solution that Requires Students to Split Their Attention

A car starting at rest reaches a speed of 20 m/s after 10 seconds. What is the acceleration of the car?

$u = 0$ m/s
$v = 20$ m/s
$t = 10$ s

$v = u + at$
$a = (v-u)/t$
$a = (20-0)/10$
$a = 2$ m/s^2

Worked Solution that Does Not Require Students to Split Their Attention

A car starting at rest (u) reaches a speed of 20 m/s (v) after 10 seconds (t): [$v=u+at$, $a=(v-u)/t=(20-0)/10= 2$ m/s^2]. What is the acceleration of the car?

From Ward and Sweller (1990).

MNEMONICS

Many students fail to do well in science class because they do not acquire key concepts and vocabulary (e.g., King-Sears, Mercer, & Sindelar, 1992). Instructing students to use mnemonics can facilitate their learning of such key concepts and terms. Mnemonics are techniques that enhance memory by requiring learners to make associations between new concepts and information that they already know. Often, these associations take the form of mental images or pictures. Creating interactive images is a strategy well known to facilitate learning (Giesen & Peeck, 1984; Levin, 1976; Paivio & Yuille, 1967; Pressley, 1976; see Chapter 2, this volume, for an explanation about how mental imagery facilitates learning). Interested readers are referred to Mastropieri and Scruggs (1991) for further examples of mnemonics, including keywords, pegwords, acronyms and acrostics, and their application across school curricula.

The keyword mnemonic requires students to generate a mental picture of a word that shares either acoustic or orthographic features of the to-be-learned item. The learner then associates attributes of the target concept with their mental image. Consider the following example used by Mastropieri and Scruggs (1991) for remembering the meaning of the term "vertebrate" and the five categories of vertebrates. First, the keyword *dirt* was selected, because it rhymes with the first syllable in vertebrate and can be readily pictured. Second, a mental picture was created where an animal with an obvious backbone was sitting on top of a pile of dirt. In order to remember the five types of vertebrates, five piles of dirt were added to the image with a representative animal from each category sitting on each pile. Imagining a sign with the phrase "Welcome to Farm B" further facilitated remembering as each letter represents one category of vertebrate (fish, amphibian, reptile, mammal, and bird; see Figure 8-2). In order to remember the defining feature of a vertebrate or examples of the five categories of vertebrates, the learner merely needs to remember his or her mental image.

The keyword mnemonic effectively enhances elementary-school students' acquisition of science concepts and vocabulary (e.g., Levin, Morrison, McGivern, Mastropieri & Scruggs, 1986). Levin et al. found that 8th-graders who were provided with keyword mnemonics about minerals and their attributes remembered more critical information than did students who were provided with "fact maps" or students who were instructed to maintain a positive attitude while studying. Although high school students' ability to use mnemonics in the science

Figure 8-2
Keyword mnemonic picture for
learning the five categories of vertebrates.

Taken from Mastropieri and Scruggs (1991).

classroom has not yet been investigated, secondary-school science teachers should be encouraged to teach their students mnemonic strategies on the basis of its success in improving both elementary-school children's and adults' learning across a variety of disciplines including sciences, social sciences, history and geography.

CONCEPT MAPS

Concept maps, otherwise referred to as semantic maps or entailment meshes (Johnson, Pittleman, & Hiemlich, 1986, and Pask, 1975; cited in Schmid & Telaro, 1990) are essentially diagrams where hierarchical relationships between ideas or "concepts" are expressed vertically and interrelations between concepts are expressed horizontally (Schmid & Telaro, 1990). Concepts are often isolated by circles and are arranged with the most general ideas listed at the top of the page. More specific and less inclusive concepts are listed below general ones. Concepts are connected by lines, which are labelled with "linking words" that describe how the concepts are related to each other. Two or more concepts that are semantically linked (related by meaning) are referred to as a proposition. In its simplest form, a concept map would consist of two linked concepts. For example the statements, "sky is blue" or "grass is a plant" contain the concepts "sky," "blue," "grass," and "green," and the link, "is" (Novak & Gowin, 1984). Learning occurs when students create and recognize new propositions. See Figure 8-3 for a definition and an example of a concept map.

Novak and his colleagues (e.g., Novak, 1976; Novak & Gowin, 1984; Novak, Gowin, & Johansen, 1983) advocate the use of concept maps in the science classroom and suggest a number of "warm-up" activities to prepare students for concept mapping. First, students must be able to identify concepts, recognizing that although basic definitions of concepts will be the same across individuals, each person's definition will be unique (i.e., each person will think of something a little different when provided concepts like *dog* and *cat*, based on their prior experiences). Students must also learn to identify linking words and be given opportunities to use them to combine concepts and form propositions. Once students demonstrate an understanding for concepts and links, they are ready for map instruction.

While Novak and Gowin (1984) caution that there is no one way to instruct students about concept maps, they and other researchers (e.g., Malone & Dekkers, 1984) have provided some general guidelines for instruction (see Table 8-2). First, teachers or students must identify a stand-alone topic (e.g., genetics, atomic theory). Students are then required to generate concepts for this topic. Concepts can be generated in a number of ways, including having students participate in brainstorming sessions or by having them read previously selected text. Ideally, no more than 20 concepts should be identified for any one topic.

Figure 8-3
Concept map diagram defining a concept map.

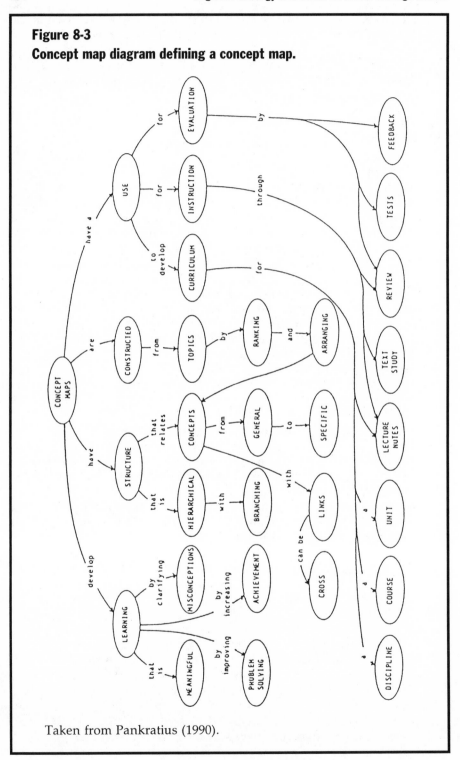

Taken from Pankratius (1990).

Table 8-2
Directions for Constructing Concept Maps

1. Identify a stand-alone topic.
2. Generate no more than 20 concepts for topic.
3. Rank concepts in order of importance or generality.
4. Physically arrange concepts in hierarchical order.
5. Edit concepts maps to ensure symmetry and accuracy between concepts.

Adapted from Malone and Dekkers (1984) and Novick and Gowan (1984).

Students must then rank the concepts in order of their importance or generality. Ranking may be done individually, in small groups, or as a class. Because it is unlikely that group consensus will be reached with respect to concept ordering, teachers should take this opportunity to reinforce the idea that there are multiple ways to conceptualize concepts. Students may also be provided with ranking aids such as the scoring procedure outlined in Figure 8-4 (Malone & Dekkers, 1984).

Concepts are then physically arranged in a hierarchical order (Novak and Gowan recommend using paper rectangles that can be moved easily), with linking words used to join concepts first vertically and then horizontally. Finally, students are encouraged to reconstruct their maps to establish better symmetry and accuracy between concept clusters. Map reconstruction is critical because many students are reluctant to edit their original concept maps. Editing and reconstructing are practices that are essential if students are to maintain concept maps over the course of unit instruction.

There is substantial evidence supporting the effectiveness of concept maps for science instruction (e.g., Jegede, Alaiyemola, Okebukola, 1990; Okebukola, 1990; Okebukola & Jegede, 1988; Pankratius, 1990; Schmid & Telaro, 1990; Soyibo, 1991; Stensvold & Wilson, 1990). For example, Pankratius (1990) found that instructing high school physics students to use concept maps significantly improved their performance on a standardized physics test (Ontario Assessment Instrument Pool: Physics–Senior Division) relative to students provided with traditional instruction. Furthermore, students who mapped concepts prior to, during, and following instruction had the highest performance scores (approximately 18% higher than students who received conventional instructions and 11% higher than students who only completed concept maps at the end of the instructional unit). However, a substantial

Figure 8-4
Ranking aid used for concept map ordering.

A CONCEPT MAP is to be prepared from the oxidation-reduction concepts listed in the
FIRST and SECOND COLUMN

FIRST COLUMN	SECOND COLUMN
electron transfer	cations
oxidation reduction process	anions
corrosion	redox titration
permanganate-titration	oxidation
electrochemical	reduction
movement of ions	electrolyte
	equilibrium
	anode
	cathode

FIRST TASK

The KEY IDEAS from the first column are listed in pairs. Score each pair as follows:

They are *not* related = 0   They are *slightly* related = 1
They are *quite* related = 2   They are *very* related = 3

oxidation-reduction process	.....	permanganate titration	=	_____
electron transfer	.....	movement of ions	=	_____
movement of ions	.....	oxidation-reduction process	=	_____
oxidation-reduction process	.....	corrosion	=	_____
corrosion	.....	permanganate titration	=	_____
permanganate titration	.....	electrochemical cell	=	_____
electron transfer	.....	oxidation-reduction process	=	_____
movement of ions	.....	corrosion	=	_____
corrosion	.....	electrochemical cell	=	_____
electron transfer	.....	corrosion	=	_____
movement of ions	.....	permanganate titration	=	_____
oxidation-reduction process	.....	electrochemical cell	=	_____
electron transfer	.....	permanganate titration	=	_____
movement of ions	.....	electrochemical cell	=	_____
electron transfer	.....	electrochemical cell	=	_____

SECOND TASK

Now add up the individual scores, crossing out each KEY IDEA as you go.

KEY IDEAS	INDIVIDUAL SCORES					TOTAL
electrochemical cells						
corrosion						
oxidation-reduction process						
electron transfer						
movement of ions						
permanganate titration						

THIRD TASK

Now write the KEY IDEAS in order of relatedness from highest score to lowest. (If some
have the same score put them on the same line.)

_____

_____

_____

_____

FOURTH TASK

Take the sheet of printed labels of KEY IDEAS and stick them LIGHTLY on the CON-
CEPT MAP (Green Paper) starting with the highest score near the top of the sheet. Leave
two or three level lines free at the bottom. Later when you have finished the whole CON-
CEPT MAP, you can press down the labels firmly.

FIFTH TASK

Now join up the KEY IDEAS and write SENTENCE WORD(s) on each connecting line between the KEY IDEAS. Try to cross link as much as possible.

SIXTH TASK

GO BACK TO THE TOP OF THE PAGE. THE SECOND COLUMN on the map using
your sheet of printed labels. TRY and place all these as the most important ones on the
higher levels and others on the lower levels. Then try to join all the key ideas up with SEN-
TENCE LINES. (Remember to put SENTENCE WORDS on each line!).

YOU HAVE NOW COMPLETED YOUR MAP

Taken from Malone and Dekkers (1984).

amount of instruction time and classroom practice was required before students were proficient at constructing maps (i.e., students were given six weeks of training).

Concept maps may not be equally beneficial for all students or for all test items. Schmid & Telaro (1990) found that map instruction was especially beneficial for low-ability high school biology students (as determined by performance on the Stanford Diagnostic Reading Test), and that learning was only facilitated for students' performance on advanced learning questions (e.g., synthesis, application and evaluation questions; Bloom et al., 1956). There were no differences between concept-map and conventionally instructed students' performance on knowledge and comprehension questions. Similar findings were reported by Stensvold and Wilson (1990).

That concept maps facilitated students' performances on high-level questions is not surprising, as these questions require learners to demonstrate an understanding of concept functions and interrelations—relationships that concept maps are designed to foster. Similarly, it is also not surprising that low-ability students gained the most from map instruction, as these students are unlikely to spontaneously use their prior knowledge to elaborate and organize new concepts.

In summary, there are several characteristics of concept maps that make them an attractive learning strategy. First, they can be used effectively by a variety of students ranging from those in elementary school (e.g., Willerman & Harg, 1991) to college (Heinze-Fry & Novak, 1990). In part, large numbers of students can successfully use concept maps because they do not require students to rely extensively on their verbal abilities. There is also evidence that using concept maps may reduce students' anxieties about science (Jegede et al., 1990). Second, concept maps allow individualized learning, as scientific concepts can be accurately represented by more than one hierarchy. Third, concept maps can be used as formative and summative evaluation tools. (See Novak and Gowin, 1984, and Malone and Dekkers, 1984, for examples of scoring procedures that can be used to grade students' concepts maps.) Fourth, students can use concept maps to organize text, lecture and laboratory materials across several content areas (Novak & Gowin, 1984). Finally, concept maps are cost-effective—they require no costly materials or elaborate teaching techniques.

The time and effort required to initially learn how to create concept maps, however, is substantial and should not be underestimated. Ideally, concept map training should occur over a period of at least six weeks (Pankratius, 1990; also see Stensvold & Wilson (1990) for an example of where insufficient instructional time minimized concept-map learning gains), although above-average students may be able to acquire mapping skills successfully in as little time as two weeks (e.g., Schmid & Telaro, 1990). In addition, students must be willing to expend considerable cognitive effort when developing concept maps. Schmid and Telaro (1990) observed that, although high-ability students assigned to either concept map or traditional instruction performed equally poorly prior to training (approximately 40%), concept-map students lagged behind their peers at midsession (60% versus 72% respectively). At post-test, however, concept-map students outperformed their traditionally instructed peers, who failed to improve from their midsession performances. Thus, although the initial time and effort that students must spend gaining mapping skills may be at the expense of acquiring scientific concepts, long term-learning is improved following the acquisition of mapping skills.

OVERCOMING STUDENTS' INACCURATE SCIENCE BELIEFS

So far, a number of effective teaching techniques and learning strategies that enhance secondary-school students' knowledge and understanding of science content have been reviewed. Collectively, these strategies enhance learning because they require learners to activate relevant prior knowledge when studying information, seek out interrelations between new concepts, and make meaningful connections between new information and old concepts.

However, learners often possess ideas about the world that clash with scientific viewpoints. Generally, these inaccurate beliefs are pervasive, resistant to change under normal classroom instruction, and often impede the acquisition of science concepts (e.g., Roth, 1990). Prior to reading a passage about photosynthesis, one student expressed the following beliefs about how plants obtain food:

> Food (for plants) can be sun, rain, light, bugs, oxygen, soil, and even other dead plants. Also warmness or coldness. All plants need at least three or four of these foods. Plus minerals.

After reading the science passage, the student continued to express these beliefs in combination with those written in the textbook. The student responded in the following manner when asked about plants and food:

> Whew, from lots of places! From the soil for one, from the minerals and water, and from the air from oxygen. The sunlight for the sun, and it would change chemicals to sugars. It sort of makes its own food and gets food from the ground. And from the air. (Roth, 1990, p. 145)

Even when students answer conventional tests and standardized assessments correctly, they may still possess beliefs that are counterintuitive to scientific thought (Arnaudin & Mintzes, 1985). Sometimes these inaccurate beliefs are revealed only after extensive interviewing and observation and, therefore, often go unnoticed by both educators and students. More often, students' misconceptions are not so subtle.

There are many different means by which students may acquire inaccurate knowledge before entering the classroom. For example, students can acquire knowledge from conversations with peers and elders, television, reading, and everyday experiences. Some misconceptions may even be perpetuated by teachers and textbooks when they do not help students differentiate between scientific concepts and everyday experiences (Barrass, 1984).

There is considerable interest in changing students' inaccurate beliefs, or what are also known as misconceptions, alternative frameworks, children's science, children's conceptual frameworks, or misunderstandings (although some researchers may debate the appropriateness of using these terms and the subtleties differentiating them, here they are viewed as synonymous). Unfortunately, the majority of studies investigating conceptual change lack rigorous empirical investigation. There are at least four techniques, however, that enjoy some empirical support, albeit their use in the secondary-school classroom has not been extensively studied. These techniques are reported here.

Conceptual Conflict Plus Accommodation

Many science educators (e.g., Hewson & Hewson, 1982; Posner, Strike, Hewson & Gertzog, 1982) believe that the processes of *assimilation*, incorporating new information with existing knowledge, and *accommodation*, restructuring and reorganizing existing knowledge on the basis of new information, constitute learning. Of the two processes, the latter is the more difficult and the one necessary for students to undergo if they are to abandon their misconceptions in favor of scientific information. Posner and colleagues (1982) argue that for accommodation to occur, learners must express some dissatisfaction with their existing beliefs and must be provided with an intelligible and plausible alternative that is clearly superior to their existing beliefs. In other words, educators need to create circumstances that convince students to abandon their inaccurate beliefs in favor of scientific ones.

Nussbaum and Novick (1982) believe that by explicitly creating conceptual conflict in the classroom, students will be made aware of their existing misconceptions and therefore be motivated to acquire scientific concepts. They specify three requirements for creating conceptual conflict. The first is an exposing event that requires students to acknowledge and rationalize their existing beliefs. The second is a discrepant event which cannot be explained by their erroneous beliefs. Finally, the educator must support students' search for scientifically accepted concepts. That is, teachers must assist students in restructuring their old understandings and comparing their new understanding with their old ones (Krajcik, 1991; see Figure 8-5 for a model of the processes underlying conceptual change).

Nussbaum and Novak have had some success in changing 6th-, 7th-, and 8th-grade students' faulty beliefs about particle theory and gases by using conceptual conflict. Many students possess misconceptions about gas particles, including the belief that substances like air, bacteria and oxygen exist between them. These statements underlie another inaccurate belief: that matter is continuous, when in fact only empty spaces exist between gas particles (Novick & Nussbaum, 1978; Nussbaum & Novick, 1982; Lee, Eichinger, Anderson, Berkheimer & Blakeslee, 1989). To facilitate students' learning of particle theory as it pertains to gases, they were shown a demonstration in which air was sucked from a flask with a hand pump. In order to promote students' awareness of their existing beliefs, they were instructed to draw before-and-after pictures of the flask (see Figure 8-6 for examples of students' drawings), with the instructor selecting several of these models as well as the scientifically correct empty-space model for class discussion.

A discrepant event was then introduced. Specifically, equal amounts of air and water were compressed in syringes. Students were asked to reflect upon why it was possible to compress the air but not the water (i.e., *What special properties do gases have that liquids and solids do not?*).

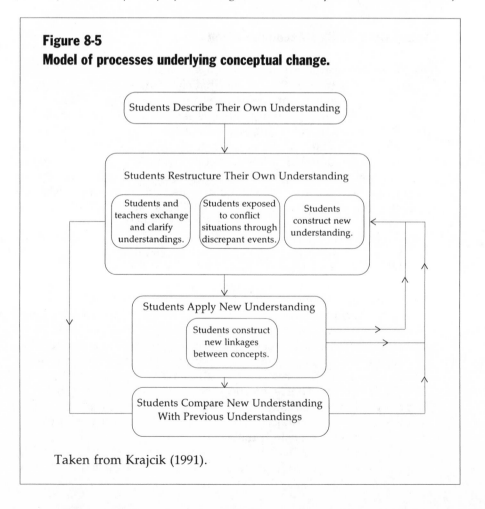

Figure 8-5
Model of processes underlying conceptual change.

Students Describe Their Own Understanding

Students Restructure Their Own Understanding

Students and teachers exchange and clarify understandings.

Students exposed to conflict situations through discrepant events.

Students construct new understanding.

Students Apply New Understanding

Students construct new linkages between concepts.

Students Compare New Understanding With Previous Understandings

Taken from Krajcik (1991).

Figure 8-6
Students' before and after drawings of gaseous particles of air being removed from a flask.

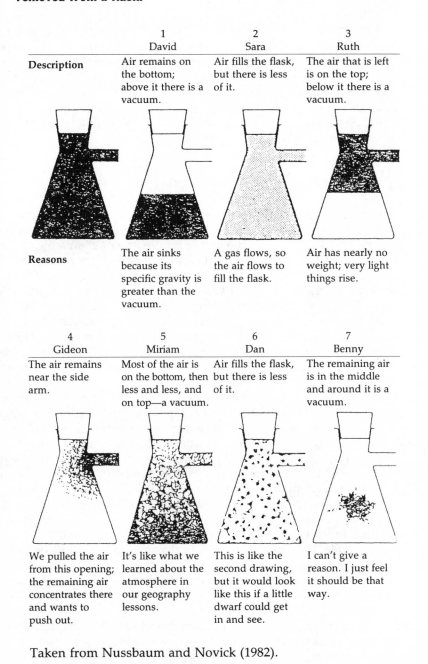

	1 David	2 Sara	3 Ruth
Description	Air remains on the bottom; above it there is a vacuum.	Air fills the flask, but there is less of it.	The air that is left is on the top; below it there is a vacuum.
Reasons	The air sinks because its specific gravity is greater than the vacuum.	A gas flows, so the air flows to fill the flask.	Air has nearly no weight; very light things rise.

	4 Gideon	5 Miriam	6 Dan	7 Benny
	The air remains near the side arm.	Most of the air is on the bottom, then less and less, and on top—a vacuum.	Air fills the flask, but there is less of it.	The remaining air is in the middle and around it is a vacuum.
	We pulled the air from this opening; the remaining air concentrates there and wants to push out.	It's like what we learned about the atmosphere in our geography lessons.	This is like the second drawing, but it would look like this if a little dwarf could get in and see.	I can't give a reason. I just feel it should be that way.

Taken from Nussbaum and Novick (1982).

Students attempted to use their own models to explain the compression of air. The instructor's task was to help students realize that, despite the strangeness of the idea, the empty space theory was the only model that could explain both the evacuation of air from the flask and the compression of air in the syringe.

Unfortunately, the accommodation model suggested by Novick and Nussbaum (1982) can only be cautiously recommended, as it has not been formally evaluated. To date, the success of the model is based on the enthusiastic reports of teachers who have used the approach and on the large number of students who accept the scientific model at the end of class sessions. Although these reports are encouraging, they are not sufficient to establish program effectiveness or to warrant large-scale classroom implementation (Pressley, Woloshyn, Lysynchuk, Martin, Wood, & Willoughby, 1990).

Refutation Text and Augmented Activation

Alvermann and her colleagues (Alvermann & Hague, 1989; Alvermann & Hynd, 1991; Hynd & Alvermann, 1986; 1987) have investigated whether specially designed text that refutes students' misconceptions (hereafter called *refutational text*) can help learners acquire scientific concepts. Unlike traditional text which only provides students with scientific information, refutational text addresses both scientific concepts and common misconceptions. Specifically, refutational text provides support for scientific concepts while refuting common misconceptions. Table 8-3 provides an example of a traditional and a refutational passage describing Newtonian theory (the refutational passage also addresses Impetus theory, a common misconception).

Working with university undergraduates, Alvermann and her colleagues have found conflicting support for the use of refutational text. While refutational text appears to have little effect on average-ability students' learning performance, it significantly improves the performance of lower-achieving students (those who enter college with less than average high school grades and/or low SAT scores). Lower-achieving students may be less confident about their background knowledge and more willing to be dissuaded from their inaccurate beliefs than average-achieving students (Alvermann & Hynd, 1991).

More positively, the success of refutational text can be readily increased for all learners by simply telling them that the ideas held by some people differ from the scientifically accepted concepts described in their text. Specifically, if students are instructed to activate their relevant prior knowledge prior to reading and to pay particular attention to text ideas that differ from their own, refutational text positively facilitates text learning.

To date, refutational text has not been used with high school students. In many ways, secondary-school students share similarities with the low-achieving students described by Alvermann and Hynd

Table 8-3
Refutational Text vs. Traditional Text

Refutational Text
Comparison Between Newtonian Theory and Impetus Theory

A central point to be made is that the medieval impetus theory is incompatible with Newtonian mechanics in several fundamental ways.... To get a sense of some of the motion studies mentioned, imagine the following situation. A person is holding a stone at shoulder height while walking forward at a brisk pace. What will happen when the person drops the stone? What kind of path will the stone follow as it falls? Many people to whom this problem is presented answer that the stone will drop straight down, striking the ground directly under the point where it was dropped. A few people are even convinced that the falling stone will travel backward and land behind the point of its release. In reality, the stone will move forward as it falls, landing a few feet ahead of the release point. Newtonian mechanics explains that when the stone is dropped, it continues to move forward at the same speed as the walking person, because (ignoring air resistance) no force is acting to change its horizontal velocity.

Traditional Text
Newtonian Theory Only

We certainly learn from our experiences. From repeated exposure to particular events, we learn to induce principles which guide our expectations for future events..... Newtonian mechanics can also be used to predict what path a stone will follow when it is dropped from shoulder height by a person walking forward at a brisk pace. Assuming no air resistance, the stone will move forward at the same speed as the person who is walking. Why? Because no force is acting upon it to change its horizontal velocity. Of course, as the stone falls forward it also moves downward at a steadily increasing speed. The forward and downward motions result in a path that closely approximates a parabola.

From Hynd and Alvermann (1986).

(1991). That is, these students are probably less confident about their prior knowledge and more readily persuaded than are college students. For these reasons, refutational text may help secondary-school students overcome their faulty science beliefs. Educators also need to be aware of the considerable effort involved in designing refutational text. Teachers who wish to use refutational text in their science classroom should do so cautiously.

ANALOGIES

Analogical thinking is one characteristic endorsed by scientists (Glynn, 1991). For instance, Kepler used a clock analogy to describe planetary motion, while Campbell argued that particles of kinetic gases behave somewhat like billiard balls (Pressley, 1995). A good analogy defines similarities between a new concept and a familiar one in order to make the new concept more meaningful. Educators can also use analogies to explain scientific concepts to novice scientists (Brown, 1992; Clement, Brown, Camp, Kudukey, Minstrill, Palmer, Schultz, Shimaburkuro, Steinberg & Veneman, 1987; Stavy, 1991). For example, the concept of a glacier may be better understood if an analogy is made to a river of ice.

Clement and his colleagues (Brown & Clement, 1989; Clement & Brown, 1984; Clement et al., 1987; Clement, Brown & Zietsman, 1989) advocate the use of analogies in the science classroom. These researchers observed that students often possess contradictory ideas, so that in one situation their beliefs are consistent with scientific knowledge, but in another, they are incompatible. For instance, 76% of the secondary-school students participating in one study responded that a table does not exert force on a resting book. However, the majority of these same students believed that a spring being pushed down by a hand exerts force on the hand (Clement et al., 1987). To scientists, the students' responses are inconsistent because the two situations are equivalent.

Clement et al. (1987) labeled students' intuitive beliefs (ones that are self-evaluated and that are in rough agreement with scientific theory) as *anchoring conceptions* and argued that instructors should use these beliefs as a starting point for instruction. Specifically, instructors must help students understand that anchoring conceptions share the same features as the misunderstood concept (e.g., just as the spring and hand exert force on each other, so do the table and book). Unfortunately, direct comparison of the target concept and the anchoring conception is often insufficient to promote students' learning. The use of bridging analogies are required.

Bridging analogies share features that are similar to both the anchoring conception and target concept. For example, a bridging analogy for the table-book/spring-hand comparison could be a book resting on a flexible board supported by two pillars (the flexible board has characteristics of both a table and a spring). Students may be led to understand that the board, like a spring, bends slightly by instructing them to imagine the board becoming sequentially thicker or thinner.

Through the use of successive bridges, students come to accept the anchoring conception and target concept as similar. In one study, Clement and his colleagues (Clement et al, 1987) provided secondary-school physics students instruction about forces exerted by static objects, frictional forces, and Newton's third law of collisions. Half the students were provided with anchoring conceptions and bridging analogies as part of their instruction, whereas the remaining students were only provided with traditional instruction. Although a great deal of discussion was required before these students accepted the bridging analogies and target concepts as analogous, they demonstrated superior learning gains relative to those students who received conventional instruction. Furthermore, these gains were maintained up to two months following instruction.

Other researchers have found similar learning advantages when students have been provided with analogies (Brown, 1992; Stavy, 1991). For example, Brown documented that the use of anchoring conceptions and bridging analogies not only enhanced high school students' performance for target questions, but also improved their achievement for related questions. After receiving instruction including the spring/hand anchoring conception and the board/book bridging analogy described by Clement and Brown (1984; see Table 8-4), 86% of the students correctly answered that a 40-pound steel block positioned under a 200-pound steel block exerts 200 pounds of force. Consider the following think aloud where a student used the bridging analogy to arrive at the correct solution:

> All right, I am having trouble with this one because I'm thinking in terms of they both should exert ... forces on each other because B [the 40-pound block on the bottom] has to ... relieve that 200-pound stress. However, it only weighs 40 pounds. Because of that number, um, I don't know whether it can do that.... Makes some sense to me. The reason [equal forces] doesn't make perfect sense to me is because block A is so much heavier than the other. Wait a minute.... I'll have to change that. I've just thought about the instances of the book and the spring and of course the spring was, weighed so much less than the book, but still the spring did bounce, the spring did bounce back. Those atoms are still springy.... Even if one weighs, even if one weighs so much more than the other because sure, the book weighed so much more than the spring, but the spring did bounce, the spring bounced back; why can't the same thing happen to this? (Brown, 1992, p. 25)

There are at least four limitations associated with using analogies in the classroom. First, a great deal of care and effort are needed when searching for anchoring and bridging analogies, as many analogies that appear intuitive to instructors do not appear so to students (Clement et al., 1987). Second, students must understand the analogue situation for the analogy to work. When students do not possess adequate knowledge about the analogy, or possess inaccurate information about it, they are likely to develop misconceptions about the target concept (see Gentner & Gentner, 1993, for an example where college students' inaccurate beliefs about water flow fostered misconceptions about electrical flow). Third, the type of analogy used influences students'

Table 4

Explanation provided to secondary school physics students containing bridging analogies

In this exercise, we will consider the question of whether a table pushes up on a book resting on it. Consider pushing down on a spring with your hand.

Now consider the case of a heavy dictionary being placed on a bedspring so the spring compresses some.

When the book is placed on the spring, the spring compresses. The further down the spring is pushed the more it pushes back. The spring is compressed by the book to the point where it pushes back with a force equal to the book's weight. For example, if the book weighs 10 pounds, the spring compresses until it exerts an equal upward force of 10 pounds. In a similar way, if you hold a 30-pound dictionary in your outstretched hand, you have to exert an upward force of 30 pounds to hold it there.

Many people say the book on the spring is different that the book on the table. They say that although neither is alive, the spring compresses but the table is rigid. But is the table rigid? Imagine a flexible board between two sawhorses. If you were to push down on this board it would bend and push back, just like pushing down on the spring. The board would also push back on a book, just like the spring. Now imagine thicker and thicker boards.

If you had a thick enough board, it would be just like a table. Both the board and the table would bend a tiny, tiny bit under the weight of a book. Another way to think of the table is like very stiff foam rubber. Even though the stiff foam rubber would not compress much under the weight of a book, it would compress some.

The table is composed of molecules which are connected to other molecules by bonds which are "springy". Thus the table has some amount of give or "bendiness" or "squishiness" to it. If you were to look closely with a microscope you would see that the book causes a slight depression in the table. The table, just like the spring, the flexible board, or foam rubber, is bent or compressed some and thus pushes back. Like the spring holding the dictionary, the table bends or compresses just enough to provide an upward force equal to the book's weight.

To summarize, many people do not think the table can exert a force since it is rigid and lifeless. However, they feel a spring can exert a force if a force is exerted on it because it "wants to get back to its original shape." Thus there seems to be a distinction between rigid objects and spring objects. However, if you look closely enough at a table it is spring because of its molecular make up. Because of this springy nature of all matter, the table can and does exert a force upward on the book. Just like a spring, the table compresses (on a microscopic scale) until it is compressed enough to provide an upward force equal to the book's weight.

From Brown (1992).

thinking about a target concept. Dupin and Joshua (1989) observed that high school students possessed different thoughts about electricity following analogy training based on heat flow versus based on a mechanical train. Fourth, the use of a single analogy may be incomplete, misleading, or insufficient to focus students' attention on critical information.

More optimistically, simply warning learners about the limitations of an analogy may be sufficient to improve their learning (Glynn, 1991). In fact, highlighting the limitations of an analogy may simultaneously focus students' attention to the unique features of the target concept (Pressley, 1995). The use of multiple analogies may also reduce some of the obstacles associated with single analogies. Multiple analogies may be more convincing to students, highlighting different attributes of the target concept and providing them with insights that a single analogy cannot (Pressley, 1994).

Elaborative Interrogation

There is substantial evidence that elaborative interrogation facilitates students' learning of factual information that is consistent with their prior knowledge (for a review see Pressley, Wood, Woloshyn, Martin, King, & Menke, 1992). Basically, elaborative interrogation requires learners to use their background knowledge to make supportive inferences and elaborations about new information by answering a *why*-question (i.e., Why is that fact true?).

In recent studies, Woloshyn and her colleagues (Woloshyn, Paivio & Pressley, 1994; Woloshyn & Stockley, in press) demonstrated that instructing intermediate students (grades 6 and 7) to answer why-questions facilitated their learning of science facts. The training instructions provided to students were simple and brief. Students were instructed to use relevant prior knowledge from their classes, readings and everyday experiences to answer why the presented science statements were true. Students were told that there was no right or wrong answer and that they should generate as many reasons as possible for each statement.

Across the series of studies, instructing students to answer the why-questions enhanced their learning of the science facts (as measured by recall and recognition tests), relative to when they were instructed to read for understanding or to select their own method of study. Question-answering learning gains were maintained regardless of whether students studied belief-consistent or belief-inconsistent materials (i.e., misconceptions), or whether they studied the science facts alone or with a partner. Impressively, these learning gains were maintained up to six months following the training session.

The quality of the students' elaborations affected learning. Overall, when students generated responses that used relevant prior knowledge which clarified why the target facts were true, learning for those items was superior to when students generated answers that did not clarify these facts or when they failed to generate a response. However, merely trying to generate a response was associated with greater learning than was reading information for understanding. Examples of good explanatory responses include the following: For the target fact, "In plants, food moves from the leaves to the roots" was, "The leaves make the food with the sun and water." For the statement, "Not all living things have blood," another explanatory response was, "It's like in plants—They have something else that food travels through."

Elaborative interrogation is a promising learning strategy for helping students overcome their inaccurate science beliefs, as it can be easily implemented in the classroom. Teachers merely need to instruct students to use their prior knowledge to answer why a given statement is true when they study science materials. However, one limitation associated with this strategy is that students must possess relevant prior knowledge about the to-be-learned concept. If students do not possess such knowledge, educators must make provisions to provide this information to students (see Woloshyn, Wood, & Willoughby, 1994, for a review of the importance of prior knowledge when using elaborative interrogation).

SUMMARY

There is general concern that students are not receiving the knowledge or skills that will enable them to be competent thinkers in an increasingly technological world. Students are electing not to pursue advanced studies or careers in the sciences—often expressing the belief that they do not possess the necessary attributes to be a scientist. However, positive change can occur in the science classroom if effective teaching techniques and learning strategies, like those reviewed in this chapter, are employed in the classroom. Teachers should be encouraged to experiment with the strategies presented here, combining and integrating approaches whenever appropriate. Teachers can also continue to read about effective science strategies in journals such as *The Journal of Research in Science Teaching*. With the commitment of both teachers and researchers, the status of science education can be improved.

REFERENCES

Ajewole, G.A. (1991). Effects of discovery and expository instructional methods on the attitude of students in biology. *Journal of Research in Science Teaching, 28,* 401-409.

Alvermann, D.E., & Hague, S.A. (1989). Comprehension of counterintuitive science text: Effects of prior knowledge and text structure. *Journal of Educational Research, 82,* 197-202.

Alvermann, D. & Hynd, C. (1991). The effects of varying prior knowledge activation modes and text structure on nonscience majors' comprehension of physics text. *Journal of Educational Research*, 213-223.

Arnaudin, M.W., & Mintzes, J.J. (1985). Students' alternative conceptions of the human circulatory system: A cross-age study. *Science Education, 69,* 721-733.

Bargh, J.A., & Schul, Y. (1980). On the cognitive benefits of teaching. *Journal of Educational Psychology, 72,* 593-604.

Barrass, R. (1984). Some misconceptions and misunderstandings perpetuated by teachers and textbooks of biology. *Journal of Biological Education, 18,* 201-206.

Basili, P.A., & Sanford, J.P. (1991). Conceptual change strategies and cooperative group work in chemistry. *Journal of Research in Science Teaching, 28,* 293-304.

Beichner, R.J. (1990). The effect of simultaneous motion presentation and graph generation in a kinematics lab. *Journal of Research in Science Teaching, 27,* 803-815.

Bloom, B., Englehart, M., Furst, E., Hill, W. and Krathwohl, D. (1956). *Taxonomy of Educational Objectives. The Classification of Educational Goals. Handbook I: Cognitive Domain.* New York: McKay.

Brasell, H. (1987). The effect of real-time laboratory graphing on learning graphic representations of distance and velocity. *Journal of Research in Science Teaching, 24,* 385-395.

Bredderman, T. (1985). Laboratory programs for elementary school science: A meta-analysis of effects on learning. *Science Education, 69,* 577-591.

Brown, D.E. (1992). Using examples and analogies to remediate misconceptions in physics: Factors influencing conceptual change. *Journal of Research in Science Teaching, 29,* 17-34.

Brown, D.E., & Clement, J. (1987). Overcoming misconceptions via analogical reasoning: Factors influencing understanding in a teaching experiment. In J. Novak (Ed.), *Proceedings of the Second International Seminar: Misconceptions and Educational Strategies in Science and Mathematics, Vol. III,* Cornell University, Ithaca, NY.

Champagne, A.B., Klopfer, L.E., & Gunstone, R.F. (1982). Cognitive research and the design of science instruction. *Educational Psychologist, 17,* 31-53.

Choi, B.S., & Gennaro, E. (1987). The effectiveness of using computer simulated experiments on junior high students' understanding of the volume displacement concept. *Journal of Research in Science Teaching, 24,* 539-552.

Clement, J., & Brown, D. (1984). *Using analogy reasoning to deal with misconceptions in physics.* Paper presented at the Annual Meeting of the American Educational Research Association (AERA).

Clement, J., Brown, D.E., Camp, C., Kudukey, J., Minstrill, J., Palmer, D., Schultz, K., Shimaburkuro, J., Steinberg, M., & Veneman, V. (1987). Overcoming students' misconceptions in physics: The role of anchoring intuitions and analogical validity. In J. Novak (Ed.), *Proceedings of the Second International Seminar: Misconceptions and Educational Strategies in Science and Mathematics, Vol. III,* Cornell University, Ithaca, NY.

Clement, J., Brown, D.E., & Zietsman, A. (1989). *Not all preconceptions are misconceptions: Finding anchoring conceptions for grounding instruction on student's intuitions.* Paper presented at the Annual Meeting of the American Educational Research Association (AERA), San Francisco, CA.

Cooper, G., & Sweller, J. (1987). The effects of schema acquisition and rule automatization on mathematical problem-solving transfer. *Journal of Educational Psychology, 79,* 347-362.

Coulter, J.C. (1966). The effectiveness of inductive laboratory, inductive demonstration, and deductive laboratory in biology. *Journal of Research in Science Teaching, 4,* 185-186.

Davidson, N., & Shearn, E. (1990). Use of small group teaching and cognitive development instruction in a mathematical course for prospective elementary school teachers. In M. Brubacher, R. Payne, and K. Rickett (Eds.), *Perspectives on small group learning* (pp. 309-327). Oakville, Ontario: Rubicon Publishing Incorporated.

Dupin, J.J. & Joshua, S. (1989). Analogies and "modelling analogies" in teaching: Some examples in basic electricity. *Science Education, 73,* 207-224.

Fuhrman, M., Lunette, V.N., & Novick, S. (1982). Do secondary school laboratory texts reflect the goals of the "new" science curricula? *Journal of Chemical Education, 59,* 563-565.

Gabbert, B., Johnson, D., & Johnson, R. (1986). Cooperative learning, group-to-individual transfer, process gain, and the acquisition of cognitive reasoning strategies. *The Journal of Psychology, 120,* 265-278.

Gayford, C. (1989). A contribution to a methodology for teaching and assessment of group problem solving in biology among 15-year old pupils. *Journal of Biological Education, 23*, 193-198.

Gayford, C. (1992). Patterns of group behaviour in open-ended only problem solving in science classes of 15-year-old students in England. *International Journal of Science Education, 14*, 41-49.

Gentner, D. & Gentner, D. (1993). Flowing waters or teeming crowds: Mental models of electricity. In D. Gentner and A. Stevens (Eds.), *Mental Models* (pp. 101-129). Hillsdale NJ: Erlbaum & Associates.

Giesen, C., & Peeck, J. (1984). Effects of imagery instruction on reading and retaining a literary text. *Journal of Mental Imagery, 8*, 79-90.

Glasson, G.E. (1989). The effects of hands-on and teacher demonstration laboratory methods on science achievements in relation to reasoning ability and prior knowledge. *Journal of Research in Science Teaching, 26*, 121-131.

Glynn, S.M. (1991). Explaining science concepts: A teaching-with-analogies model. In S.M. Glynn, R.H. Yeany, & B.K. Britton (Eds.), *The psychology of learning science* (pp. 219-240). Hillsdale NJ: Erlbaum & Associates.

Hackling, M.W., & Treagust, D. (1984). Research data necessary for meaningful review of grade ten high school genetics curricula. *Journal of Research in Science Teaching, 21*, 197-209.

Hall, D.A., & McCurdy, D.W. (1990). A comparison of a biological sciences curriculum study (BSCS) laboratory and a traditional laboratory on student achievement at two private liberal arts colleges. *Journal of Research in Science Teaching, 27*, 625-636.

Heinze-Fry, J.A., & Novak, J.D. (1990). Concept mapping brings long-term movement toward meaningful learning. *Science Education, 74*, 461-472.

Hewson, P.W., & Hewson, M.G. (1982). The role of conceptual conflict in conceptual change and the design of science instruction. *Instructional Science, 13*, 1-13.

Hofstein, A., & Lunette, V.N. (1982). The role of the laboratory in science teaching: Neglected aspects of research. *Review of Educational Research, 52*, 201-217.

Humphreys, B., Johnson, R.T., & Johnson, D.W. (1982). Effects of cooperative, competitive, and individualistic learning on students' achievement in science class.

Journal of Research in Science Teaching, 19, 351-356.

Hynd, C.R., & Alvermann, D.E. (1986). The role of refutation text in overcoming difficulty with science concepts. *Journal of Reading, 29*, 440-446.

Hynd, C.R., & Alvermann, D.E. (1987). Prior knowledge activation in refutation and non-refutation text. In J.A. Niles & L.A. Harris, (Eds.), *Thirty-fifth Yearbook of the National Reading Conference*. Rochester, NY: National Reading Conference.

Jegede, O.J., Alaiyemola, F.F., & Okebukola, P.A.O. (1990). The effect of concept mapping on students' anxiety and achievement in biology. *Journal of Research in Science Teaching, 27*, 951-960.

Johnson, D., & Johnson, R. (1990a). What is cooperative learning? In M. Brubacher, R. Payne, and K. Rickett (Eds), *Perspectives on small group learning* (pp. 80-96). Oakville, Ontario: Rubicon Publishing Incorporated.

Johnson, D., & Johnson, R. (1990b). Cooperative classrooms. In M. Brubacher, R. Payne, and K. Rickett (Eds.), *Perspectives on small group learning*. (pp. 80-96). Oakville, Ontario: Rubicon Publishing Incorporated.

Johnson, D., & Johnson, R. (1991). Classrooms instruction and cooperative learning. In H. Waxman and H. Walber (Eds.), *Effective teaching: Current research* (pp. 277-294). Berkeley, CA: McCutchan Publishing Company.

Jones, M.G. (1990). Action zone theory, target students and science classroom interactions. *Journal of Research in Science Teaching, 27*, 651-660.

Kagan, S. (1990). Cooperative learning for students limited in language proficiency. In M. Brubacher, R. Payne, and K. Rickett (Eds.), *Perspectives on small group learning*. (pp. 202-223). Oakville, Ontario: Rubicon Publishing Incorporated.

King-Sears, M.E., Mercer, C.D., & Sindelar, P.T. (1992). Toward independence with keyword mnemonics: A strategy for science vocabulary instruction. *Remedial and Special Education, 13*, 22-33.

Kinzie, M.B., Sullivan, H.J., & Berdel, R.L. (1992). Motivational and achievement effects of learner control over content review within CAI. *Journal of Educational Computing Research, 8*, 101-114

Krajcik, J.S. (1991). Developing students' understanding of chemical concepts. In S.M. Glynn, R.H. Yeany, & B.K. Britton (Eds.), *The psychology of learning science* (pp. 117-147). Hillsdale NJ: Erlbaum & Associates.

Lederman, N.G., & O'Malley, M. (1990). Students' perceptions of tentativeness in science: Development, use, and sources of change. *Science Education, 74,* 225-239.

Lee, O., Eichinger, D.C., Anderson, C.W., Berkheimer, G.D., & Blaskeslee, T.D. (1989). *Changing middle school students' conceptions of matter and molecules.* Paper presented at the Annual Meeting of the American Educational Research Association (AERA), San Francisco, CA.

Levin, J.R. (1976). What have we learned about maximizing what children can learn? In J.R. Levin & V.L. Allen (EDs.), *Cognitive learning in children.* New York: Academic Press.

Levin, J.R., Morrison, C.R., McGivern, J.E., Mastropieri, M.A., & Scruggs, T.E. (1986). Mnemonic facilitation of text-embedded science facts. *American Educational Research Journal, 23,* 489-506.

Linn, M.C., & Songer, N.B. (1991). Teaching thermodynamics to middle school students: What are appropriate cognitive demands? *Journal of Research in Science Teaching, 28,* 885-918.

Lloyd, C.V. (1990). The elaborations of concepts in three biology textbooks: Facilitating student learning. *Journal of Research in Science Teaching, 27,* 1019-1032.

Malone, J., & Dekkers, J. (1984). The concept map as an aid to instruction in science and mathematics. *School Science and Mathematics, 84,* 220-231.

Mastropieri, M.A., & Scruggs, T.E. (1991). *Teaching students ways to remember: Strategies for remembering mnemonically.* Brookline Books, Cambridge: MA.

McIntosh, W.J., & Zeidler, D.L. (1988). Teachers' conceptions of the contemporary goals in science education. *Journal of Research in Science Teaching, 25,* 93-102.

Mergendoller, J.R., Marchman, V.A., Mitman, A.L., & Packer, M.J. (1988). Task demands and accountability in middle-grade science classes. *The Elementary School Journal, 88,* 251-265.

Mokros, J.R., Tinker, R.F. (1987). The impact of microcomputer-based labs on children's ability to interpret graphs. *Journal of Research in Science Teaching, 24,* 369-383.

Morrell, P.D. (1992). The effects of computer assisted instruction on student achievement in high school biology. *School, Science and Mathematics, 92,* 177-181.

Nachmias, R., & Linn, M.C. (1987). Evaluations of science laboratory data: The role of computer-presented information. *Journal of Research in Science Teaching, 24,* 491-506.

National Center for Education Statistics (1990). *Who majors in science? College graduates in science, engineering, or mathematics from the high school class of 1980.*

Nastasi, B. & Clements, D. (1991). Research on cooperative learning: Implications for practice. *School Psychology Review, 20,* 110-131.

Novak, J.D. (1976). Understanding the learning process and effectiveness of teaching methods in the classroom, laboratory, and field. *Science Education, 60,* 493-512.

Novak, J.D., & Gowin, B. (1984). *Learning how to learn.* Cambridge University Press: Cambridge.

Novak, J.D., Gowin, B., & Johansen, G.T. (1983). The use of concept mapping and knowledge vee mapping with junior high school science students. *Science Education, 67,* 625-645.

Novick, S., & Nussbaum, J. (1978). Junior high school pupils' understanding of the particulate nature of matter: An interview study. *Science Education, 62,* 273-281.

Nussbaum, J., & Novick, S. (1982). Alternative frameworks, conceptual conflict and accommodation: Toward a principled teaching strategy. *Instructional Science, 11,* 183-200.

Odubunmi, O., & Balogun, T.A. (1991). The effect of laboratory and lecture teaching methods of cognitive achievement in integrated science. *Journal of Research in Science Teaching, 28,* 213-224.

Okebukola, P.A. (1985). The relative effectiveness of cooperative and competitive interaction techniques in strengthening students' performance in science classes. *Science Education, 69,* 501-509.

Okebukola, P.A. (1990). Attaining meaningful learning of concepts in genetics and ecology: An examination of the potency of the concept-mapping technique. *Journal of Research in Science Teaching, 27,* 493-504.

Okebukola, P.A., & Jegede, O.J. (1988). Cognitive preference and learning mode as determinants of meaningful learning through concept mapping. *Science Education, 72,* 489-500.

Okebukola, P.A., & Ogunniyi, M.B. (1984). Cooperative, competitive, and individualistic interaction patterns - effects on students' achievements and acquisition of practical skills. *Journal of Research in Science Teaching, 21,* 875-884.

Paivio, A., & Yuille, J.C. (1967). Mediation instructions and word attributes in paired associate learning. *Psychonomic Science, 8*, 65-66.

Pankratius, W.J. (1990). Building an organized knowledge base: Concept mapping and achievement in secondary school physics. *Journal of Research in Science Teaching, 27*, 315-333.

Posner, G.J., Strike, K.A., Hewson, P.W., & Gertzog, W.A. (1982). Accommodation of a scientific conception: toward a theory of conceptual change. *Science Education, 66*, 211-217.

Pressley, M. (1976). Mental imagery helps eight-year-olds remember what they read. *Journal of Experimental Psychology, 68*, 355-359.

Pressley, M. (1995). Science. *Advanced educational psychology for educators, researchers and policy makers.* New York: Harper Collins.

Pressley, M., Woloshyn, V. Lysynchuk, L.M., Martin, V., Wood, E., & Willoughby, T. (1990). Cognitive strategy instruction: The important issues and how to address them. *Educational Psychology Review, 2.* 1-58.

Pressley, M., Wood, E., Woloshyn, V., Martin, V., King, A., & Menke, D. (1992). Encouraging mindful use of prior knowledge: Attempting to construct explanatory answers facilitates learning. *Educational Psychologist, 27*, 91-109.

Russell, J. & Chiapetta, E. (1981). The effects of a problem solving strategy on the achievement of earth science students. Journal *of Research in Science Teaching, 18*, 295-301.

Sanford, J.P. (1987). Management of science classroom tasks and   effects on students' learning opportunities. *Journal of Research in Science Teaching, 24*, 249-265.

Saunders, W.L. & Dickinson, D.H. (1979). A comparison of community college students' achievement and attitude change in a lecture-only and lecture-laboratory approach to general education biological science courses. *Journal of Research in Science Teaching, 16*, 459-464.

Schmid, R.F., & Telaro, G. (1990). Concept mapping as an instructional strategy for high school biology. *Journal of Educational Research, 84*, 78-85.

Schneider, W., & Pressley, M. (1989). *Memory development between 2 and 20.* New York: Springer-Verlag.

Sharon, S. (1990). The group investigation approach of cooperative learning: Theoretical foundations. in M. Brubacher, R. Payne and K. Rickett (Eds.), *Perspectives on Small Group Learning* (pp. 168-184). Oakville, Ontario: Rubicon Publishing Inc.

Sherman, L.W. (1989). A competitive study of cooperative and competitive achievement in two secondary biology classrooms: The group investigation model versus an individually competitive goal structure. *Journal of Research and Science Teaching, 26*, 55-64.

Shymansky, J.A., Hedges, L.V., & Woodworth, G. (1990). A reassessment of the effects of inquiry-based science curricula of the 60's on student performance. *Journal of Research in Science Teaching, 27*, 127-144.

Shymansky, J.A., Kyle, W.C., & Alport, J.M. (1983). The effects of new science curricula on student performance. *Journal of Research in Science Teaching, 20*, 387-404.

Shymansky, J.A., & Penick, J.E. (1981). Teacher behavior does make a difference in hands-on science classrooms. *School Science and Mathematics, 81*, 412-422.

Simmons, P.E. (1991). Learning science in software microworlds. In S.M. Glynn, R.H. Yeany, & B.K. Britton (Eds.), *The psychology of learning science* (pp. 241-256). Hillsdale NJ: Erlbaum & Associates.

Slack, S.J., & Stewart, J. (1990). High school students' problem-solving performance on realistic genetics problems. *Journal of Research in Science Teaching, 27*, 55-67.

Songer, N.B., & Linn, M.C. (1991). How do students' views of science influence knowledge integration? *Journal of Research in Science Teaching, 28*, 761-784.

Soyibo, K. (1991). Impacts of concept and vee mappings and three modes of class interaction on students' performance in genetics. *Journal of Educational Research, 33*, 113-120.

Staver, J.R., & Small, L. (1990). Toward a clearer representation of the crisis in science education. *Journal of Research in Science Teaching, 27*, 79-89.

Stavy, R. (1991). Using analogy to overcome misconceptions about conservation of matter. *Journal of Research in Science Teaching, 28*, 305-313.

Stensvold, M.S., & Wilson, J.T. (1990). The interaction of verbal ability with concept mapping in learning from a chemistry laboratory activity. *Science Education, 74*, 473-480.

Sweller, J., & Cooper, G.A. (1985). The use of worked examples as a substitute for problem solving in learning algebra. *Cognition and Instruction, 2*, 59-89.

Tobin, K. (1987). Forces which shape the implemented curriculum in high school science and mathematics. *Teaching and Teacher*

Education, *3*, 287-298.

Tobin, K., & Fraser, B.J. (1990) What does it mean to be an exemplary science teacher? *Journal of Research in Science Teaching*, *27*, 3-25.

Watson, S.B. (1991). Cooperative learning and group educational modules: Effects on cognitive achievement of high school biology students. *Journal of Research in Science Teaching*, *28*, 141-146.

Ward, M., & Sweller, J. (1990). Structuring effective worked examples. *Cognition and Instruction*, *7*, 1-39.

Welch, W.W., Klopfer, L.E., Aikenhead, G.S., & Robinson, J.T. (1981). *Science Education*, *65*, 33-50.

Willerman, M., & Harg, R.A. (1991). The concept map as an advanced organizer. *Journal of Research in Science Teaching*, *28*, 705-711.

Woloshyn, V.E., & Stockley, D.B. (in press). Helping students acquire belief-inconsistent and belief-consistent science facts: Comparisons between individual and dyad study using elaborative interrogation, self-selected study and repetitious reading. *Applied Cognitive Psychology*.

Woloshyn, V.E., Paivio, A., & Pressley, M. (1994). Use of elaborative interrogation to help students acquire information consistent with prior knowledge and information inconsistent with prior knowledge. *Journal of Educational Psychology*, *86*, 79-89.

Woloshyn, V.E., Wood, E., & Willoughby, T. (1994). Considering prior knowledge when using elaborative interrogation. *Applied Cognitive Psychology*,

Woodward, J., & Noell, J. (1991). Science instruction at the secondary level: Implications for students with learning disabilities. *Journal of Learning Disabilities*, *24*, 277-284.

Yager, R.E. Engen, H.B., & Snider, B.C. (1969). Effects of the laboratory and demonstration methods upon the outcomes of instruction in secondary biology. *Journal of Research in Science Teaching*, *6*, 76-86.

Yager, R.E., & Penick, J.E. (1987). Resolving the crisis in science education: Understanding before resolution. *Science Education*, *71*, 49-55.

Zhu, X., & Simon, H.A. (1987). Learning mathematics from examples and by doing. *Cognition and Instruction*, *4*, 137-166.

CHAPTER 9

Computers and Cognitive Strategies

Jim Kerr • Brock University

It is estimated that in North America, more than one household in three has a personal computer, with people continuing to buy computers in record numbers; but what ratio of computers to students is best in the classroom? The question of this optimum ratio has been argued by educational specialists, business and industrial sectors, parents and students. Some argue that the best scenario might be to have one computer in front of each child. In the mid-1980s, it was estimated that there were over 200,000 microcomputers in elementary and secondary schools in the U.S. (Ingersoll, Elliott and Smith, 1983). By 1992, data returned from 85% of all public, private and Catholic schools in the United States indicated that there were more than 2.5 million computers in the schools (The survey of microcomputers in schools, 1992). Today, educators have been striving for a ratio that approaches one computer for every ten students. However, this ratio has been achieved in only some districts. For example, in 1991-1992, Alaska had one computer for every 10 students, while Mississippi only had one computer for every 30 students (The survey of microcomputers in schools, 1992). Although the ratio of computers to students varies across schools, it is obvious that there are classrooms and schools that provide successful programs with limited computer support. It is important to examine how computers can be best used to facilitate learning and enhance the classroom environment, especially when resources are limited.

Despite the variation in the number of computers found across schools, many teachers use the computer in their classrooms to enhance the delivery of the curriculum. Others use it as a remediation or enrichment device, and some send students to the computer when they have finished their assignments or as a reward for good behavior. Other educators employ the computer when they are devising lesson plans. When it is time to calculate grades, many teachers use grade management software or a utility that they have developed on a spreadsheet or database. No matter what the application, computers are used regularly by many educators in the classroom as a tool for effective delivery of the curriculum.

THE COMPUTER AS AN EDUCATIONAL TOOL

Students regularly verbalize and demonstrate their interest in working with the computer and, for that matter, technology in general (Roth & Beck, 1987; Torgesen, 1986). Some teachers even relate that students are inclined to display enthusiasm, rather than the common resentment, for school activities when computers are used to augment instruction. This is supported by researchers such as Roth and Beck (1987), who argue that the computer can deliver exercises in an "instructionally appropriate game format" to students and, therefore, may improve students' academic motivation as well as learning skills. Some software companies even suggest that they have computer programs that have the potential to "treat" a variety of learning disabilities. Many software packages are currently available that introduce and reinforce necessary skills, such as basic reading skills, in novel formats (Muth, 1988).

Others warn of potential pitfalls that might await the unsuspecting educator. Ragsdale (1988) reviews many of the social implications that accompany the development of microcomputers, and the values that support or constrain computer applications and the evolution of computers in the classroom. He cautions that many innovations, including computer applications, are accepted with very little critical assessment. Ragsdale (1988) and Torgesen (1986) speculate that many computer applications are often sanctioned for their romantic appeal, rather than for their ability to fill a specific void in our educational or societal environments.

Torgesen (1986) argues that educators have viewed the introduction of computers into the classroom with mixed feelings. While some have approached it with excitement, others are neutral or even negative in their attitude. Both the technical and the pedagogical aspects of this information-processing instrument have experienced growing pains. Weizenbaum (1984) also declares that false assumptions exist about the use of computers in education: that computer literacy guarantees employment, that learning to program computers is essential, and that technology can solve all problems. In general, though, computer programs have become more accessible to the classroom teacher, and computers are gaining acceptance as functional educational tools in various milieux (Askov, 1986).

The purpose of this chapter is to examine computer-based interventions and to isolate where, and for whom, interventions have proven successful for enhancing learning.

DEVELOPING EFFECTIVE LEARNING ENVIRONMENTS

There is no doubt that the computer has a place as an educational tool, but there are factors that educators should consider before they design learning materials or decide to use a particular strategy to enhance learning. Clancey (1986) contends that to create an effective curriculum, three important components must be considered: the characteristics of the student, the current curriculum, and pedagogy. Clancey (1986) argues that the characteristics of the learner are the most important elements for consideration when educators develop curricula. Therefore, if the computer appears to provide some students with an incentive for learning, it should be included as a functional component or alternative in the curriculum design.

Educational steering committees, boards of education, and governing bodies are recommending that educators should use contemporary teaching techniques that focus more on concrete and activity-based systems. This activity-based environment complements the holistic approach that is widely accepted and promoted in schools today. The curriculum should include cross-curricular strategies that encourage active learning environments and involve all members of the class. Course structures should also accommodate small-group activities and individual endeavors. When these conditions exist, children are "encouraged to investigate, think, judge, appreciate, imagine, feel, enjoy, and create" (Deineka, Hunt & Pogue, 1986, p. 1).

The Effects of Computers in The Classroom

Microcomputers have been in the classroom for over a decade and have been used in education for more than 25 years. Despite this passage of time, the effects of computers on adolescent learning are still substantially unknown. However, as schools are faced with increasing financial constraints, more data are being demanded to support purchasing resolutions.

In a meta-analysis of 38 published and unpublished studies and 44 dissertations, Roblyer (1989) concluded that computer applications had a significantly positive effect in most of the areas that were reviewed. Computer applications were found to be most effective at the post-secondary level and for the adult learner. The research also suggests that there were slightly, although not significantly, better results with mathematics and science than with language arts and reading. General cognitive processing skills, such as problem solving and critical thinking skills, also increased as much as mathematics and language arts competencies. However, Roblyer (1989) cautions educators about the small number of studies and the wide variation in focus and methodology, recommending that more research be carried out before conclusive recommendations can be proposed.

An examination of the types of computer-assisted instruction suggests that more research should be initiated to investigate any differences that might exist between drill, tutorial, simulation, and other models of computer-assisted instruction.

Drill

Programs that have been designed to drill facts usually present questions for which there is one correct answer, e.g.: 12 times 11 equals ___? The drill proceeds without much feedback and usually only reports whether an answer is right or wrong. Many early programs were based on a model of drill and practice. This model was particularly functional because the computer was and is an excellent vehicle for delivering questions or instructions in a repetitive mode. Because it never tired of the methodology nor ran out of patience while waiting for the student to master the concepts, drill and practice exercises were very common applications and can still be purchased from software suppliers.

Tutorial

A program based on the tutorial model presents information to the student and then asks questions to check for comprehension. If remediation is required, the program reviews previous materials and provides information to augment the student's understanding. If the student demonstrates understanding, the tutorial continues to present 'new' information. For example, the computer might display a lesson and the rules for adding, subtracting, multiplying, and dividing integers. After the lesson, to check for comprehension, questions would then be presented for all four operations. If the student could correctly answer 75 percent of all questions, the computer would then advance to the next lesson. However, if the student achieved less than 75 percent on the section for subtraction of integers, the computer would present supplementary lesson material for this one component. More questions would then be asked to determine if the student had now mastered the work. If the student had not mastered the work, the computer would again present more information to help the student comprehend this section and would again offer more questions. This pattern would repeat until the student achieved the criteria for advancing to the next lesson or until the teacher decided to allow the student to go on.

Simulation

Simulation software is designed to provide a computer experience that will closely match "real-life" experience. Probably the oldest and best-known simulation is the operation of an aircraft. This type of simulation provides experienced or novice pilots with all of the advantages of real aircraft handling without the accompanying dangers.

Choosing the Right Package

Some studies imply that drill might be better for lower-order skills, such as for learning mathematics times-tables, but tutorials may be more appropriate for addressing higher-order skills, like comprehension (e.g., Patterson, 1986; Pitsch & Murphy, 1992; Ryba & Anderson, 1990). Since drill is based on the principle of repetition, very little understanding of the subject matter is needed by the learner; in fact, memorization of the facts will usually be sufficient to yield success for the student. However, to attain full comprehension of subject material, learners must rely on their own cognitive abilities and strategies for formulating the complex links that lead to personal understanding and knowledge-building. Because tutorials can present critical information in a logical sequence, the students are empowered to design a landscape for comprehension of the theme and not just memorization.

It is important to note that effective lessons can only be created at the hands of the skilled educator. Computers alone cannot conceive a lesson, develop it, or implement it in the curriculum. Ultimately, it is the responsibility of the educator, who understands the nature of the learner, to determine what technology to apply and when it is appropriate to use it. That is, educators need to be able to locate quality software and to determine whether the software corresponds to the ability level of the student(s). Many factors must be considered when deciding the quality of a software package. To help with the evaluation of software, an evaluation instrument is listed in Table 9-1. This instrument, when completed, will provide essential information about the software, including manufacturer, price, and an evaluation of the effectiveness of the package.

Much of the current software goes well beyond drill and practice. Packages today not only determine the skill and ability level of the student through comprehensive evaluation instruments, they also diagnose and present remediation for students with specific needs.

The word "diagnose" may seem inappropriate to assign to a computer program, yet when the process is examined, the almost mechanical dimensions of any diagnosis are evident. That is, the diagnostician must determine what characteristics are present, make an assessment, choose a suitable treatment, implement the treatment, evaluate the results, and start the cycle again. Since computers are able to perform mathematical computations and compare values, the computer can give the appearance that it is diagnosing and prescribing treatment. For example, a computer can establish formative evaluation scores as a student progresses through a learning module. Then, based on programmer- or teacher-designated minimum achievement, the computer can guide the student to the next appropriate module level. This could involve a remediation exercise, reinforcement for the current work, sequential placement in higher level, enrichment exercises, or perhaps a test.

In fact, of course, it is the programmer who specifies all of the logic for the computer program. Therefore, if the programmer uses incorrect information or logic, the computer will provide erroneous analysis and remediation. Software is only as effective as its design. Fortunately, most educational packages today have been written in consultation

Table 9-1
Educational Software Evaluation

Title: Price:
Company: One User=>
Address: Site Licence=>
                                        NOTES:

Type of Computer: Peripherals:

Subject Area: Delivery Methods:
                                          Lessons/tutorial
                                          Drill
Frequency of Use: Review
  Daily   Simulation
  Weekly   Testing
  Other:_____   Other:_____

Use with: Primary
  Class   Junior
  Small Group   Intermediate
  Individual   Secondary
  Without teacher   Other:_____

Rating Code: 5-Excellent 4-Good 3-Satisfactory 2-Fair 1-Poor
Educational Value and Pedagogy

Program is flexible for intended user(s)	5	4	3	2	1
Appropriate for classroom setting	5	4	3	2	1
Meets relevant educational needs	5	4	3	2	1
New terms are defined	5	4	3	2	1
Student has chance to correct errors	5	4	3	2	1
Help is available	5	4	3	2	1
Material is presented clearly and interestingly	5	4	3	2	1
Branches to new information, reviews old information and adjusts feedback	5	4	3	2	1
Follows progression of skills	5	4	3	2	1
Student response input is in a familiar manner	5	4	3	2	1
Student advances at appropriate speed	5	4	3	2	1
Criteria for advancing can be adjusted by teacher	5	4	3	2	1

Ease of Use

Clear, complete teacher documentation	5	4	3	2	1
Clear, complete student documentation	5	4	3	2	1
Instructions can be bypassed	5	4	3	2	1
Easy to exit from program	5	4	3	2	1
Easy to set up program	5	4	3	2	1

Effective Use of Computer

Computer presentation is more effective/efficient than other methods	5	4	3	2	1
Video display is pleasing and functional	5	4	3	2	1
Audio is effective	5	4	3	2	1
Other peripherals are employed when needed	5	4	3	2	1
Computer maintains useful information for records	5	4	3	2	1

SUMMARY EVALUATION   Excellent   Good   Satisfactory   Fair   Poor
Comments:

with professionals who are expert educators and with others who understand the full implications of testing and remediation. When these programs are used effectively in the classroom, teachers can allow students to work independently or with a peer tutor. When students are engaged at a computer, the teacher is able to direct attention to students in the class who may need more individualized instruction. In some schools, more advanced students work with younger students or with those with fewer skills, in a tutor-tutee relationship or in a reciprocal teaching relationship.

SUBJECT-DEPENDENT COMPUTER APPLICATIONS

Mathematics

Throughout the evolution of the computer, one fact remains constant— the computer is very good at performing quick, accurate mathematics. Since arithmetic was and always has been the underlying function of the computer, mathematics programs were the initial applications that were developed for the computer. Bitter and Hatfield (1989) describe a model for integrating the computer into the mathematics curriculum; they examine the elements of development, understanding, higher-order thinking skills, and applications, and present software suggestions for each component. They also survey other computer applications including telecommunication, spreadsheets, databases, and graphics.

Today, excellent computer programs are available in all subject areas and at many levels. The programs can deliver lessons on everything from the four basic mathematical operations of addition, subtraction, multiplication and division to simulating complex chemical reactions in the laboratory or chemistry class (see Table 9-2 for some examples of available software).

Writing/Language Arts

In the language arts classroom, many educators see the computer as a mere writing tool. Others use the computer to assist and encourage students in creative writing (Griffin, 1991). The question of whether to use word processors has been debated by educators and researchers since word processing packages were first introduced (Dusewicz & Beyer, 1990). Research evidence supports the use of word processors to promote revision in the writing process (e.g., Cochran-Smith, 1991; Grejda & Hannafin, 1992; Porter, 1992). For instance, Outhred (1989) contends that word processors help students with learning disabilities to write with fewer spelling errors and to increase the length of their written work.

Table 9-2
Examples of software companies and some software packages.

Subject Area	Title	Company	Grade Level
ESL	English Express	Davidson & Associates	Pre to 12
	ESL Companion	Creative Pursuits	2 to 12
Foreign Language	Bilingual Writing Center	The Learning Company	2 to 12
	Bilingual Reading Comprehension	Educational Publishing Concepts	6 to 12
Language Arts	Story Club	Davidson and Associates	2 to 12
	Once Upon a Time Series	Compu-Teach	4 to 12
Mathematics	Gears	Sunburst	6 to 12
	Math Blaster Mystery	Davidson and Associates	5 to 12
	Number Munchers	MECC	4 to 12
Science	SimLife	Maxis	6 to 12
	Operation Frog	Scholastic	4 to 12
Social Studies/ Geography	Where in the World/ the USA/Time/America's Past is Carmen Sandiego?	Broderbund	5 to 12
	MacGlobe/PC Globe	Broderbund	6 to 12
Spatial Visualization	The Factory	Sunburst	4 to 12
Word Processing	The Writing Center	The Learning Company	2 to 12
	Children's Writing and Publishing Center	The Learning Company	2 to 12
	WordPerfect	WordPerfect	7 to 12

Some other companies that develop and/or sell software are:
Adobe, Aldus, Barnum, Baudville, Berkeley, Central Point, Claris, Central Point, Curtis, Didatech, Educational Resources, Excel, Hartley, Lotus, MediaTECH, Merit, Microsoft, Orange Cherry, Sierra On-Line, Spinnaker, Stickybear, Ventura, Wordstar. These represent just a few of the companies in the educational software business.

From Educational Resources, 1994.

Student attitude toward writing is affected positively by using a computer to complete written work (Evans, 1991; Tone & Winchester, 1988; Zeni, 1990). Studies indicate that the amount of written material increases when students use computers. New studies suggest that computer-assisted instruction strengthens students' enjoyment of writing, that teachers also enjoy the process more, and furthermore that the quality of student work improves (e.g., Dusewicz & Beyer, 1990; Griffin, 1991; Owston, 1989). Owston (1989) found that when students wrote on the computer, they scored higher in writing competence, focus, support, and mechanics than when they wrote with pen and paper.

Different strategies have been suggested to help optimize the utility of the word processor in the language arts classroom. For example, progressive stories are used frequently and successfully. For this method to be most effective, students use the computer(s) individually or in small groups. A story is started by the teacher or a student, and other students further expand and enhance it. Through this process, a passage is created that reflects the writing style and inventiveness of many students.

This method of creating a progressive story is advantageous when there are many students and few computers. The computer becomes a focal point for expression of imagination. Students can elect to participate when they feel that they have something to add to the product.

The following is an example of a starting passage created by a teacher to initiate the writing process.

> On that day, as I moved cautiously through the steaming jungle, the gigantic shape that approached me had not yet registered in my sleep-deprived mind. Suddenly it hit me! I had come face to face with the mighty TYRANNOSAURUS REX!!! If I did not act quickly, ...

Students go to the computer center and add their imaginative touch to the evolving story. Here is the way one group of students proceeded with the story.

> ... If I did not act quickly, the T.R. would turn me into a 16-year old pancake—me, THE PANCAKE! So what was there left to do? I whipped out my favorite guitar, that I just happened to have on my back, and started singing Elvis ballads. "LOVE ME TENDER, LOVE ME TRUE, NEVER LET ME GO. OH MY DARLIN'..." I couldn't believe it. That huge beast, the King of the jungle, actually realized that this was a tune by another king—the King of Rock and Roll. Well, fortunately, the King of the jungle turned out to be the Queen of the Jungle and that just happened to be my salvation, or so I thought.
>
> Miss T.R. enjoyed Elvis tunes so much that when I stopped and tried to move away and into the jungle, she almost caused an earthquake as she pursued me through the trees. Once again, the only solution to prevent instant pulverization was to play her favorite tune—"LOVE ME TENDER, LOVE ME TRUE..." Can you imagine my mother's

face when she saw me and my new girlfriend coming up the driveway!

Many options exist that will allow students access to the word processor and remain involved in the scheduled classroom activities. For example, the teacher may want to design an agenda that involves students in the writing process only when instruction is finished. Another format would let students migrate to the computer as soon as they feel inspired to write. Other teachers might prefer to define set times when students are expected to move to the computer writing center.

Computers and Decoding

Even before the widespread availability of microcomputers in the classroom, Samuels (1979) suggested strategies that teachers could use to help students achieve automaticity in word recognition/decoding. According to Samuels, teachers must first instruct students how to accurately recognize words. One method that may provide an initial impression of this skill competence is to have the learner read written excerpts orally. Many researchers assert that proficiency in phonological processing and a reasonably large sight-word vocabulary facilitate the ability to process connected text. It also appears that extended practice, and the accumulation of skills that are appropriate to phrase and sentence processing, enhance fluent text processing skills. After instruction, time for extensive practice must be provided until this skill becomes an automatic part of the students' reading.

Stanovich (1980) suggests that poor readers rely heavily on context to help them with meaning. Context reliance becomes the compensatory process to offset a deficit in word recognition skills. However, he believes that context reliance does not aid comprehension. Perfetti (1985) refers to a process he calls the *verbal efficiency theory*, which extends from letter recognition to comprehension and content-based exploration competence. He concludes that some reading functions must become rehearsed to the degree of automaticity to allow for unobstructed comprehension procedures. Many other researchers also believe that repetitive activities promote decoding automaticity, which helps students develop reading comprehension skills (LaBerge, 1973; LaBerge & Samuels, 1974; Perfetti, 1985; Perfetti & Lesgold, 1977; Samuels, 1988; Siegel, in press; Stanovich, 1982a; Stanovich, 1982b). Since people tend to become weary of repetitive tasks, the computer appears to be an effective alternative for presenting instructional material repetitively.

Fiedorowicz and Trites (1987) conducted a systematic study of the effectiveness of their computer program, *Autoskill*. They selected their subjects from a group of students who, after several years of reading training, were experiencing deficits in their reading ability (mean age =

11.0 years). Kerr (1993) also completed a study with adolescent subjects (mean age for the experimental group = 16.8).

Fiedorowicz and Trites's (1987) rationale for program design corresponds closely with research that has been done by LaBerge and Samuels (1974). Practice, which theoretically leads to automaticity, is the foundation for the *Autoskill* program. They designed the computer program to assist in developing greater automaticity in letter to word recognition through repetition.

In *Autoskill*, the student proceeds through levels of recognizing letters, pseudowords, and authentic letter/word combinations that are aurally and visually presented by the computer through speakers/headphones or on the computer monitor. In one segment of the program, the *auditory-visual matching* module, students were presented with three letters, phonemes, pseudowords or real words on the monitor, and an auditory prompt that represented one of the three. Headphones were used to alleviate noise and consequent distractions. The student pressed the "1," "2," or "3" key to match the position of the display with the sound. For example, if the target was at the screen position farthest to the left, the student pressed "1". If the response was correct, a large plus (+) sign appeared over the appropriate target. If an error was made, a rectangle formed around the correct target. An adjustment could be made to the amount of time that the (+) and the rectangle remained on the screen. Other program parameters could also be modified. The default was set so that the rectangle stayed on longer than the plus sign. As soon as the student pressed a key, the reaction time (latency) was also measured and recorded. Computer-recorded pretesting, to establish a baseline measure of skills, combines with ongoing testing to maintain an accurate record of the student's progress, which is used to guide the student through custom-designed learning sequences.

Fiedorowicz and Trites (1987) found that their computerized-component reading-skills program had positive effects for poor readers. After 30 hours of training, Fiedorowicz and Trites reported the *Autoskill*-trained group showed significant progress in reading: word recognition skills, accuracy and speed at the anticipated grade level. In addition, both teachers and students felt positively about the program.

Roth and Beck (1987) reported on the effectiveness of two micro-computer programs called *Construct-a-Word* and *Hint and Hunt*. These programs were designed to improve the accuracy and speed of decoding and word recognition skills of students with below-average reading performance by improving their orthographic knowledge. These programs also have their theoretical basis in the verbal efficiency theory (Perfetti & Lesgold, 1979).

Construct-a-Word uses a setting in which students are required to assemble words from sets of subwords in a limited amount of time. The students are challenged to determine which consonants and consonant clusters combine to form real English words. Roth and Beck (1987) argue that the computer provides a motivational game-like atmosphere and helps to maintain concentration for extended practice sets.

Like *Construct-a-Word, Hint and Hunt* requires students to consider subwords for word identification. However, *Hint and Hunt* uses aural presentation of words and pseudowords. Students must then find or fashion a string of letters that duplicates the one that they heard. Roth and Beck (1987) found significant learning gains for the low- and medium-reader groups. Other findings indicated that exposure to the computer program, for the group classified as low readers, significantly increased their speed of response and their accuracy. By contrast, students who did not use the computer program improved their speed of response by only 4 percent and accuracy by only 5 percent. (For additional examples of computer programs appropriate for language arts, see Table 9-2.)

Social Studies

In another project that was designed for high school students, computer-based activities were fashioned to help the students to become well-informed voters (*Voteline: A Project for Integrating Computer Databases...*, 1992). The first of the four modules in this project was aimed at the 1992 Presidential elections; it consisted of media research and a spreadsheet used to examine demographics and opinions. Voter registration, role-playing an election, and analysis of election results were also included in the first module. A database containing demographics for counties in North Carolina was the focus for the second module. To decide political election results in the third module, students used higher-order thinking skills, demographics, and a spreadsheet. The fourth module was generalized, to allow students to use their problem-solving abilities to predict results for any election based on a spreadsheet analysis of survey results from various voting districts.

Specific Computer Software

The preceding examples are just a few of the thousands of programs that can be used to help students master specific subject material from mathematics to family studies. Examples of companies and some of their software packages are listed in Table 9-2.

CROSS-SUBJECT COMPUTER APPLICATIONS

Many programs are not designed with a single subject area as their focus and can therefore be applied to a wide range of subjects. The first example is the database.

The Underused Database

The database is probably one of the most underused computer utilities in the classroom. Although not often thought of as an educational tool, it can easily be adapted to classroom applications. From mathematics to geography to art to history, most curriculum material is an accumulation of data. The effective teacher, with the support of well-designed texts or other learning aids, is able to present this database of material in a way that is both enjoyable and instructive for students.

For example, if a class is studying the geographical regions of a country, the teacher will have prepared a set of objectives that will guide the accumulation of knowledge. The teacher might have students list questions that they feel they should be able to answer after they have studied the geography of an area. In this way, students indirectly restate the teacher's objectives, and a sense of ownership is developed. For example, the students will likely articulate questions like:

- What are the major cities?
- How many people live there?
- What are the industries?
- What areas grow wheat?
- Describe the climate.
- What are the major bodies of water?

Once objectives have been identified, the students can then choose a particular region for which they will be responsible for gathering information. They might form groups based on states or provinces, or by other natural areas like the Southeast, the Midwest, or the lake basin. After the students have chosen the regions that they will study, they proceed to the library or resource area where the information is maintained. Students gather the facts, answer the questions they have generated and then return to the classroom with the information their group has accumulated. These data can then be recorded on recipe cards to form a concrete database. New questions can be constructed, and then all questions and answers can be transferred to a computer database to compare speed and ease of retrieving answers.

By working with information contained in databases, students can enhance skills that are necessary in every subject. That is, they learn and practice classification, grouping, selection, and sorting. Of course, even when students leave the school building and go to the grocery store or to their job as a gas station attendant, it becomes apparent that these skills are important.

A simple example of a database lesson for studying text is presented in Table 9-3. In this example, students develop their own database of facts from available references. However, there are also many comprehensive databases that have been prepared by other teachers, or commercially, from which students can gather information. One com-

Table 9-3
Database Activity

ACTIVITY TITLE: LETTERS... WORDS... SENTENCES
LEVEL: Introductory

OBJECTIVES:

1. Collect, organize and analyze data from a newspaper and create a card database.
2. Answer a series of questions about the data.
3. Transfer the data to a computerized database.
4. Answer a similar series of questions to those of number 2.

Activity:
Students work together to collect data from printed materials that will be organized and analyzed.

Example Questions:
Each student will examine four paragraphs from selected stories and answer the following questions.

1. How many verbs in the passive tense did you find?_____

   1a. List them.

2. How many verbs in the active tense did you find?_____

   2a. List them.

3. What type of words do the sentences begin with?

   3a. List them.

4. List all adjectives.

5. List all adverbs.

   Add more questions for further skill building.

   Discuss with the students the best method of collecting the data.

Once the data have been collected, the students answer questions as a group. For example:

• What passive verb appears most often?
• Which adjective is used most often?
• Which adverb is used most often?
• What is the most common beginning for a sentence?

Again, add more categorization questions of your own.

mon source of formatted database information is the very durable CD-ROM (compact disk read-only memory).

CD-ROM and Videodisk Technology

Compact disks can store huge quantities of data, and the information can be accessed very quickly. They are similar in size to computer diskettes, but the information is in a laser-readable format, whereas data on a diskette is stored magnetically. One compact disk is capable of amassing over six hundred megabytes of data. This is the equivalent of approximately three thousand books of one hundred pages each.

Searches can involve more than one parameter, and therefore, Boolean techniques can be applied. Boolean strategies allow the student to apply restrictions on their search. For example, the student might be learning about dinosaurs and chooses the CD that contains information in encyclopedia format to gather data. By adding the phrase *and vegetarian* to the original search for *dinosaur*, the search can be narrowed to include dinosaurs that eat vegetables only. Also, since the information is digitized, this medium can store both text and graphic images. Therefore, in a database that contains information about prehistoric creatures, pictures and drawings of the beasts can be included along with the textual descriptions.

Caissy (1989) believes that CD-ROM will help students develop research skills and understand the importance of careful planning to extract valuable information. A precise search will yield results more quickly, and the data is more likely to relate to the information that the researcher/student actually wanted to locate. She also suggests that the strategies used for searching databases really do not differ between databases available on CD-ROM or printed materials. Technology allows users to take charge of the direction and rate of information gathering, which in turn builds their knowledge base. Also, information can now be retrieved, managed and manipulated so quickly that people are able to experiment with many alternate and unique solutions to problems instead of a limited number.

Interactivity

Another exciting facet of compact disk (CD) and videodisk technology is the realization that these media create excellent avenues for interactivity. The convergence of the computer with CD and videodisk unravels an educational potential with nearly unlimited promise.

Currier (1983) explores the qualities of interactive videodisk and argues that it is the "ultimate educational tool." This unique medium combines the television's strength in graphic representation with the interactive power of the microcomputer. Instructors should perceive this equipment as a tool that can enhance instruction, in much the same way that a video production might provide experiences to their students. With video technology, students are afforded visions of far-off lands and various cultures, the excitement of seeing animals in their natural habitat, or the thrill of a skydiving adventure. A CD-ROM or videodisk also allows students to *manipulate* simulations, to experience conditions and emulate experiments in the classroom and laboratory that might otherwise be impractical and potentially dangerous. For example, students can take a trip via computer software to a rain forest or to the bottom of an ocean. They can also mix toxic or explosive chemicals and view an emulation of the effect of their combination on a computer monitor without risking uncontrolled physical consequences.

Since the computer has the capability of executing calculations very rapidly, it can predict results for experiments or simulations in a time frame that may not otherwise be achievable in classroom hours. Weather predictions, soil erosion, population effect, water pollution and asteroid collisions are a few examples of computerized models that yield, to students and scientists alike, the ability to contemplate the consequences of many simulated events (see Table 9-2 for examples of specific programs).

Internet

The Internet is a relative newcomer among the resources that are available to educators, but has quickly been adopted as a major player in the classroom for thousands of teachers in many school districts (Carroll & Broadhead, 1994; Krol, 1993). It is described as a "network of networks" and reaches people worldwide in over 170 countries. Additional users are being added at a rate of about 10 percent each month. There are estimates that the Internet is composed of as many as 5,000 networks connecting more than 15 million people (Gaffin, 1993). Businesses are also quickly discovering the power of the 24-hour capabilities of the Internet. For example, cable television companies are exploring methods of extending Internet access to their subscribers. Book companies are listing their publications and accepting orders through the Internet, and even florists now offer worldwide ordering options.

Educators have not lagged behind in embracing the Internet as a new means of access to educationally relevant material. Many discussion groups can be reached through the Internet, allowing collaboration between teachers and students in countries around the globe. For example, students from New York can interact with students from Yellowknife to gather information comparing the lifestyles of people in the city to people who reside in remote areas. Others join exchanges that engage the participants in conversations about stamps, space exploration, the rainforest, the Olympics, puppets, car parts, computer programs, snow days, and virtually any topic that interests two or more people. More recently, full-credit secondary school, college, and university courses are being offered electronically as distance education courses.

Educational references have also been added to the Internet and can be found by anyone who has an Internet address. For example, the Educational Resources Information Center (ERIC) can be accessed to conduct full searches on-line, or requests for references can be sent by electronic mail (e-mail) to these centers. This means that educators and students now have the capability to conduct extensive literature searches from their home computer. Many other resources are also available through the Internet for most fields in education (see the Appendix to this chapter). Even the full text of various works is available on the Internet. For example, the complete works of Shakespeare, Sherlock Holmes novels, dictionaries, thesauri, and newsfeeds from major newspapers can be reached from Internet sites.

There are many sites that offer extensive collections of public domain software, shareware, and freeware. By following a few simple procedures, the software can be downloaded to your personal computer. Usually the software must be uncompressed before it can be executed and evaluated. The reasons for compressing software are that files will occupy less disk space and many files can be reduced into one. It is generally a simple procedure to uncompress the file(s) to their original state, so that they 'run' on your computer. With current budget constraints that restrict software purchases among many others, the availability of relatively inexpensive software is appreciated in most classrooms.

The discussion groups that have evolved for educators are growing almost as fast as the number of users on the Internet. Some e-conferences and discussion groups that are ongoing are: Kidsphere, K12Net, SchoolNet, K12Admin, ECENET, The Electronic Classroom, Academy One (which initiated TeleOlympics), and EDNet. Communities are planning and developing their own networks that allow all members of the district free access to resources and expertise. These networks have been established so that the local population can obtain information about community activities such as sports and weather, search for materials at the library, send an 'e-letter' to the editor, and even talk to their local politicians. Simultaneously, another benefit of these local networks is that they provide communications vehicles for those who have difficulty in travelling outside their home. For those who cannot leave their home, the ability to interact with others regularly from the comfort of their home is extremely beneficial. Local networks provide many of the advantages of the Internet, and some even allow users to gain passage through a 'gateway' to the full-featured Internet.

Attitudes Toward Learning

It appears that modification of the curriculum is essential to allow students with learning difficulties and a history of school failure to gain the feelings of success that lead to the healthy development of self-esteem and self-confidence (Askov, 1986; Fagan, 1990). Brown, Collins, and Duguid (1989) propose that many methods of instruction are inappropriate because they assume a high degree of commitment by students. However, experience seems to indicate that, often, there is a lack of commitment.

The computer has already been endorsed as an effective educational tool, and it appears to hold a natural attraction for many students. It can enhance learning materials for some students who would otherwise lose interest in subjects that are taught by traditional methods (Turkle, 1984). Numerous studies indicate that with properly designed activities, motivation actually increases when computers are used for instruction (e.g., Malouf, 1988; Relan, 1992; Yang, 1992).

When students use the computer to learn a new skill or concept or strengthen old ones, motivation usually increases, and some school-related problems, such as attendance and behavioral dysfunctions, tend to decrease (Yang, 1992). Therefore, if the computer can be used to effect a positive change in some of our students and increase their self-esteem, the money spent on this device is money well spent.

CONCLUSIONS

Computer-assisted learning, multimedia applications, interactive video, and virtual reality are just a few of the techniques that have become more readily available to teachers as the technological race accelerates. Combinations of devices such as laser videodisk, compact disk, digital cameras and scanners combine to offer multimedia options for instruction. Interactive video is becoming more accessible, and these tools can allow users to actively participate in decisions that affect the outcome of a video-presented scenario rather than passively viewing the production. Virtual reality (VR) is an extension of interactive video. Usually a headset is worn, which permits the participant to view scenes and hear the accompanying sound effects with real-life authenticity. As with interactive video, the user can provide input that may alter the scenario. These are only some of the gadgets that our students can now experience that perhaps were not even imaginable a few years ago.

These powerful technological tools are available now for educators and for their students. There will be arguments for and against the subsequent evolution of this technology in the educational forum. However, it will be the mandate of the individual teacher to decide whether or not to use the technology to enhance the learning environment. Thus, teachers need to critically evaluate both the pedagogical implications and the value-laden relevance of these devices. To this end, educators are faced with the continuous task of appraising the value of the technology and of formulating strategies for the implementation of this tool. "Microcomputers and optical recording technology have provided a powerful set of tools for educators; it is now up to us to learn how to use these tools effectively in the betterment of the educational process" (O'Connor, 1989). Educators today should no longer be contemplating whether or not to use the technology. The question should be *when* to use it to produce the most effective learning environment.

REFERENCES

Askov, E. (1986). *Evaluation of computer courseware for adult beginning reading instruction in a correctional setting: Final report*. Institute for the Study of Adult Literacy, Pennsylvania State University.

Bitter, G., & Hatfield, M. (1989). Computing and mathematics. *Journal of Reading, Writing, and Learning Disabilities International, 5*(1), 1-21.

Brown, J. S., Collins, A., & Duguid, P. (1989). Situated cognition and the culture of learning. *Educational Researcher, 1*, 32-42.

Caissy, G. (1989). Computers and Information Processing Skills. *Computers in Education, 6*(7), 17-18. Toronto: Mooreshead Pub.

Carroll, J., & Broadhead, R. (1994). *Canadian Internet Handbook*. Scarborough, ON: Prentice Hall.

Clancey, W.J. (1986). Qualitative student models. *Annual Review of Computer Science, 1*, 381-450.

Cochran-Smith, M. (1991). Word processing and writing in elementary classrooms: A critical review of related literature. *Review of Educational Research, 61*(1), 107-155.

Currier, R.L. (1983). Interactive Videodisc Learning Systems. A new Tool for Education Creates powerful Visual Lessons. *High Technology, 22*, 25-27.

Deineka, M. Hunt, G. & Pogue, L. (1986). *Ages 9 through 12: A resource book for teachers*. Ministry of Education: Ontario Public School Teachers' Federation.

Dusewicz, R.A. & Beyer, F.S. (1990). *The Delaware middle level computer writing project first year evaluation report*. Unpublished paper. Syracuse, NY: ERIC Clearinghouse on Information Resources. ED329991.

Educational resources catalogue (1994). Vineland, Ontario.

Evans, K.S. (1991). *The effects of a metacognitive writing tool on classroom learning environment, student perceptions and writing ability*. Syracuse, NY: ERIC Clearinghouse on Information Resources. ED 344212.

Fagan, W. (1990). *The L-I-T-E-R-A-T-E program: A resource book for literacy instructors*. Alberta: University of Alberta.

Fiedorowicz, C. A. & Trites, R. L. (1987). *An evaluation of the effectiveness of computer-assisted component reading subskills training*. Toronto: MGS Publication Services for the Ontario Ministry of Education.

Gaffin, A. (1993). *Big Dummy's Guide to the Internet*. Washington, DC: Electronic Frontier Foundation.

Grejda, G.F. & Hannafin, M.J. (1992). Effects of word processing on sixth graders' holistic writing and revisions. *Journal of Educational Research, 85*(3), 144-149.

Griffin, J.C. (1991). *The effects of computers on secondary remedial writing*. Syracuse, NY: ERIC Clearinghouse on Information Resources. ED 340018.

Ingersoll, G., Elliott, P. & Smith, C. (1983). Microcomputers in American public schools. *Educational Computer, 3*(6), 28,30-31.

Kerr, J. (1993). *Computerized reading skills remediation for reading disabled adolescents: a compensatory supplement to instructional strategies*. Unpublished doctoral dissertation, University of Toronto, Toronto.

Krol, E. (1993). *The Whole Internet Catalog and User's Guide*. Sebastopol, CA: O'Reilly & Assoc.

LaBerge, D. (1973). Attention and the measurement of perceptual learning. *Cognitive Psychology, 1*, 268-276.

LaBerge, D. & Samuels, S. (1974). Toward a theory of automatic information processing in reading. *Cognitive Psychology, 6*, 293-323.

Malouf, D. (1988). The effect of instructional computer games on continuing student motivation. *Journal of Special Education, 21*(4), 27-38.

Muth, W.R. (1988). *Federal prison system reading*

programs. Paper presented at the National Adult Literacy Symposium, Washington.

O'Connor, R. (1989). CD-ROM Technology: A New Teaching Tool. *The Computing Teacher*, November.

Outhred, L. (1989). Word processing : Its impact on children's writing. *Journal of Learning Disabilities*, 22(4), 262-264.

Owston, R. (1989, Summer). *Computers and writing at Sam Sherratt School*. Available from R. Owston, Director, Centre for the Study of Computers in Education, Faculty of Education, York University, 4700 Keele St., North York, Ont., M3J 1P3.

Patterson, J. (1986, May, October). Computers and complex thinking. *Computers and Complex Thinking*, pp. 1-24.

Perfetti, C.A. (1985). *Reading ability*. New York: Oxford University Press.

Perfetti, C.A. & Lesgold, A.M. (1977). Discourse comprehension and sources of individual differences. In M. Just & P. Carpenter (Eds.), *Cognitive processes in comprehension* (pp. 141-183). Hillsdale, NJ: Erlbaum.

Perfetti, C.A. & Lesgold, A.M. (1979). Coding and comprehension in skilled reading and implications for reading instruction. In L.B. Resnick & P.A. Weaver (Eds.), *Theory and practice of early reading* (pp. 269-297). Hillsdale, NJ: Erlbaum.

Pitsch, B. & Murphy, V. (1992). Using one computer for whole-class instruction. *Computing Teacher*, 19(6), 19-21.

Porter, B. (1992). In between trapezes: Living gracefully between old and new. *Writing Notebook: Creative Word Processing in the Classroom*, 9(3), 10-12.

Ragsdale, R. (1988). *Permissible computing in education: Values, assumptions and needs.* New York: Praeger.

Relan, A. (1992). *Motivational strategies in computer-based instruction: Some lessons from theories and models of motivation*. Syracuse, NY: ERIC Clearinghouse on Information Resources. ED 348017.

Riggins, D. (1993). *Gopher jewels*. Austin, TX: Riggins/dw@dir.texas.gov .

Roblyer, M.D. (1989). *The impact of microcomputer-based instruction on teaching and learning: A review of recent research*. Syracuse, NY: ERIC Clearinghouse on Information Resources. ED 315063.

Roth, S. & Beck, I. (1987). Theoretical and instructional implications of the assessment of two microcomputer word recognition programs. *Reading Research Quarterly*, 22(2), 197-218.

Ryba, K. & Anderson, B. (1990). *Learning with Computers: Effective Teaching Strategies.*

Syracuse, NY: ERIC Clearinghouse on Information Resources. ED 327157.

Samuels, S.J. (1979). The method of repeated readings. *The Reading Teacher*, 32, 403-409.

Samuels, S.J. (1988). Decoding and automaticity: Helping poor readers become automatic atword recognition. *The Reading Teacher*, 4, 756-760.

Siegel, L. (in press). Phonological processing deficits as the basis of developmental dyslexia: Implications for remediation. In J. Riddoch & G. Humphreys (Eds.), *Cognitive neuropsychology and cognitive rehabilitation*. New Jersey: Lawrence Erlbaum.

Stanovich, K. E. (1980). Toward an interactive-compensatory model of individual differences in the development of reading fluency. *Reading Research Quarterly*. 16(1), 32-71.

Stanovich, K. E. (1982a). Individual differences in the cognitive processes of reading: I. Word Decoding. *Journal of Learning Disabilities*, 15(8), 485-493.

Stanovich, K. E. (1982b). Individual differences in the cognitive processes of reading: II. Text-Level Processes. *Journal of Learning Disabilities*, 15(9), 549-554.

The survey of microcomputers in schools (1992). *ERIC Clearinghouse on Information Resources*. ED352930.

Tone, B. & Winchester, D. (1988). *Computer-assisted writing instruction*. Unpublished paper. Syracuse, NY: ERIC Clearinghouse on Information Resources. ED 293130.

Torgesen, J. K. (1986). Using computers to help learning disabled children practice reading: A research-based perspective. *Learning Disabilities Focus*, 1(2), 72-81.

Turkle, S. (1984). *The second self: Computers and the human spirit*. New York: Simon and Schuster.

Voteline: A Project for Integrating Computer Databases, Spreadsheets, and Telecomputing into High School Social Studies Instruction (1992). *ERIC Clearinghouse on Information Resources*. ED350243.

Weizenbaum, J. (1976/1984). *Computer power and human reason*. San Francisco: W. H. Freeman and Co.

Yang, Y. (1992). The effects of media on motivation and content recall: Comparison of computer and print-based instruction. *Journal of Educational Technology Systems*, 20(2), 95-105.

Zeni, J. (1990). *Writing lands: Composing with old and new writing tools*. Unpublished paper. Syracuse, NY: ERIC Clearinghouse on Information Resources. ED 323556.

APPENDIX: GOPHER SITES

NOTE: Gophers disappear just about as fast as they are created. Therefore, do not be too upset if you try one or several of these addresses and the Gopher seems to have scurried away.

Acadia University Gopher
    Host=gopher.acadiau.ca
Apple Computer Higher Education gopher server
    Host=info.hed.apple.com
AskERIC (Educational Resources Information Center)
    Host=ericir.syr.edu
Australian Defence Force Academy (Canberra, Australia)
    Host=gopher.adfa.oz.au
Baylor College of Medicine
    Host=gopher.bcm.tmc.edu
Brock University, St. Catharines, Ontario, Canada
    Host=spartan.ac.BrockU.CA
Centre for Scientific Computing, Finland
    Host=gopher.csc.fi
Clearinghouse for Subject-Oriented Internet Resource Guides (University of Michigan)
    Host=una.hh.lib.umich.edu
Communications Research Centre Gopher
    Host=debra.dgbt.doc.ca.
Consortium for School Networking (CoSN)
    Host=cosn.org
Dept. of Information Resources, State of Texas (experimental)
    Host=ocs.dir.texas.gov
Go M-Link
    Host=vienna.hh.lib.umich.edu
Gopher Jewels
    Host=cwis.usc.edu
Internet Wiretap
    Host=wiretap.spies.com
InterNIC: Internet Network Information Center
    Host=rs.internic.net
Library of Congress (LC MARVEL)
    Host=marvel.loc.gov
McGill Research Centre for Intelligent Machines, Montreal, Canada
    Host=lightning.mcrcim.mcgill.edu
Merit Software Archives
    Host=gopher.archive.merit.edu
Ministry of Environment, Lands and Parks, BC, Canada
    Host=gopher.env.gov.bc.ca
National Center on Adult Literacy
    Host=litserver.literacy.upenn.edu

National Science Foundation Gopher (STIS)
    Host=stis.nsf.gov
North Carolina State University Library gopher
    Host=dewey.lib.ncsu.edu
Ontario Institute for Studies in Education (OISE)
    Host=gopher.oise.on.ca
PeachNet Information Service
    Host=gopher.peachnet.edu
Queen's University
    Host=gopher.queensu.ca
Ryerson Polytechnic University CCS Gopher
    Host=hermes.acs.ryerson.ca
SchoolNet Gopher
    Host=gopher.schoolnet.carleton.ca
South African Bibliographic and Information Network
    Host=info2.sabinet.co.za
Texas A&M University
    Host=gopher.tamu.edu
The Faculty of Health Sciences Gopher, McMaster University
    Host=fhs.csu.mcmaster.ca
The World *(Public Access UNIX, featuring the Online Book Initiative)*
    Host=world.std.com
University of British Columbia
    Host=gopher.ubc.ca
University of Calgary
    Host=acs6.acs.ucalgary.ca
University of California–Irvine
    Host=gopher-server.cwis.uci.edu
University of California - Santa Barbara Library/
    Host=ucsbuxa.ucsb.edu
    Port=3001
University of Illinois at Chicago
    Host=gopher.uic.edu
University of Michigan Libraries
    Host=gopher.lib.umich.edu
University of Nevada
    Host=gopher.unr.edu
University of Prince Edward Island
    Host=Gopher.cs.upei.ca
University of Toronto
    Host=gopher.utoronto.ca
Whole Earth 'Lectronic Magazine—The WELL's Gopherspace
    Host=gopher.well.sf.ca.us
Yale University
    Host=yaleinfo.yale.edu

Taken from Riggins, 1993.

CHAPTER 10

Using Cognitive Strategies to Enhance Second Language Learning

Maria Myers • Queen's University

Second language learning is a common requirement of the secondary school curriculum and has been so for over a century. Although second language instruction is increasingly more prevalent in the elementary grades, there are still many adolescents who encounter second language instruction for the first time in secondary school. One advantage that secondary school learners experience over their younger peers is that they approach second language acquisition with all the skills, knowledge, and conceptual development of an experienced language learner because, by secondary school, they are well versed in their first language.

Within the secondary school classroom, students vary greatly in their knowledge of second languages. Some students emerge from elementary school with well-developed second language skills, some have limited knowledge gained through personal experiences, and some adolescents have no prior knowledge or experience with a second language. In addition, due to financial constraints and new directives encouraging destreaming, learners with varied backgrounds and ability levels are often grouped together in the same classroom. This means that educators must plan for an array of different goals and appropriate strategies for students who differ in their experience with a second language. This chapter examines the unique learning experiences and instructional procedures that facilitate second language acquisition in adolescent populations.

In general, second language training for adolescents has a dual purpose. On the one hand, there are academic objectives aimed at developing students' knowledge of linguistic components, such as expanding the lexicon (vocabulary), and grammatical structure; on the other hand, there are *sociopragmatic* and *pragmalinguistic* developments which involve social, communicative, and experiential objectives that enable students to become competent members of social groups and to learn the role of language in society (Schieffelin & Ochs, 1986). In addition to language training, it is also important for learners to be made more aware of their language learning process. Research suggests that training secondary school students to become independent language learners is most effective when tasks that foster independent learning account for 30% of course content for intensive introductory courses and 10-15% of course content for less intensive introductory courses (Ellis & Sinclair, 1989). This chapter presents strategies that will help educators and students to achieve both language and process goals.

The acquisition of language learning strategies, and the rate of second language learning, are contingent upon the amount of time and experience the instructional environment provides for second language learning. Students generally experience second language learning in one of two instructional settings:

1) *core language instruction,* where students are allotted a specific amount of instruction hours per week in the second language class with their remaining courses in the first language, or *enriched core instruction* format where one or more subject matters like History or Geography are taught in the second language; or
2) *immersion programs* where all instruction, activities and events are conducted in the second language.

Most secondary school students are exposed to the core course form of instruction. For example, in 1991-92, 50.6% of the student population in Canada was enrolled in core French programs at the secondary level, versus 5.3% in French immersion. One constraint of this type of language instruction is the limited amount of time that students spend engaged in the second language. Clearly, time management is important in second language learning, as progress has been equated with the number of secondary language teaching hours. Therefore, using strategies that maximize the use of available time may have direct implications on achievement.

Second language programs vary so greatly that it is almost impossible to give average amounts of time spent in language instruction; however, some generalizations can be drawn from general school formats. For example, students in semester-system classes may have daily classes lasting up to 76 minutes, with the possibility of no contact with a second language for one semester or more, whereas classes running the whole year may vary from 40 to 55 minutes per day. To provide an idea of the total amount of exposure this provides, consider that each secondary school credit course in French/Second Language in Ontario is counted as 120 hours of instruction (total of approximately 1,080 by the end of the secondary program). In contrast, extended French students will have accumulated 2,100 hours of French instruction, and immersion French students will have 5,000 hours of instruction.

Although strategic interventions for students in both core and immersion programs would be similar for students at the rudimentary stage of second language learning, the interventions differ when students are more advanced. For example, core students, who have a sound knowledge of grammar, have to work on discourse, both in the production and comprehension of language in a sociocultural setting. Immersion students, on the other hand, face problems because they *sound* fluent but display some lack of awareness of sentence structure, grammar, and the rules that govern the function of language. This chapter examines strategies that can be used for students in both of these programs.

DEFINING SECOND LANGUAGE LEARNING

Success in second language learning can be defined at many levels. The following section defines the basic components of language that are used to describe where errors or successes occur as students progress through their second language learning.

Language is often divided into two major skill groups: *receptive* language skills (reading, listening and comprehension), and *productive* skills: writing and speaking. It is not uncommon for second language learners to be more adept at one set of these skills over the other. Even within these skill groups, learners are likely to display some variation in the fluency of the subskills (Taylor & Taylor, 1990). For example, a learner may find writing easier than speaking or vice versa.

Sometimes language skill is assessed as a function of the structural level of language acquired or the structural level at which a learner demonstrates errors. The structure of language includes: phonemes, morphemes, syntax, semantics and pragmatics.

- *Phonology* examines the value of speech sounds. Proficient language users can distinguish the phonemes that are appropriate to the target language. For example, a native speaker of Chinese would have to learn the appropriate *r* sound for English (Taylor & Taylor, 1990).

- *Morphology* looks at minimal units with meaning. For example, a native speaker of English would have to learn that approximately the same sounds used in English for 'women' mean 'we' or 'us' in Mandarin Chinese. In English this would be similar to the situation for knowing that the prefix *un-* has two meanings: when combined with an adjective it means 'not,' e.g., *unlucky*; when combined with a verb it means 'to do the opposite of,' e.g., *unlock* = 'doing the opposite of locking'.

- *Syntax* has to do with sentence structure and the rules for constructing sentences. Words cannot be looked at in isolation. Their function in a whole sentence has to be considered. Compare, for instance, 'the little girl jumped' and 'the little girl hit.' The latter sentence sounds incomplete, but 'the little girl hit *the wall*' is complete. Word order, also, changes from language to language but tends to be consistent within a language: for example, whether modifiers come before heads or heads before modifiers.

- *Semantics* involves the study of meaning. Words that share meaning in the native language may not be equally interchangeable in the second language. For example, in English the words *sofa* and *couch* are synonymous. In French, although these same words share meaning, they contain added connotations which describe the style of the furniture and the time period to which it corresponds.

- *Pragmatics:* Once students become more fluent, they then need to look at pragmalinguistic and sociopragmatic components of language. These two components define how language is used in the cultural and social context of the second language culture.

  Pragmalinguistics represents the way discourse is organized, taking into account the linguistic context and the physical context. It allows learners to decide what language structure is the appropriate one to use in a specific context. For example, pragmalinguistic competence involves knowing that English-speaking North Americans interchange color labels for the caution light of a traffic light (e.g., yellow, orange, or amber) equally, whereas in France, the only acceptable term is "orange light" (*un feu orange*). It also means knowing that words can take on different meanings in popular culture over a period of time. In North America, for example, the word *awesome* is often used by adolescents to mean "great."

  Sociopragmatics deals with the correct way of doing certain things in a certain social context, taking into consideration both the background knowledge shared by speakers and hearers, and the social relationship and setting of the speakers and hearers. For instance, it provides information on how to write an invitation that will convey both the content and the desired tone. Here, a learner may have to decide how the recipient would respond if the invitation is written in long windy sentences as opposed to getting straight to the point. It is important to encourage learners to consider the cultural inferences and not to assume that something makes sense simply because it follows structural rules of the language.

Apart from the individual components of language, it is also important to consider the pattern of language learning in order to understand whether students are succeeding or demonstrating difficulty. One of the most salient features of second language learning is that it is not linear. Students need time to assimilate data. In the holistic approach, this time is called the *incubation period* (Miller, 1992). The incubation period is when students have been taught certain language items but have not assimilated them into their own active usage. Learners should be made aware of the time needed to assimilate new data (which can be weeks or months). As well, they have to know the steps leading to what researchers call the *inductive leap*, which signifies that some deconstruction might take place (Dirven, 1974). That is, before a new item is added to second-language knowledge, existing information has to be "pulled apart" and reorganized in order to fit in the new elements. Learners sometimes seem to be going backwards before taking a leap ahead. Research on brain activity (Haier, 1992) shows that when new knowledge is first acquired, there is a high level of mental activity. Therefore, a strategic effort is made. By contrast, after a week or two of learning the new information, decreases in mental effort are observed. At the same time, learners continue to successfully complete tasks related to the same topic at increasing levels of difficulty. Strategies also have to be time-effective in order to prevent students from getting distracted. To maximize appropriate use of strategies and time, students need to identify the strategies which work best for them. This requires a great deal of patience and flexibility.

A COGNITIVE FRAMEWORK FOR SECOND LANGUAGE INSTRUCTION

Although some researchers have argued that languages are learned independently, the majority of studies support the opposing position— that once one language is learned, it provides an underlying framework for learning and understanding subsequent languages (McCormack, 1977; Nation & McLaughlan, 1986). Students, therefore, have skills and knowledge that they can transfer when learning the new language (Cummins, 1983). This is especially relevant for adolescents, who have already developed a strong language base in their native language. In order to acquire their native language, they had to develop procedures and skills which they can later apply when learning the second language. For example, they approach the new language with a knowledge base rich in both conceptual and abstract information, as well as an array of learning strategies that vary from specific language-learning techniques to more global metacognitive study skills. The advanced knowledge base reduces some of the workload; where younger learners must struggle to acquire a concept and a label, adolescents may already have the concept and need only acquire a new label. Similarly, where younger children face the demands of using strategies, adolescents may have experience with using strategies and hence find them easier to learn and execute.

The proximity of the second language to the native language also dictates how easily acquisition will occur. Languages from the same "families" (e.g., English and Dutch) are more likely to permit easier acquisition than more distant languages (e.g., German and Romance languages). Nevertheless, even between more distant languages, some transfer of general cognitive and metacognitive skills can make second language acquisition more efficient for the adolescent learner.

Both schema theory and information processing models have been used by cognitive theorists to explain how adolescent learners are able to use existing knowledge to facilitate second language acquisition. In general, schema theory assumes that knowledge is organized into "packets of information" (Galotti, 1994) where concepts, situations, events, and actions are stored together in memory. Each "packet" of information, or *schema*, represents both general knowledge about the world and information about specific events that are constructed from life experiences with events in the relevant domain. For example, the concept of *bird* would include general information about all birds—they are avian, have wings, two legs, and feathers, lay eggs, etc.—as well as more specific information regarding particular breeds of birds (e.g., budgies, eagles, sparrows), variety in size, color, and names of pet birds that the learner had encountered. Some schemata are simple and represent only single concepts (such as the *bird* schema). Schemata also can be very complex and arranged within hierarchies of other schemata. The construction and use of schemata is not a passive experience. Instead, learners are assumed to be constantly revising, editing, and elaborating existing schemata as they encounter new information and compare it with the information that they already have available.

According to the supporters of schema theory, there are rich ties between language, vision and cognition which prompt learners to seek out commonalities between all aspects of cognition (Koehler, 1947; Rivers & Temperley, 1978). In new situations, learners can use their knowledge and perceptions to guide their behavior. This feature is important for second language acquisition because it allows learners to use existing knowledge to understand both the academic and social complexities of the second language. Adolescents can use "scripts" that they have developed in their first language (for example, the conventions that define letters to friends versus formal invitations, or casual versus formalized conversations) to identify and to learn the social "rules" of the second language. Such learning implies that the learner internalizes the schemata and that the teacher must devise strategies which make the principles of the target language accessible.

The challenge to teachers is that a learner's internal schemata are often difficult to identify and are sometimes only apparent when the learner makes a mistake, such as extending the rules from the native language to the second language. Such errors are most often detected through written work or verbal interactions. In order to have an effect on subsequent production, teachers have to be able to relate these errors to the principles of the language being learned and the student's native language. In this way, the teacher can identify the source of the error and convey that rule/principle to the student. One conclusion that can be drawn from schema theory is that strategies aimed at comparing, modifying, operating on, and reorganizing language should prove successful for promoting both understanding and production of the second language.

Information-processing models also provide a means for understanding the acquisition process for learners of a second language. These models have been used to explain what language is and how learners can efficiently organize and store linguistic information. Information-processing models usually follow the computer metaphor, where information passes through a series of systems, ranging from superficial processing systems that function at a sensory level to sophisticated processing that functions at a semantic level. For a brief overview of one of these generic processing systems, see Figure 10-1.

The first system, often called the *sensory store* or *sensory memory*, is

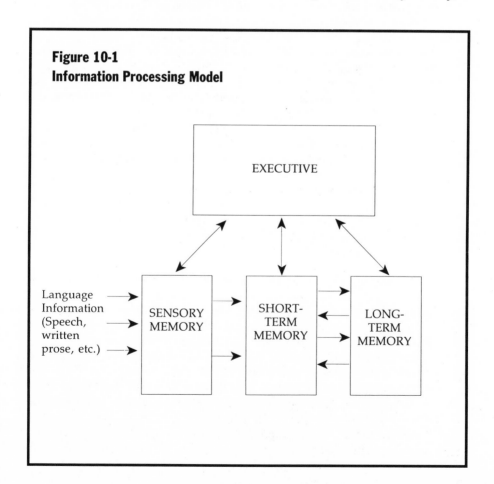

Figure 10-1
Information Processing Model

responsible for all sensory information, such as the detection of sound. The last system is more advanced and is often referred to as the *long-term store* or *long-term memory*. This extensive and intricate system handles all accumulated knowledge about language, and language is represented here in terms of meaning. Information-processing models generally assume that verbal and nonverbal linguistic information is eventually stored in long-term memory in some common abstract form different from the original mode in which the information was received (Kolers & Roediger, 1984).

Between the storage systems mentioned above there are other active systems which are responsible for managing the information. In our figure, these are represented as one system called the *short-term memory*. A critical step for storing information involves the ability of the learner to sort out and to hold onto important information when it is detected by the sensory memory, until it can be coded for long-term storage. In this interim system, learners can employ strategies that help them to organize and code information so that it can be stored. Strategies are generally executed in the short-term store (another name for this store is *working memory*). In addition, strategies can also be used to retrieve information from long-term memory to be used in ongoing tasks. To facilitate communication among the systems, most models include a component referred to as the *executive*. This component is responsible for ongoing monitoring and management of information among the different processing systems. The executive and short-term memory components are critical because they provide learners with the opportunity to manage their own language learning.

Students can be provided with a full range of cognitive strategies that promote effective and efficient monitoring, management, organization and rehearsal of information, which will later permit greater access when they wish to retrieve information.

STRATEGIES FOR SECOND LANGUAGE LEARNING

By carefully monitoring the strategies that students are presently using and keeping in mind the implications from theory, more extensive strategic repertoires can be tailor-made for adolescents. Bialystok's (1985) research indicates that students may not be aware of the strategies they use and, hence, need help to develop their awareness of strategies. Similarly, Garner (1990) suggests that students often rely upon lower-level strategies even when more sophisticated strategies are available. As a corollary then, we can say that *students have to be taught how to learn a second language*. To do this, teachers not only have to make students aware of the vast array of strategies available to them, they must also encourage strategy use, perhaps through trial and error practice.

Strategies for Vocabulary

One important step in second language acquisition is to acquire some rudimentary vocabulary items. Once students have access to a working vocabulary, even a very limited one, they can become involved in the classroom. They can recognize and respond to information conveyed by teachers and peers, and they can begin to express their own ideas. Ideally, vocabulary items should be expanded to more than one word. Preference should be given to expressions that take into account idioms and the development of pragmatic competence. When teaching vocabulary items, four steps have to be observed: (a) convey the correct meaning, (b) ensure the correct pronunciation, (c) give the correct spelling, (d) make sure that the item, phrase, or sentence is used correctly in the structure or the paragraph. Teach useful phrases as whole items. This can help to prevent structural mistakes. Most importantly teachers should make sure that learners are familiar with current conversational vocabulary items.

Cognates

When students are learning a second language that belongs to the same family as their native language, the meaning of a new word can often be derived through comparison and inference because the new word will be a *cognate* to a word in the native language. Cognates are words that stem from the same origin and, hence, share similar sounds, appearances, and meanings. For example, because English and Danish come from the same language family, they share cognates. The Danish equivalent for *mother* is *moder* (Taylor & Taylor, 1990). This comparison strategy lets students use their existing knowledge to understand and learn new vocabulary items. To employ this strategy students need to be made aware of whether their native language is related to the second language, and if so, they should be instructed to search for cognates.

Other related strategies encourage learners to make inferences about word stems and derivations. For example, to convey the similarities and differences between the following French verbs: *mener, amener, emmener, ramener, apporter, emporter, rapporter,* one can look at the stems: *mener*=to give direction, to take along, *porter*=to carry (in the specific context we are looking at here); and the prefixes: *a*- meaning to a place or a destination, *em*- meaning with, or away from the place, and *r*- implying a repetition. This gives the following: *mener*=to give direction, *amener*=to bring along to a place, *emmener*=to take away with you from the place you are at, *apporter*=to carry a thing to a place, *emporter*=to carry a thing away to another place. Using these kinds of inferences can promote greater facilitation of vocabulary.

Mnemonic Strategies

Although it is always ideal to present vocabulary in context, it is often difficult to do this with the first words acquired by students. For speed and efficiency, it is often useful to employ mnemonic strategies to facilitate acquisition of vocabulary items, in order to provide students with a repertoire so that they can understand and participate in subsequent classroom interactions. Mnemonic techniques are associative strategies that encourage learners to create links (i.e., associations) in order to help them remember new information. When using these strategies, learners are often asked to create mental images or use rhymes or other verbal sequences to link a new vocabulary word and the meaning of the word. Mnemonic strategies result in better recall by integrating new material into existing information and by providing retrieval cues. Some examples of these strategies are listed below.

The keyword method involves creating an image-based link between a new vocabulary word in the second language and an acoustically similar item in the first language. For example, if an English-speaking student were learning the Spanish word for "duck," *pato*, she would do the following: First, the student would need to find an English word that both sounded like the word *pato* (or part of the word) and was easily imaginable (e.g., concrete). One possible choice would be *pot*. The student would then create an interactive image of the duck and the pot, as in Figure 10-2. To remember the meaning of the word *pato*, the learner would be able to use the keyword *pot* as a link to her image, which in turn would enable her to retrieve the meaning "duck."

This technique has consistently proven effective with elementary

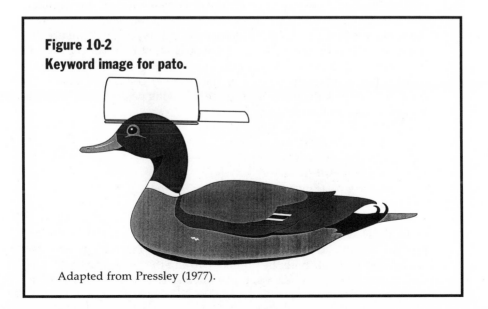

Figure 10-2
Keyword image for pato.

Adapted from Pressley (1977).

school children (e.g., Pressley, 1977), adolescents (Delaney, 1978; Dickel & Slack, 1983), and adults (Atkinson, 1975). The method works best if the learners themselves generate the keywords. However, research findings suggest that educators should be sensitive to the skill level of the learner when using this strategy. Younger learners, less knowledgeable learners, and novices to the strategy may acquire and use this strategy best if they are supported (at least initially) by being provided with a good keyword before generating the image (Paivio & Begg, 1981).

The pegword method was specifically designed for second language vocabulary learning and has a long history of success (see Mastropieri & Scruggs, 1991). This associative strategy uses both imagery and memorized verbal lists or routines (for example, rhymes or the number system) as *pegs* or "hooks" to retrieve new vocabulary words. To use the pegword technique, the learner must first identify a memorized verbal "routine" that will serve as the pegs. It is important that this routine be completely memorized and that the learner be able to accurately reproduce it without effort. For our example, we will use the number system (1, 2, 3, 4, 5). Then, for each number, the learner pairs one (or two) consonants that match the number on visual or acoustic similarity. For example, consider the following number-consonant pairs suggested by Lorayne (1974):

> 1 = *t*, *d* because each of the consonants has one downstroke
> 2 = *n* because the letter has two "legs"
> 3 = *m* because the letter has three "legs"
> 4 = *r* because *r* appears in many languages for the number 4
> 5 = *l* because a capital L is the Roman numeral for 50

After establishing a well-defined number-consonant pair, the learner is given a list of words that serve as the hooks or pegs for the new vocabulary items. There are three criteria that must be met to insure that these *pegwords* are appropriate. The words must be from the second language; they must easily yield an image; and the first letter of each word must correspond to one of the number-consonant pairs. For example, Paivio & Begg (1981) used the following pegwords to promote French language learning:

> 1 = t, d = *thé* (tea)
> 2 = n = *noeud* (knot)
> 3 = m = *mât* (mast)
> 4 = r = *roi* (king)
> 5 = l = *loi* (law)

Once these relations are overlearned to the extent that students can produce any one of three elements from only one cue (i.e., given *n*, the student can generate both the number two and the image of a knot), then they are ready to learn new vocabulary items. The final step involves the learner creating an interactive image of the pegword with the new vocabulary item. The student matches one new vocabulary item to each peg and creates the interactive image of the new word and the peg. For example, if one new vocabulary word was the French word *tasse* ("cup"), a student could generate an image of a teabag (image for *thé*) in a cup. Later, when the student wants to remember the new word, they first go through the numbers and access the consonant, which gives them the peg for the image. The image then yields them the new vocabulary word.

Frameworking

Minsky (1975) claims that in our memory we have sets of stereotypical situations, or "remembered frameworks," which we call up when necessary. These *frames* or scenarios constitute the backdrop into which we fit the details of the present situation. Galisson (1984) first used frameworks by taking an inventory of the most commonly used French words. He then grouped them into thematic charts. For instance, to chart the human body, a stick figure was constructed and labeled with all necessary vocabulary items corresponding to parts of the body. Commonly used adjectives and verb phrases were written next to the corresponding body. The stick figure, therefore, organizes information and encourages learners to construct relations among related items (Bogaards, 1988), which facilitates memory by providing a cue for retrieval.

Strategies for Grammar and Syntax

Relexification

Butterworth (1972), one of the earliest researchers to study language acquisition by adolescents, showed the importance of reducing structure to simple syntax and then comparing the use of words in the first and second language (a strategy called *relexification*). This means that students use second-language words in the syntactic patterns of their first language. By comparing the first and second languages and showing students what structures are the same, one can then have students use second-language words they know in order to make complete and accurate sentences.

The key here is to develop a sense of familiarity of what second-language syntactic patterns correspond to first-language patterns, as students often fear that if something looks too familiar in second language, it must be wrong (Deckert, 1994).

First-Letter Mnemonics

Verbal elaboration methods through grouping word chains and narrative chains are also effective. For instance, the acronym B.B.A.G.S. (*Beauty, Badness, Age, Goodness, Size*) can be used to recall the position of the categories of short adjectives of up to two syllables to be placed before nouns in French, knowing that adjectives for color come after the noun.

The start of a word serves as a base for the retrieval of the subsequent part; hence, first-letter mnemonics can serve as a good cue for organizing words in memory. Fay and Cutler (1977) found that the retention rate for the first vowel of words was higher than for other parts of the word, and researchers agree that the beginnings of words are more prominent in storage than other parts. Marslen-Wilson and Tyler (1980, 1981) suggest that a whole army of words marches up each time a word begins to be spoken. On hearing a sequence *st*, a listener accesses the whole set of words with this beginning. The hearer then cuts down the range of possibilities by restricting the choice to the grammatical category in question and then further according to the immediate context.

Strategies for Semantics

Grids and Trigger-Type Activities

The purpose of grids and trigger-type activities is to provide visual support for problem solving and organizing information. Grids can consist of filled-in charts giving attributes of objects or people/charac-ters, with blank squares to be checked if the object or character of the list possesses certain attributes. The same is possible for events or language functions and structures. A sample of a grid activity is contained in Figure 10-3. In this exercise, students in a German class would be placed into small groups, such that each member has a map and only one unit of information about a grid. In the example in Figure 10-3, the students must work cooperatively to complete the grid. Their task is to determine the home city and vacation city of each character mentioned in the units. The grid is used to summarize and organize the information that is gathered when group members share information.

Grids and trigger-type activities help to put emphasis on meaning. The purpose of the grids can vary. They can create interest, and enhance organization skills which are needed in oral interaction or note-taking.

Lexical Chains

Lexical chains can be made with word families. In addition, it is possible to make long lists of words with associated meanings (Carter & Long, 1987). Words with logical connections between them can also be developed into a circular rather than a horizontal or vertical pattern.

Strategies for Sociopragmatics and Pragmalinguistics

Interaction provides an opportunity for social understanding. If the course objective includes a component for developing oral skills, it is

Figure 10-3
Grid Activity

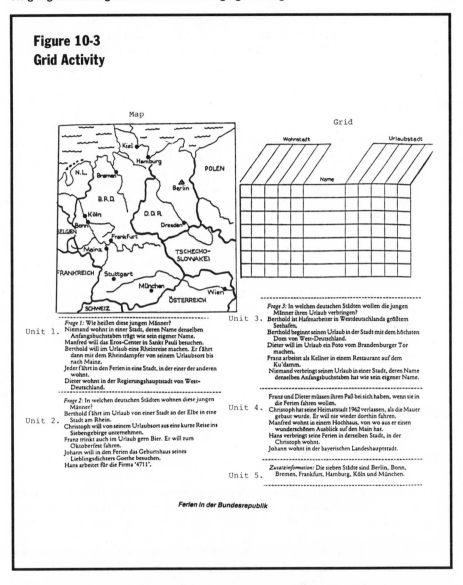

Map

Grid

Frage 1: Wie heißen diese jungen Männer?

Unit 1.
Niemand wohnt in einer Stadt, deren Name denselben Anfangsbuchstaben trägt wie sein eigener Name.
Manfred will das Eros-Center in Sankt Pauli besuchen.
Berthold will im Urlaub eine Rheinreise machen. Er fährt dann mit dem Rheindampfer von seinem Urlaubsort bis nach Mainz.
Jeder fährt in den Ferien in eine Stadt, in der einer der anderen wohnt.
Dieter wohnt in der Regierungshauptstadt von West-Deutschland.

Frage 2: In welchen deutschen Städten wohnen diese jungen Männer?

Unit 2.
Berthold fährt im Urlaub von einer Stadt an der Elbe in eine Stadt am Rhein.
Christoph will von seinem Urlaubsort aus eine kurze Reise ins Siebengebirge unternehmen.
Franz trinkt auch im Urlaub gern Bier. Er will zum Oktoberfest fahren.
Johann will in den Ferien das Geburtshaus seines Lieblingsdichters Goethe besuchen.
Hans arbeitet für die Firma '4711'.

Frage 3: In welchen deutschen Städten wollen die jungen Männer ihren Urlaub verbringen?

Unit 3.
Berthold ist Hafenarbeiter in Westdeutschlands größtem Seehafen.
Berthold beginnt seinen Urlaub in der Stadt mit dem höchsten Dom von West-Deutschland.
Dieter will im Urlaub ein Foto vom Brandenburger Tor machen.
Franz arbeitet als Kellner in einem Restaurant auf dem Ku'damm.
Niemand verbringt seinen Urlaub in einer Stadt, deren Name denselben Anfangsbuchstaben hat wie sein eigener Name.

Unit 4.
Franz und Dieter müssen ihren Paß bei sich haben, wenn sie in die Ferien fahren wollen.
Christoph hat seine Heimatstadt 1962 verlassen, als die Mauer gebaut wurde. Er will nie wieder dorthin fahren.
Manfred wohnt in einem Hochhaus, von wo aus er einen wunderschönen Ausblick auf den Main hat.
Hans verbringt seine Ferien in derselben Stadt, in der Christoph wohnt.
Johann wohnt in der bayerischen Landeshauptstadt.

Unit 5.
Zusatzinformation: Die sieben Städte sind Berlin, Bonn, Bremen, Frankfurt, Hamburg, Köln und München.

Ferien in der Bundesrepublik

recommended that students spend at least 20% of all class time actively involved in oral interaction via a communicative or experiential activity. Pattison (1987) recommends many activities of an interactive nature, including *information gap activities* and *matching activities*. Information gap activities encourage students to engage in dialogue because each partner possesses information that the other partner needs in order to complete the task. For example, each partner may have a different list or a different version of a picture. By finding out the missing items, or completing their picture, they arrive at a representation of the whole situation.

Matching activities are also designed to get learners to increase communication. For instance, in a split dialogue task, learners match given phrases. This makes them aware of the use of the phrases in order to communicate different meanings.

Production

The most common problem with language production generally involves getting passive vocabulary to be included into active use. A way suggested by Prokop and Hartmetz (1984) is to encourage students to react to situations by using new language items out loud, if they are alone, or subvocalizing them otherwise. In the past it was suggested that students speak in front of mirrors to improve their articulation of the second language; it appears that carrying on conversations with oneself in front of a mirror while trying to recall new language items is a very effective means to ensure the transition from passive to active use (Prokop & Hartmetz, 1984).

In addition, many other strategies help to improve oral communication (Pattison, 1987), including information gap activities, practicing information giving and information getting, and having genuine telephone conversations (perhaps with the help of ham radio operators) with native speakers of the second language.

GENERAL STRATEGIES

Organizational Strategies

Woodward (1992) favors getting people interested in information by reacting to it and advocates the construction of *mind-maps*. Mind-maps start from a central title or theme, with main branches and secondary branches drawn out from it, all labeled. Arrows, side details and additional colored lines serve to add extra points that arise. Mind-maps are nonlinear, allowing students to follow whatever comes up and yet retain organization and overview. In addition, the strategy permits less important questions and comments to fit into the scheme. For an example of a mind-map, see Figure 10-4.

Mind-maps can be used before introducing information on a subject, while information is given, or as a post-activity. As a pre-activity, it implies guessing, inductive inferencing of what will come about. One often mentions advance-organizing as corresponding to this type of anticipation. Mapping during an activity helps to organize thoughts. After the activity, mapping is useful for verification and (re)organization of data. Talk and visual support, as well as organization with the possibility of rewriting and reorganizing, are used to pass on

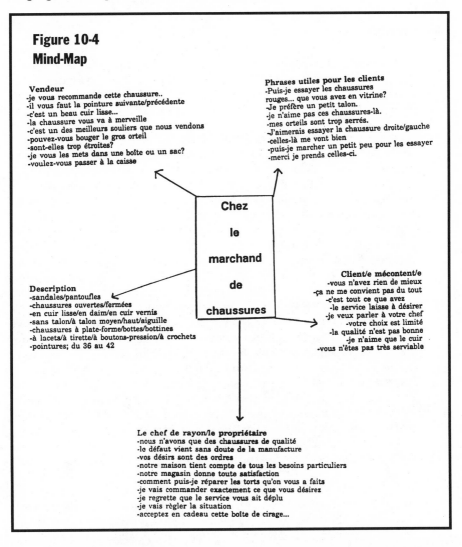

Figure 10-4
Mind-Map

Vendeur
-je vous recommande cette chaussure..
-il vous faut la pointure suivante/précédente
-c'est un beau cuir lisse...
-la chaussure vous va à merveille
-c'est un des meilleurs souliers que nous vendons
-pouvez-vous bouger le gros orteil
-sont-elles trop étroites?
-je vous les mets dans une boîte ou un sac?
-voulez-vous passer à la caisse

Phrases utiles pour les clients
-Puis-je essayer les chaussures
rouges... que vous avez en vitrine?
-Je préfère un petit talon.
-je n'aime pas ces chaussures-là.
-mes orteils sont trop serrés.
-J'aimerais essayer la chaussure droite/gauche
-celles-là me vont bien
-puis-je marcher un petit peu pour les essayer
-merci je prends celles-ci.

Chez
le
marchand
de
chaussures

Description
-sandales/pantoufles
-chaussures ouvertes/fermées
-en cuir lisse/en daim/en cuir vernis
-sans talon/à talon moyen/haut/aiguille
-chaussures à plate-forme/bottes/bottines
-à lacets/à tirette/à boutons-pression/à crochets
-pointures; du 36 au 42

Client/e mécontent/e
-vous n'avez rien de mieux
-ça ne me convient pas du tout
-c'est tout ce que avez
-le service laisse à désirer
-je veux parler à votre chef
-votre choix est limité
-la qualité n'est pas bonne
-je n'aime que le cuir
-vous n'êtes pas très serviable

Le chef de rayon/le propriétaire
-nous n'avons que des chaussures de qualité
-le défaut vient sans doute de la manufacture
-vos désirs sont des ordres
-notre maison tient compte de tous les besoins particuliers
-notre magasin donne toute satisfaction
-comment puis-je réparer les torts qu'on vous a faits
-je vais commander exactement ce que vous désirez
-je regrette que le service vous ait déplu
-je vais régler la situation
-acceptez en cadeau cette boîte de cirage...

the message simultaneously in two different media. Mapping also demonstrates priorities, allowing students to see which areas are more important, as well as networks of connections between points. Mind-maps enable students to connect words grammatically as well as thematically. For example, if your central theme is "at the shoe shop," the map should include relevant vocabulary having to do with shoe types (from slippers to boots), sizes, colors, and styles, and should also include expressions or lexical phrases likely to be used by the salesperson, the manager, a happy customer, and an unhappy customer (see Figure 10-4).

Collaboration

Cooperative work seems to be beneficial for mixed-ability teams. Language socialization is developed in cooperative work situations and learners see how to improve their performance. O'Malley, Chamot, Stewner-Manzanares, Kupper, and Russo (1985) refer to these as "social-mediating" or "socioaffective" strategies. Moreover, research has shown that helping other learners (here, explaining some language data) forces the individuals involved to go through all the steps checking for thorough knowledge, thus reinforcing the knowledge gained.

Peer intervention during work on vocabulary items also proves to be very useful. Students explaining meanings to each other and helping one another provide a form of cognitive elaboration which enhances students' own understanding. Similarly, group work also facilitates grammar tasks. In many cases, group work enables students who have just passed the stage of understanding the grammar points themselves to explain them to peers. This makes understanding easier (Slavin, 1983).

The best collaborative strategy for skill use consists of pairing a native speaker with a language learner, or arranging to have a native speaker agree to act as a resource person for a group of learners (Nunan, 1992). The most strategically tempting model for cooperative teaching seems to be team-teaching with one native speaker, as in the Koto-ku project (Stein, 1989). This project is a cooperative venture between the British Council Cambridge English School and the Board of Education in the Koto ward of southeast Tokyo. Qualified and experienced ESOL teachers worked with their Japanese counterparts to team-teach. Each week a one-hour liaison period was arranged. The team teaching worked because of three principles of what they called "flexible equality":

1. Material and methods had to be acceptable and appropriate to both ESOL and Japanese teachers in a way that was sensitive to the Japanese teachers' relationship with students.
2. During the liaison periods exact roles at each stages were determined, taking care that the Japanese teacher actually agreed with the final decisions rather than just appearing to.
3. Native English teachers had to adapt to Japanese ideas and be very sensitive when trying to persuade the Japanese teachers to change things they were apprehensive about. Working cooperatively as a student or as a teacher can promote substantial advantages for second language learning.

CONCLUSION

Overall, this chapter highlighted strategies that increase the knowledge and understanding within specific skill areas, ranging from vocabulary acquisition to sociopragmatic competence. In addition, steps which help to promote and improve language production were outlined. Because good production presupposes good listening and comprehension skills, it is important to include strategies that organize information (for example, mind-maps). Throughout the chapter we have focused on the complementary aspects of language learning: the structure of sentences (i.e. syntax, the grammatical and orthographic codes), and the interaction involving meaning, pragmatics and communicational objectives.

At the outset, the emphasis was put on the need for learners to understand the learning process. This is especially crucial given the variety of settings in which adolescents learn a second language. As a corollary of this awareness, learners will also see what skills they excel at and which are the ones they have to improve upon. The use of individual strategies, however effective, will not lead further into language development unless there is a continuous evaluation of experience, reflection, conceptualization, and active experimentation. The level of difficulty should be manageable; the best way to ensure this is to have students choose the task from a series presented by the teacher. The next aim is to develop students' strategies for choice-making as regards the different tasks and to vary the context of learning to include collaborative learning opportunities.

These strategies were presented in order to provide students with the tools to learn and understand the second language they have chosen to study.

> *If you give a man a fish, you feed him for a day.*
> *If you teach a man to fish, you feed him for a lifetime.*
> Confucius (551-479 B.C.)

In the same vein as the famous proverb: strategies that permit students to learn language independently permit them to be lifelong learners.

REFERENCES

Atkinson, R.C. (1975). Mnemotechniques in second-language learning. *American Psychologist, 30*, 821-828.

Bialystok, E. (1990). *Communication Strategies.* Oxford: Basil Blackwell Ltd.

Bogaards, P. (1988). *Aptitude et affectivité dans l'apprentissage des langues étrangères.* Paris: Hatier-Crédif.

Butterworth, G. (1972). A Spanish-speaking adolescent's acquisition of English syntax. M.A. thesis, University of California at Los Angeles.

Carter, K., & Long, M. (1987). *The web of words.* Cambridge: Cambridge University Press.

Cummins, J. (1983). Language proficiency, biliteracy and French immersion, *Canadian Journal of Education, 8*, 117-137.

Deckert, H. (1994). Mental translation in advanced second language learners' grammaticality judgement. Paper given at the Second International Conference of the Association of Language Awareness. Plymouth, April.

Delaney, H. (1978). Interaction of individual differences with visual and verbal elaboration instructions. *Journal of Educational Psychology, 70*, 306-318.

Dickel, M., & Slack, S. (1983). Imagery vividness and memory for verbal motivation. *Journal of Mental Imagery, 7*, 121-125.

Dirven, R. (1974). The relevance of generative semantics for language teaching. In *Linguistic Insights in Applied Linguistics* (pp. 23-44). Brussels: AIMAV.

Ellis, G. & Sinclair, B. (1989). *Learning to learn English.* Cambridge: Cambridge University Press.

Fay, D., & Cutler, A. (1977). Malapropisms and the structure of the mental lexicon. *Linguistic Inquiry, 8*, 505-520.

Galisson, R. (1984). Pour un dictionnaire des mots de la culture populaire. *Le Français Dans Le Monde, 188*, 57-63.

Galotti, K. (1994). *Cognitive Psychology In and Out of the Laboratory.* California: Brooks/Cole Publishing.

Garner, R. (1990). When children and adults do not use learning strategies: Toward a theory of settings. *Review of educational Research, 60*(4), 517-529.

Haier, R. (1992). Talk given at a conference, U. C. Irvine, Brain Imaging Center.

Koehler, W. (1947). *Gestalt Psychology.* New York: Liveright.

Kolers, P.A., & Roediger, H.L. (1984). Procedures of mind. *Journal of Verbal Learning and Verbal Behavior, 23*, 425-449.

Lorayne, H. (1974). *How to develop a super-power memory.* New York: NAL, Signet Books.

Marslen-Wilson, W. & Tyler, L. (1980). The temporal structure of spoken language understanding. *Cognition, 8*, 1-71.

Marslen-Wilson, W. & Tyler, L. (1981). Central processes in speech understanding. *Psychological Mechanisms of Language.* London: The Royal Society and the British Academy.

Mastropieri, M., & Scruggs, T. (1991). *Teaching students ways to remember: Strategies for learning mnemonically.* Cambridge, MA: Brookline Books.

McCormack, P.D. (1977). Bilingual linguistic memory: The independence-interdependence issue revisited. In P.A. Hornby (Ed.), *Bilingualism: Psychological, social and educational implications.* New York: Academic Press.

Miller, J. (1992). *The holistic curriculum.* Toronto: OISE Press.

Minsky, M. (1975). A framework for representing knowledge. In P. Winston (Ed.), *The psychology of computer vision.* New York: McGraw Hill.

Nation, R. & McLaughlan, B. (1986). Experts and novices: an information-processing approach to the good language learner problem. *Applied Psycholinguistics, 7*, 41-56.

Nunan, D. (Ed.) (1992). *Collaborative Language Learning and Teaching.* Cambridge: Cambridge University Press.

O'Malley, J., Chamot, A., Stewner-Manzanares, G., Kupper, L., & Russo, R. (1985). Learning strategy applications with students of English as a second language. *TESOL Quarterly, 19*(3).

Paivio, A., & Begg, I. (1981). *Psychology of Language.* NJ: Prentice-Hall.

Pattison, P. (1987). *Developing Communication Skills.* Cambridge: Cambridge University Press.

Pressley, M. (1977). Children's use of the key-word method to learn simple Spanish vocabulary words. *Journal of Educational Psychology, 69*, 465-472.

Prokop, M., & Hartmetz, F. (1984). *Effective Strategies for Second Language Learning.* Unpublished manuscript.

Rivers, W., & Temperley, M. (1978). *A practical guide to the teaching of English as a second or foreign language.* New York: Oxford University Press.

Schieffelin, B.B., & Ochs, E. (1986). Language socialization. *Annual Review of Anthropology, 15*, 163-91.

Slavin, R. (1983). *Cooperative Learning.* New York: Longman.

Stein, L. (1989). Some comments on "Team teaching in Japan: The Koto-ku Project." *JALT Journal, 11*(2), 239-244.

Taylor, I. & Taylor, M. (1990). *Psycholinguistics: Learning and using language.* New Jersey: Prentice-Hall.

Woodward, T. (1992). *Ways of training.* Harlow, UK: Longman.

CHAPTER 11

Cognitive Strategies for Test-Taking

Eileen Wood • Wilfrid Laurier University
Teena Willoughby • University of Waterloo

Exams, tests, and pop quizzes are a prominent feature of the secondary school classroom. Tests come in many forms; some are formal and others informal, their presence can be expected or a surprise, and they can vary in length from short quizzes that take a few minutes to complete to extensive exams that take hours. Regardless of form or length, a quick sweep across any group of students taking a test reveals an array of responses among the students, ranging from near panic to apathy. In the majority of classrooms, no single task raises as much anxiety, stress, and general concern as does the taking of an exam or test. Tests tend to be perceived, however, as a necessary (albeit unpleasant) feature of the curriculum.

There is considerable variability in the purpose for testing. Both formal and informal tests are given to assess student achievement (Foos & Fisher, 1988). Often these tests serve a prescriptive function by allowing teachers to adapt their lessons to accommodate students' areas of weakness. Tests also can be used to determine student assignment to different instructional opportunities (advanced versus general programs) and future academic pursuits (e.g., the SAT scores for university access). Some schools have also introduced formalized "common" exams. Common exams test curriculum that is shared across different instructors and/or schools.

In general, students face heavier demands from testing as they progress through school. In some cases, the proportion of the students' grade that is derived from test scores increases from 57% in junior high school to 72% in senior years (e.g., Putnam, 1992). The form of testing also varies from pop quizzes, to tests and formal exams. Given the prevalence of tests within the secondary curriculum and their implications for academic progression, it is important to consider cognitive strategies that might improve students' test performance.

COGNITIVE UNDERPINNINGS OF TEST PERFORMANCE

Students' test performance is really a product of two related cognitive processes: encoding and retrieval. *Encoding* relates to the cognitive processes that are engaged when a student first encounters information. Most study strategies could be called encoding strategies because they help the learner to "store" information in memory. According to information processing models, this encoding procedure involves two memory systems: *short-term memory* (sometimes called working memory) and *long-term memory* (see Chapters 3 and 10 for a diagram of this basic memory model). When students want to remember information that they hear in class or read in a book, they must first make sure that they attend to the information. This initial attention to, and processing of, the information allows the material to be held in short-term memory, the memory system that involves active thinking (hence the term "working memory"). The goal, however, is for the material to be transferred to long-term memory, the system which holds information for extensive periods of time. In order for information to be stored in the long-term memory, it has to be coded. This process is similar to the type of coding that occurs in a computer. Although the text we type into the computer is in the form of alphabetical letters, the computer stores this information in a completely different form—in a binary code which can be compared to a series of "off" and "on" signals, or a series of zeros and ones. Although the code no longer physically represents its original form, it can still be "retrieved" in the form that we understand at a later time when we call up the file from memory. A similar process occurs within our own memory when we 'call up' information from our long-term memory. The information is retrieved in its coded form and translated.

Retrieval is the process that most of us consider when we think about test-taking. This process involves transferring known information from our long-term memory into our short-term memory so that it can be used to respond to present demands—namely test questions. Retrieval is partly contingent on encoding processes because the success of "finding" the stored information will depend on both the effectiveness and the kind of strategy used to "learn" the information. The effectiveness of the strategy will determine how much of the original information was stored, whereas the kind of strategy will affect how the information was stored. For example, some strategies encourage the learner to manipulate new information by elaborating, summarizing, or attaching the information to existing knowledge, whereas other strategies encourage verbatim processing. If the original information is manipulated at study, for example being placed within a hierarchy of other related concepts—it could be transformed into a semantically related form at retrieval. The following example demonstrates this type of alteration:

In a geography course, a student is learning about natural population management among the chickaree. The student is not familiar with the chickaree but is told during the course of the lesson that the chickaree is a mammal and is part of the squirrel family. The student then categorizes the chickaree as a squirrel. On a subsequent test, the student produces the more general answer "squirrel" rather than chickaree when asked about population management.

A Few Words About Encoding

As mentioned above, encoding strategies affect retrieval. Before discussing specific retrieval strategies it is important to understand how different kinds of strategies affect memory. Throughout this book there are references to mnemonic or elaboration strategies. These kinds of strategies fall under the general heading of associative strategies because they encourage the learner to relate (associate) one piece of information with another piece of information by creating some kind of link between the two items. These encoding procedures provide the learner with a "hook" or code to help them to "find" information when they look for it at retrieval (test). They serve two purposes: 1) to reduce and organize the amount of information encoded, and 2) to provide a cue to retrieve the information. The cue provided at retrieval can be a letter as in first-letter mnemonics (for example, HOMES to remember the Great Lakes: Huron, Ontario, Michigan, Erie, and Superior), an image (such as the interactive images generated for the keyword method—see Chapter 2), or part of the information (as picture adjuncts, story grammar). Whatever the cue, the strength of the association predicts whether the remaining piece of information will be retrieved. For example, when using imagery it is best if the learner generates a particularly salient or unusual image, rather than one that is underdeveloped, vague, or general. Organization can also facilitate retrieval by establishing interconnections among pieces of information. At retrieval calling up one piece of information can provide a means for accessing other related information (similar to the concept maps and network models presented in chapters 3 and 10). The encoding strategies that are reported throughout the other chapters of this book produce strong learning gains because they promote strong associations which make it easier to "find" information at retrieval.

Retrieval is also affected by the types of retrieval strategies that the student uses to access and find information in the long-term memory. Some strategies are more efficient and effective than others. This chapter will specifically examine retrieval strategies that facilitate performance in test-taking situations.

In addition, test taking is often accompanied with emotional responses that may or may not facilitate performance. This chapter will also review briefly cognitive factors related to test anxiety.

Retrieval

Although encoding and retrieval are closely related, and often interdependent, there are occasions when these two components can be separated. For example, often we find ourselves unable to generate a name, label, or word even though we know that the item was familiar, learned, and should be easily recalled. This retrieval error can often be facilitated by providing prompts. For example, if someone were trying to remember the name of the nautical instrument that is used to determine direction, you might prompt them by saying "Does it start with an S?" A simple prompt like this usually will be enough for the individual to recall the label *sextant*. Retrieval strategies are often more complicated than providing simple prompts. The retrieval strategies that facilitate memory in the classroom are usually related to the type of test that the student must write. The following section considers retrieval strategy as a function of the type of test.

RETRIEVAL TASKS: TYPES OF TESTS

Not all tests are the same. Testing formats can include any combination of the following types of questions; multiple choice, forced choice (true and false), short answer, or essay questions. The perceived difficulty of these different kinds of questions matches their cognitive demands. For example, many students perceive multiple choice and forced choice questions to be easier than essay questions (Pintrich, McKeachie & Lin, 1987; Foos & Fisher, 1988). In many cases, this belief accurately reflects lower cognitive demands imposed by multiple choice questions relative to essay questions. In other cases, the demands across these tasks are not so easy to distinguish. When "choice" questions appear to be easy, they most often reflect the cognitive demands that researchers associate with *recognition* tasks, whereas the more difficult essay questions approximate *free recall* tasks (Schmidt, 1983). Recognition memory tasks occur when the learner is provided with all of the relevant information that was presented at study and is required to identify the correct answer from a selection of available choices. Recall tasks require the learner to generate information in the absence of any cues (Pauk, 1987). Many experimental studies have demonstrated higher performance for learners who are asked to complete a recognition task relative to a recall task (e.g., Gregg, 1976), even when great effort is taken to ensure that the same information is tested in both tests. This is not to say that "choice" tests are not challenging. One concern regarding most of the literature comparing recognition and recall tests is that these studies are conducted in a laboratory setting and may not reflect the kinds of questions used in the classroom.

For example, recognition tasks conducted in the lab first present learners with information and then later test the identical information. In the classroom, however, the alternatives for multiple choice tests do not always contain verbatim presentations of the information presented at study (Lundeberg & Fox, 1991). Instead, teachers may paraphrase the information, generate an applied example, or require the students to generalize beyond the original information given. Any of these variations increase the cognitive demands of the "choice" task to the level more often associated with essay questions. Any question aimed at a verbatim level is "easier" than one at an inferential level (Foos & Fisher, 1988). Given the variability in the demands between types of questions and the level of questions, learners need to be prepared for varied retrieval demands (Schmidt, 1983). Regardless of which kind of test the learner encounters, there are some general test-taking behaviors that the student should acquire in order to enhance performance. Putnam (1992) generated the following list of general test behaviors based upon the findings of a number of researchers who tested elementary and high school students. The points suggest that students should be instructed to

   a) use their time wisely
   b) read all directions and questions carefully
   c) attempt to answer every question
   d) feel free to ask for clarification at any time that they are
      uncertain or do not fully understand a question

                                                    (Putnam, 1992, p. 20)

Multiple Choice and Other Choice Questions

Although there are many study guides that describe various procedures for enhancing performance on multiple choice tests, there is very little research that systematically examines the impact of the procedures advocated in these study guides. The specific procedures that have been tested are presented here. Two test-taking packages that have received considerable attention are SCORER (e.g., Lee & Alley, 1981) and PIRATES (Hughes, Schumaker, Deshler & Mercer, 1988). The acronyms SCORER and PIRATES represent the steps that learners should take when employing these strategies (see Table 11-1).

There is considerable overlap in the two programs although the order of steps does vary. For example, in both programs students are encouraged to prepare in advance by organizing study time and notes. Both programs encourage the student to read all of the instructions and each question carefully. Students are also encouraged to attempt to answer all questions but if they encounter difficulty when attempting an answer they are encouraged to skip the question until all of the "easier" questions are answered first. They can return to the more difficult questions later when they review their work. Secondary school students, especially those experiencing learning difficulties, benefit when taught to use either of these systematic procedures for tackling multiple choice questions (Hughes & Schumaker, 1991; Putnam, 1987). The two test-taking strategies are effective because they provide students with a systematic set of procedures to use when approaching test questions. In both strategies, the first step is for the student to generate the first-letter mnemonic that serves as the cue for the test-taking procedures. The advantage of the PIRATES program over the SCORER program is that the mnemonic also reflects the order of the steps that students should follow. In the SCORER program, students must learn the sequence of the steps in addition to the mnemonic. For example, it is important that students know that they should *Read* before they *Omit*. In general, however, the progression of procedures is the same for both programs. For simplicity, the PIRATES model is outlined here.

In the PIRATES program, the "P" stands for *Prepare to succeed*. To *prepare*, students write down the acronym (PIRATES). Students also generate a positive thought regarding their ability to do well on the test. Finally, students scan the test to determine the types of questions, ranking the sections of the exam (if there are more than one) from least to most difficult. These preparation procedures should be completed within three minutes of starting the test (Hughes & Schumaker, 1991). Students turn to the least difficult questions and are ready for step two: *inspect* the instructions. Students read the instructions and search for cue words that will help them to understand HOW and WHERE to answer the question (Hughes & Schumaker, 1991). Students then *read* the question for meaning. At this point they should search their available knowledge for relevant information (*remember*) that will help them to eliminate responses that are clearly incorrect (*reduce*). After this step students may have remembered enough information to correctly respond to the question (*answer*). If so, they select the correct response

---

Table 11-1

Comparing the SCORER and PIRATES test-taking programs.

S—schedule your time	P—prepare to succeed
C—use clue words	I—inspect the instructions
O—omit difficult questions	R—read, remember, reduce
R—read carefully	A—answer or abandon
E—estimate your answer	T—turn back
R—review your work	E—estimate
	S— survey

Adapted from Hughes (in press) and Hughes & Schumaker (1991).

(*answer*) and proceed to the next question. If not, students mark the question with an identifying symbol to indicate that they should come back to that question at a later point (*abandon*). Once on the next question, students repeat the steps that correspond to the I, R, and A of the acronym. These steps are repeated until all questions have been attempted once. Students then *turn back* to the beginning of the test and start to go through the questions that they abandoned. Sometimes the activity of completing the test will provide sufficient reminders or cues that students are now able to select an appropriate response. If students are still unable to answer the question, they use the *estimate* procedure. Estimating involves the use of guessing strategies (avoiding absolute answers, eliminating answers that have similar options, etc.) to reduce the number of options to the point where students can select one response. The final *survey* step has students review the test to ensure that all questions were answered. Although this series of steps may appear complex at first glance, secondary school students can easily acquire and execute the procedures. When tested, students instructed to use these techniques demonstrate significant grade improvements (Hughes, in press; Hughes and Schumaker, 1991).

The steps within the SCORER and PIRATES programs are also captured by a model of test-wiseness proposed and tested by Rogers and Bateson (1990). They found that test-wise secondary school students followed a particular pattern when attempting to solve multiple-choice questions. First, test-wise students read the stem of the multiple-choice question and try to connect that information with their prior knowledge. After activating relevant prior knowledge, students should examine the possible alternatives and make a surface level decision about whether any of the alternatives match with their prior knowledge. At this point, if there is no direct match, students reexamine the alternatives to see if their are any available cue words that are familiar, or if there is some partial recognition of information in the alternatives. This is a cyclical process with the learner reevaluating alternatives individually and in comparison with one another. The goal for the student is to eliminate as many alternatives as possible. Eventually, the student minimizes the choices, hopefully to one alternative. If more than one alternative remains, the learner usually selects the choice based on a match with at least some existing partial knowledge. Although some study books recommend various "guessing" strategies as an alternative to using partial knowledge (using the longest answer, when in doubt pick C, etc.) research suggests that these guessing strategies are no more effective than chance or random selection of an answer (Shatz, 1985), and this type of guessing is not the strategy of choice for test-wise students (Farr, Pritchard & Smitten, 1990; Rogers & Bateson, 1991).

Educators can facilitate students' performance on multiple choice tests by providing students some practice with the same types of questions that students should expect to find on a subsequent exam. There is evidence of practice effects when students are exposed to study questions that parallel the kinds of questions that will appear on later tests (Lundeberg & Fox, 1991). For example, if a history test involves verbatim recognition of dates, events, etc., then verbatim questions should be presented in a practice quiz or study questions. If students are required to analyze or interpret historical events, then the practice test or study questions should involve analysis or interpretation questions. In other words, it is not sufficient to tell students to expect a multiple choice test. Students must have exposure to the types of questions that will be used in order to demonstrate improved performance (Lundeberg & Fox, 1991).

Educators might also consider organizing multiple choice questions and providing students with an orienting heading for related groups of questions. Townsend, Moore, Tuck and Wilton (1990) provided university students with headings on their tests. The students found the heading useful for orienting them to the correct knowledge base, however, their overall performance was not much higher than students who did not receive headings. The effectiveness of headings on a test seems to depend on whether students have access to similar headings while encoding information. A large body of literature supports the use of headings as an organizational cue when students study (Wilhite, 1989). It is presumed that the learner can reinstantiate these headings at test as a cue for recall. Given that students recognize the value of the headings for accessing appropriate information, and that related studies demonstrate higher performance when cues are provided both at study and recall, headings may be beneficial for facilitating student performance on "choice" tests, especially if the same headings are used at study.

Short Answer/Essay Questions

Essay questions are typically perceived as being more difficult than "choice" questions (Zeidner, 1987). As a result, many students adopt more sophisticated encoding strategies at study when they expect an essay question exam rather than a multiple choice exam (Foos, 1991). When explicitly tested, students expecting a difficult essay question performed better than students expecting a difficult multiple choice exam or an easy essay or multiple choice exam. This outcome was consistent regardless of the type of test the student eventually wrote. Students who expected the hard essay question did better than all other students, even when they were actually given the other kinds of tests (easy essay, or hard or easy multiple choice) after study. It appears, then, that knowledge of essay tests encourages learners to work harder and employ more sophisticated learning strategies when studying (Foos, 1991). Specifically, experienced test writers assume that they must employ strategies that require deeper and more meaningful processing when they are expected to respond to essay questions. However, when students have limited experience, or are not given information that would lead them to expect essay questions, they must rely primarily on retrieval strategies rather than encoding strategies.

There are few retrieval strategies for essay questions that have been tested experimentally. One strategy that has received some attention is the value in constructing plans prior to writing essay answers. Plans or outlines are organized sequences of information. Students read an essay question and determine the critical information that is necessary to answer the question. Prior to writing the answer, students write out the main points and then add relevant supplementary information under these major headings. These plans/outlines can be used as a reference while writing to ensure that all relevant information is eventually included and that the information is presented in a cogent manner. When asked, students themselves acknowledge that plans/outlines are useful when writing answers because they provide structure and ensure that relevant rather than irrelevant ideas are presented (Torrance, Thomas & Robinson, 1991). The experimental support for plan/outline construction is less conclusive. When university students were given the option of constructing plans for their course exams, about 53% of the students chose to generate plans (Torrance, Thomas & Robinson, 1991). There was some evidence that the essay answers written by these students were more structured and contained fewer irrelevant details than essay answers written by students who did not construct a plan. There was, however, no difference in overall grade for students who wrote plans and those who did not. Before assuming that plans do not affect performance, it is important to note that this study did not assess whether students generated mental plans. Presumably some students at this level would be practiced enough in plan construction to generate and follow a mental plan instead of writing it down. Similarly, it is important to assess how much weight is given to structure and organization on an essay test. If structure is considered in the grading process, then plans/outlines can facilitate performance. On the other hand, if structure and the appearance of occasional irrelevant items is not important, then there may be few observable benefits from instructing students to construct plans. The structural benefits from constructing plans also matches to related research that examines the impact of organization on study and test behaviors. Generally, strategies that enhance organization are associated with increments in performance (Weinstein & Mayer, 1986). It seems then that instructing students to construct plans can be beneficial for facilitating essay answer performance.

General Points About Tests

Researchers examining students' test-taking strategies suggest that students survey exams by going through and identifying easy-to-answer questions and answering them prior to attempting more difficult questions (Lee & Alley, 1981; Hughes, Schumaker, Deshler, &

Mercer, 1988). There is also research supporting a preference for answering easy questions prior to difficult ones. Allison and Thomas (1986) compared elementary, junior and senior high school students and university students in their preference for answering items that varied in difficulty. The majority of students, at all ages, preferred easy questions first followed by difficult ones, or questions presented in a random order, relative to the presentation of difficult questions before easy ones. To make tests more comfortable and to remove one step in the test-taking routine, educators could arrange test items in an ascending order from easier to more difficult items.

ANXIETY

Test-taking performance also may be influenced by anxiety. Anxiety or stress can have a detrimental impact on test performance. Although almost all students experience some anxiety when taking tests, concern is directed toward those students who experience very high levels of anxiety. At first glance it may seem that all students who experience any anxiety should be assisted to ensure that anxiety does not impede performance. Even though anxiety often is perceived as a negative state, in small doses anxiety can assist rather than detract from performance (the Yerkes-Dodson law; Yerkes & Dodson, 1908). In fact, it appears that students who experience low levels of anxiety perform much better than students who experience no anxiety or those who experience high levels. Whereas non-anxious students fail to become involved in tasks and often perceive tasks as less important (Sarason, 1984), the presence of low levels of anxiety serves to energize and focus learners. Highly anxious students, however, are least likely to do well on tests (Deffenbacher & Deitz, 1978). Sarason (1972) argues that highly anxious students become preoccupied with thoughts about themselves and their emotions rather than attending to the test. Instead of engaging in thoughts and behaviors that are task-appropriate, highly anxious students are distracted and are unable to focus on the test they are taking (Tryon, 1980). Research divides the distractive behaviors of individuals with high anxiety into two components (Defenbacher & Dietz, 1978). The first component is the physiological response that often accompanies test-taking situations. These include elevated heart rate, sweating palms, shaking hands and nausea (Defenbacher & Deitz, 1978). This first component is often called *emotionality*. The second component, called *worry*, involves the cognitive component of anxiety. Worry describes the thoughts that students have about their performance. These thoughts can range from comparisons of their own performance with their peers to negative comments about their own memory, ability or general thoughts about failure (Sarason, 1981). Students who score high on measures of worry and emotionality also tend to score high on measures of test anxiety. Researchers suggest that it is the cognitive interference that accounts for low performance of highly anxious students (Sarason, 1984). It seems that the evaluative context of the test acts as a trigger to start test-anxious responses.

Sarason (1984) manipulated test instructions by making the test situation appear less evaluative to see if this would counteract the onset of test anxious responses. When highly anxious students were given instructions that directed them to attend to the test—for example, "Concentrate all your attention on the problems. Don't let yourself get distracted from the task" (Sarason, 1984, p. 935), they did much better than similar students who were just told that they would be tested. Even this simple reminder to stay on task facilitated performance. These instructions proved more effective globally than those intended to reassure and downplay the evaluative context of the test. Although highly anxious students did benefit somewhat from reassuring statements (e.g., "Don't worry"), these same comments had a negative impact for students with low levels of anxiety. Performance in the low-anxiety group was much lower when given reassuring comments than when they received directive comments, most probably because the reassuring comments served to minimize the importance of the test to the extent that students did not perceive it as important. Overall, simple directive statements, given prior to or throughout tests, can be used in classroom settings with students who vary in levels of anxiety. While primarily directed toward highly anxious students, these prompts also help other members of the class. Related studies have also supported the benefits of encouraging test-anxious individuals to attend to task-appropriate behaviors (e.g., Meichenbaum & Butler, 1980). In particular, this research has examined the benefits of getting students to generate their own directive prompts to modify their anxiety rather than relying on teacher-provided prompts.

Recent research, however, has suggested that the most effective interventions for test-anxious students are those that combine both the test anxiety issues mentioned above and training in study skills (Paulman & Kennelly, 1984). This line of research considers the possibility that test-anxious students are anxious because they have poor study skills and hence, know that they will perform poorly (Tobias, 1985). Their test anxiety therefore stems from the knowledge that at some point in the processing 'chain', encoding or retrieval, their skills will not permit them to perform at a high level (Benjamin, McKeachie, Lin, & Holinger, 1981). To combat the cyclical progression of anxiety and poor skills, researchers now suggest that programs should include anxiety-reduction techniques (e.g., stress inoculation, desensitization, relaxation, etc.), redirection of attention (prompts to orient students to task behaviors), and training in study skills. These three components each address one concern about test-anxious students. The anxiety-reduction techniques decrease the physiological interference, whereas redirection prompts correct for interference from intrusive thoughts. Study-skills training provides students with support by extending their strategic repertoires and encouraging them to become more effective learners. Highly anxious students typically select low-level strategies (i.e., verbatim repetition) rather than strategies that encourage deeper and more meaningful processing of information (Benjamin et al., 1981). Therefore, their learning is less efficient at encoding and less effective at retrieval. Elaborative, organizational, and mnemonic strategies that promote deeper processing (e.g., Weinstein, 1983), like those presented throughout this book, serve to enhance the skills of highly anxious learners, which in turn makes the testing situation less worrisome.

SUMMARY

It is not uncommon for students to base their study behavior on the perceived difficulty of the type of test they are expecting. The literature would suggest that students typically expect greater difficulty from essay exams than they do from choice exams, and that this results in differential study techniques for the different kinds of tests. The problem with this thinking is that choice exams are not necessarily easier than essay exams. In fact, when questions involve application and inference, choice questions can parallel the level of difficulty most often associated with essay exams. Educators need to be sensitive to students' perceptions about the level of difficulty and should encourage their students to consider the *level* of difficulty of the questions more than the *type* of questions. Knowing the level of difficulty will make students better able to select appropriate study strategies. In this chapter we highlighted retrieval/test strategies rather than focusing on the encoding strategies presented in other chapters in the book. Ideally, students should have a repertoire of strategies that include both encoding and retrieval techniques to maximize learning gains.

In addition, effective test-taking strategies should include techniques that reduce anxiety as well as facilitate cognitive performance. Ideally, the more information students have about the test that they will take, the easier it will be for them to execute appropriate encoding and retrieval strategies and the less anxiety they will experience. Educators also should encourage students to regulate both their cognitive and affective test behaviors with the goal of becoming more self-directed in their learning.

Suggested Readings

For constructing exams:
> Scruggs, T.E. & Mastropieri, M.A. (1992). *Teaching test-taking skills: Helping students show what they know*. Cambridge, MA: Brookline Books.

For improving student study skills:
Scheid, K. (1993). *Helping students become strategic learners: Guidelines for teaching.* Cambridge, MA: Brookline Books.

REFERENCES

Allison, D., & Thomas, D. (1986). Item-difficulty sequence in achievement examinations: Examinees' preferences and test-taking strategies. *Psychological Reports, 59,* 867-870.

Benjamin, M., McKeachie, W., Lin, Y-G., & Holinger, D. (1981). Test anxiety: Deficits in information processing. *Journal of Educational Psychology, 73,* 816-824.

Deffenbacher, J., & Deitz, S. (1978). Effects of test anxiety on performance, worry, and emotionality in naturally occurring exams. *Psychology in the Schools, 15,* 446-450.

Farr, R., Pritchard, R., & Smitten, B. (1990). A description of what happens when an examinee takes a multiple-choice reading comprehension test. *Journal of Educational Measurement, 27,* 205-226.

Foos, P. (1991). Test performance as a function of expected form and difficulty. *Journal of Experimental Education, 60,* 205-211.

Foos, P., & Fisher, R.P. (1988). Using tests as learning opportunities. *Journal of Educational Psychology, 80*(2), 179-183.

Gregg, V. (1976). Word frequency, recognition, and recall. In J. Brown (Ed.), *Recall and recognition* (pp. 183-216). New York: Wiley.

Hughes, C.A. (in press). Memory and test-taking strategies. In G. Alley & D. Deshler (Eds.), *Strategies and Methods for Adolescents with Learning Disabilities.* Denver, CO: Love.

Hughes, C.A., & Schumaker, J. (1991). Test-taking strategy instruction for adolescents with learning disabilities. *Exceptionality, 2,* 205-221.

Hughes, C.A., Schumaker, J., Deshler, D., & Mercer, C. (1988). *The test-taking strategy.* Lawrence, KS: Excellenterprises, Inc.

Lee, P. & Alley, G. (1981). *Training junior high LD students to use a test-taking strategy* (Research Report No. 38). Lawrence, KS: University of Kansas Institute for Research in Learning Disabilities.

Lundeberg, M., & Fox, P. (1991). Do laboratory findings on test expectancy generalize to classroom outcomes? *Review of Educational Research, 61,* 94-106.

Meichenbaum, D., & Butler, L. (1980). Toward a conceptual model for the treatment of test anxiety: Implications for research and treatment. In I. Sarason (Ed.), *Test anxiety: Theory, research and applications* (pp. 187-208). Hillsdale, NJ: Erlbaum.

Pauk, W. (1987). *Study skills for community and junior colleges.* Clearwater, FL: Reston-Stuart.

Paulman, R.G., & Kennelly, K.J. (1984). Test anxiety and ineffective test taking: Different names, same construct? *Journal of Educational Psychology, 76,* 279-288.

Pintrich, P.R., McKeachie, W.J., & Lin, Y-G. (1987). Teaching a course in learning to learn. *Teaching of Psychology, 14,* 81-86.

Putnam, L. (1992). The testing practices of mainstream secondary classroom teachers. *Remedial and Special Education, 13,* 11-21.

Rogers, W., & Bateson, D. (1991). Verification of a model of test-taking behavior of high school seniors. *Journal of Experimental Education, 60,* 331-350.

Sarason, I. (1972). Experimental approaches to test anxiety: Attention and the uses of information. In C.D. Spielberger (Ed.), *Anxiety: Current trends in theory and research,* Vol. 2. New York: Academic Press.

Sarason, I. (1981). Test anxiety, stress, and social support. *Journal of Personality, 49,* 101-114.

Sarason, I. (1984). Stress, anxiety, and cognitive interference: Reactions to tests. *Journal of Personality and Social Psychology, 46,* 929-938.

Schmidt, S. (1983). The effects of recall and recognition test expectancies on the retention of prose. *Memory and Cognition, 11,* 172-180.

Shatz, M. (1985). Students' guessing strategies: Do they work? *Psychological Reports, 57,* 1167-1168.

Tobias, S. (1985). Test anxiety: Interference,

defective skills, and cognitive capacity. *Educational Psychologist, 20,* 135-142

Torrance, M., Thomas, G., & Robinson, E. (1991). Strategies for answering examination essay questions: Is it helpful to write a plan? *British Journal of Educational Psychology, 61,* 46-54.

Townsend, M., Moore, D., Tuck, B., & Wilton, K. (1990). Headings within multiple-choice tests as facilitators of test performance. *British Journal of Educational Psychology, 60,* 153-160.

Tryon, G. (1980). The measurement and treatment of test anxiety. *Review of Educational Research, 58,* 352-372.

Weinstein, C. (1983). *Learning and study strategies inventory.* Austin, TX: University of Texas.

Weinstein, C.E., & Mayer, R.E. (1986). *The teaching of learning strategies.* New York: Macmillan.

Wilhite, S. (1989). Headings as memory facilitators: The importance of prior knowledge. *Journal of Educational Psychology, 81,* 115-117.

Yerkes, R.M., & Dodson, J.D. (1908). The relation of strength of stimulus to rapidity of habit formation. *Journal of Comparative Neurological Psychology, 18,* 459-482.

Zeidner, M. (1987). Essay versus multiple-choice type classroom exams: The students' perspective. *Journal of Educational Research, 80,* 352-358.

CHAPTER 12

Strategies for Students with Learning Disabilities

Zoe L. Hayes • St. Francis Xavier University

Many of the suggestions in this chapter have been developed from interviews with academically successful learning disabled students, students who have reached the university level and are coping and passing. They have described their struggles, and successes, and tried to articulate the strategies and circumstances which have made it possible for them to reach college in spite of their learning problems. By listening to their stories, it is possible to gain a sense of those factors which were important in the success of these students. By keeping those factors in mind we may be able to encourage and help more such individuals to reach for post secondary education and others to reach something closer to their full potential. Because the students interviewed have been promised anonymity, the descriptions which appear in this chapter are composites, and the names are false, although the words quoted are as they were spoken by individuals.

To Set the Stage

Let us consider three adolescents as they might appear in your class:

- Robert seems bright and articulate and is an active participant in class, answering questions thoughtfully. You are astonished to find that his written work is not only almost illegible, but is disorganized, difficult to follow, and often not even of passing quality.
- Ken has very hesitant speech, and appears to be slow to take in what you say. He has great difficulty remembering lecture information. He is uncoordinated, and has trouble with directions, frequently getting lost. You wonder if he may be a slow learner. However, when asked to research information in the library, he can produce well thought-out written work, with an obvious grasp of key principles,

although his spelling and grammar may require correction.
- Sherry is a gifted musician, sight reading music fluently and showing a depth of understanding of the music beyond her years. She has been very good with arithmetic and is expected to be an above-average math student in high school. However, she has had remedial help with reading since the second grade, and takes a very long time to gather information from print. She often misunderstands what she reads and is very reluctant to read aloud in front of others. However, she seldom forgets what she hears in class or directions given orally.

All three of the students described above have learning problems and may be considered learning disabled. However, the term learning disabled means different things to different people.

Since the 1960s, the professional literature has reflected an interest in children who appear to be of normal intelligence but somehow have significant difficulty with some aspect of learning—reading, writing, spelling, or arithmetic—with no apparent explanation for their difficulties. Many parents and professionals began to argue that although these children manifested many of the problems which were seen in children who had been labelled mentally retarded, they were not retarded and, therefore, should be treated differently within the educational system. When Samuel Kirk suggested the term *learning disabled* in 1963 to describe such children, parents adopted it with enthusiasm, and the Association for Children with Learning Disabilities was born in Chicago (Kirk, 1976). Since that time a great deal of research has accumulated, and psychologists and educators certainly have a much greater understanding of the processes involved in learning, but there is still confusion about what we mean by the term *learning disability*. In addition, there are many other terms which have been used to describe such students: *dyslexic, brain injured, suffering from minimal brain dysfunction* or *attention deficit disorder*, *perceptually handicapped*, and so on. Although these terms hold special and precise meaning for certain professionals, for many laypersons they are ill-defined, adding to the confusion.

What is clear is that there is a subset of students who perform adequately or better in many areas, appear to be of normal intelligence and cannot be termed educationally or socially disadvantaged, but have significant difficulties with some forms of learning. This discrepancy between aptitude and achievement is a key characteristic of learning disabled students. When these students are tested by professionals, they frequently display an uneven pattern of development, with good skills in some areas and dramatically poor skills in others. The definitional problem arises because the pattern of strengths and weaknesses varies from child to child. Many learning disabled students have reading difficulties, but not all. Others have problems with oral or written expression, or difficulty memorizing, or weaknesses in attending or perceiving, or perhaps combinations of various difficulties. The term *learning disability* thus encompasses many different kinds of learning problems, and its victims are a widely disparate group. If we assume that the term refers to only one kind of learning problem, we will fail to recognize many of these students. However, if we take as our defining feature for a learning disability difficulty in some aspect of learning with an uneven pattern of development, coupled with the appearance of normal intelligence and little evidence that might explain the difficulties that the student exhibits, we will much more readily identify these students.

In the examples above, Robert has a good spoken vocabulary and seems to think on his feet, but has serious difficulty organizing ideas for a written presentation. People are surprised to find he has difficulty writing. Ken has the reverse problem: he is able to produce reasonable written work, but has serious difficulty when required to produce or take in orally presented information. Ken may be tagged as slow and written off by someone who does not look far enough, yet his performance IQ on a standardized test was above average. Sherry has a reading problem, experiencing difficulty in extracting information from printed text, although she can read music with ease, is comfortable with numbers and arithmetic operations, and has a better than average memory for orally-presented information. If each of these students were formally tested, the reports would undoubtedly indicate a much more detailed pattern of strengths and weaknesses, suggesting things such as difficulty with written expressive language, spatial orientation, auditory memory, or verbal receptive language, with strengths in other areas. Whether they are officially labelled learning disabled, and whether they receive specialized assistance, will depend on the serious-ness of their difficulties and possibly the availability of services for such children in their particular educational jurisdictions. Further, the effects of their difficulties on their academic performance will be differentially influenced by personal and social factors.

Rawson (1978) organized the factors that contribute to human learning in a very helpful hierarchy. This hierarchy can still assist us to understand the various ways that a child may be learning disabled and alert us to the types of difficulties these students may exhibit. Given that basic physical and social needs are met, basic sensory capacities must be there; that is, vision, hearing and motor control must be adequate to take in information from the world around us and produce a response. However, some children do not take in information as we might expect them to, even though their senses may not show deficits. For example, they may seem to have difficulty with perceptual tasks although their visual or hearing acuity tests within normal bounds. Rawson indicated that this may "have to do with perceptual intake, motor ability, activity level, emotional response, or a combination of these and other factors" (p. 53). Although these are considered noncognitive, such difficulties may have an impact on the learning in any area. Children classed as perceptually disordered, or hyperactive, or suffering from attention deficit disorder would be placed at this level.

At another level, interferences with learning that occur at the thinking, rather than the perceptual level, may not be language-related (e.g., difficulties with spatial organization, poor directional sense, difficulty with auditory sequencing, or memory problems) but frequently affect language abilities. Ken, described above, is just such an individual. His testing showed that he had serious difficulty with auditory sequencing as well as a poor auditory memory. You can understand why he would have trouble taking in lecture information. His memory for orally presented material is not good, and he has trouble sorting out the order in which such material is presented.

Finally, Rawson (1978) discussed learning problems which are specific to language. Figure 12-1 is an adaptation of a diagram offered by Rawson which helps to clarify the interactive role of the various capacities which must be in place for adequate learning and language function. The diagram lists many of the inner perceptual-cognitive processes which underlie all functioning. You can see that the inner processes can influence language function, but that problems with inner processes can also influence performance that is not language-related. Some learning disabled individuals may have difficulty with directions, or spatial tasks, or some aspects of remembering, but be able to read, write, speak and listen reasonably well. These students may have less serious problems in the classroom than those who have difficulties with language. It could also be that those with language-related problems may have no difficulty with perceptual tasks. In the model in Figure 12-1, verbal language is subdivided into two dimensions, *auditory-visual* and *receptive-expressive*, creating the four aspects of verbal language: listening, speaking, reading and writing. It is possible to have difficulty with only one modality, say the auditory, which would then affect listening or speaking. Similarly, a person who has trouble with expressive language would be most handicapped when speaking or writing. Ken is unfortunate to be handicapped in both the receptive and expressive auditory dimensions. Sometimes, the difficulty will be much greater in, or confined only to, one modality. Robert appears to have his greatest difficulty in the area of visual, expressive language (i.e., writing).

In your classroom you may have students who present such varied patterns of skill, although they have not been formally labelled as learning disabled. Some of those diagnosed as learning disabled may have had access to special assistance for some years and be quite sophisticated about the techniques and strategies which will work for them. Others may be limping along, with little idea how to deal with their problems although they have had some remediation help in the past. Still others may not have been formally identified because their difficulties are only just becoming apparent as educational demands are increased, or they are not seriously enough affected to have been appropriate candidates for special services. Ideally, there will be information available on those students who have been previously

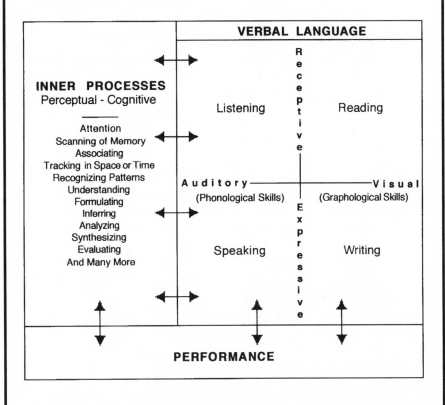

Figure 12-1
The Relationship Between Inner Processes,
Verbal Language and Performance.

identified as learning disabled, and often an individual program plan will have been drawn up. Often students will have experienced resource withdrawal in their elementary schools. This involves having a teacher trained to deal with the specialized problems of the educationally handicapped take the student from the regular classroom for sessions which are focused on the student's particular difficulty, be it reading, arithmetic, or perception. These resource teachers assist the students with their regular work so that the skills that are taught are transferred to classroom learning. Often resource teachers teach the student strategies for getting around certain problems. Unfortunately, this kind of assistance is not always available, particularly at the secondary level. This chapter is focused particularly on suggestions for helping adolescent students who appear to have specific difficulties that prevent them from performing as they should, even though they may not be diagnosed as learning disabled. It is intended for the content area teacher who wishes to help as many students as possible.

Environment for Adolescents with LD

As students enter adolescence, they are often faced with major changes in the school system. Typically, elementary school children have one main teacher who carries the responsibility for organizing the curriculum, coordinating the lessons, and maintaining contact with home. Home base is a classroom that contains all the students' books, supplies, and resource materials. Suddenly, not only are teachers expecting more, but transition to a junior high or high school may mean rotating classes for the first time and having to deal with several different teachers, rather than one key teacher with a few resource teachers who come into the home classroom. Every new teacher has a different style of interaction, different expectations, and different methods of organizing material. They all demand a portion of the student's day, and cannot be dealt with through one key teacher. In addition, students may be expected to move from room to room, and maintain a schedule as they do so. Further, the move to junior high or high school may mean that the specialized services that were available to learning disabled students are no longer there. Many jurisdictions have mainstreamed their special classes, and a student who is accustomed to being in a special class may now be involved in mixed classes. Others may experience resource withdrawal for the first time. Not only is adolescence a time of great physical, personal, and social change (Powers, Hauser, & Kilner, 1989), but this is frequently occurring within a changing environment.

Imagine yourself as a Robert, Ken or Sherry, moving into a larger school with other students who are strangers, and facing new teachers who have increased academic expectations at a time when peer influence is paramount, and when you are anxious to be popular, confused and excited by your feelings toward members of the opposite sex, and perhaps subject to wild emotional swings. At a time when conformity is extremely important, the possibility that your learning difficulties may lead to you being thought of as different can be very intimidating and may affect both your social interactions and your performance at school. If you are easily distracted or unable to attend to important stimuli, the potential to be distracted may have increased exponentially and your performance will suffer accordingly. Adolescence is even more trying for these students.

Several of the students interviewed talked with emotion about their first weeks in secondary schools.

> "I missed several classes because I got lost and was late and afraid to go in after the door was shut. I felt like an idiot. Thank goodness for my English teacher. He figured out what was happening and helped me understand the layout of the

school by drawing some maps."

"The first few weeks were agony. I couldn't remember the schedule, brought the wrong books to class, couldn't find the gym. I was sure that everyone thought I was a real dummy. It was hell."

"The teachers expected us to do things that we had never been taught. I couldn't remember what my assignments were and didn't know enough to keep a list. I tried to sit at the back of classes and shrank down in the seat when the teacher was asking questions. I wanted to drop out of school several times a day."

These difficulties are typical of those faced by many secondary students in the first few weeks. The difference for many learning disabled students is that they may have a much more difficult time adjusting to change in routine and in learning from these new experiences. Note the comment in the first quotation which refers to a teacher who identified the problem the student was having in finding his way around the school and provided valuable assistance. This student might have continued to have directional difficulties for some time without that assistance.

COGNITIVE CHALLENGES

The increased academic demands which all adolescents face on entering secondary school may be exceptionally difficult for those with learning disorders. It is assumed at this level that every child can carry out rapid, independent and accurate reading, and write and spell adequately. The student is expected to process volumes of information rapidly and efficiently, and often, to teach him or herself details. There is often an assumption that all students have adequate study skills and know how to tackle the assignments and tasks assigned to them. The rules of school have changed dramatically. Even with average intelligence and a strong desire to master the information, learning disabled adolescents may find that it seems almost impossible to perform at the same level as their peers in content-based subjects such as science, math, history and English taught at the secondary level. They need help to understand what is required of them, guidance in the best ways to tackle the tasks, and assistance in using the strengths they have to get around their weaknesses. Students who are not learning disabled can also benefit from this kind of instruction. For example, many students who attain admission to university start to flounder because they use inappropriate study strategies. Many secondary teachers assume that students will learn how to study without instruction. Unfortunately this is not a safe assumption, and we frequently see students performing well below their capabilities because they do not know the most effective way to tackle the material (Garner, 1992). Efforts to assist all students to improve study strategies will not be wasted.

GENERAL STRATEGIES TO IMPROVE PERFORMANCE

The strategies discussed here may benefit all students in content-based classes, but can be particularly effective for learning disabled students. Dillon (1986) has indicated that low and average performers benefit most from strategy instruction and that good students may be hindered if the strategies introduced conflict with their already competent tactics. This finding addresses the need to introduce strategies with concern for the individual strengths of the students. Keeping this in mind, Jeff's story serves to illustrate some general strategies that all teachers might introduce to appropriate students. When Jeff was interviewed, he was just finishing his second year of college. His grades were in the 60 to 70 range.

Jeff was diagnosed as dyslexic in the fifth grade. His parents, who were professionals and ambitious for their children, were told that he might not be able to complete secondary school and to prepare him for a low-level blue collar job. The report indicated that he had a below-average verbal IQ, although his performance IQ was slightly above average. He had great difficulty in comprehending order or sequence, and his reading skills were over two years below his grade level. He was placed in a special class over the protests of his parents, who were convinced that his understanding and interests were well above both the level of his reading and the level of instruction he would receive in that class. At that point, he became an increasingly difficult student, and there were two years where the records indicate that Jeff was considered a troublesome, slow student. During this period, his mother coached him at home, searching out reading material that was easier but that provided the required content. She also worked especially hard to help him with sequencing problems: number series, time, dates, instructions. This additional help paid off: By the eighth grade Jeff was passing, although he had to spend much longer studying than his fellow students. His reading skills still tested well below his grade level.

He entered secondary school with a great deal of apprehension. It was Jeff who missed classes because he couldn't find the classrooms fast enough. It was Jeff's English teacher who rescued him, in several ways.

> Mr. B. was great. After he realized that I had a problem with directions he sat down and talked to me about school. I told him I was dyslexic and he really seemed to be interested in what that meant. He even called my mom and talked to her. After that, he always made sure that I understood what the

assignments were without making a big deal about it. I seemed to be able to follow what was going on in his classes. He listed the day's lecture topics on the board in the order he was going to talk about them. He always gave us a handout with instructions for assignments, and explained them too. The handouts always seemed easier to read than some from other classes, maybe because he used drawings and jokes. We didn't just read the stories, he read some to us, and we acted out parts, and did a whole bunch of stuff that really helped me understand what was going on. Sometimes he brought in videotapes of the plays or had us pretend to be a character in a story. He gave us a way of working on the stories and we used that over and over so that now I use it even when I see a movie. I ask myself questions like 'What are the internal influences acting on that character?' I always had a hard time keeping up with the reading assignments but I didn't mind doing extra work 'cause I really felt that I was learning. He made me feel that I could do it. I might not have finished high school if Mr. B. hadn't been around in ninth grade.

Jeff's story illustrates several strategies which were helpful to Jeff, and probably to all the students in that English class. Mr. B took the trouble to spend some time getting to know Jeff and discussing his problems. Once he had an idea what Jeff's difficulties were, he made a point of checking to make sure that Jeff had appropriate understanding to carry out assignments. But he did other things that were helpful too. He emphasized the structure of his lectures by listing the lecture topics. He also attempted to maintain interest by varying the classroom activities and providing more than one approach to the material being studied. And he provided a pattern for analyzing the stories and used it repeatedly. Even dyslexic Jeff was gradually able to assimilate that pattern to the point that he can apply it to material from a different medium, films, several years later. Much of what this teacher did was part of his regular teaching style, but it was particularly helpful to Jeff.

From this account we can derive several general strategies for helping all students, and learning disabled students in particular, to succeed in your classes.

(a) Get to know the special idiosyncrasies of your students. If you can understand the particular difficulties that the learning disabled students have, you are in a position to step in before they get in to serious trouble. Knowing past educational history, the learning style, the strengths and weaknesses of every student, but particularly students with learning difficulties, makes it easier to plan classes which involve the students and take into account their special needs. Knowing that Jeff is dyslexic alerted Mr. B to potential problem areas.

(b) All students get restless, but some learning disabled students have particularly short attention spans (Krupski, 1986). Vary activities within a classroom period. This is typically done with younger children but by the time students reach secondary school we often expect them to remain alert and interested while we talk at them for 40 to 60 minutes. Moving to discussion groups or an activity will often revive flagging interest, and bring back attention to the topic. Varying activities also gives students who may learn better in other than a lecture situation an opportunity to grasp the material more quickly. Morgan (1983) argues for a multisensory approach which stimulates all channels, auditory, visual and tactile, and provides examples of hands-on activities which help the students at any level, and in a variety of subjects, move from the concrete to the abstract. Mr. B used a varied approach to the stories on his curriculum so that students like Jeff, who had trouble reading, could pick up information. One way to vary activities is to use different types of media (print, audio, television and film, and computers, including video games) in your teaching (see Chapter 9, this volume, for computer applications). Greenfield (1987) makes a strong case that each form of medium emphasizes and develops particular cognitive skills and that our emphasis on print does not recognize that there are other kinds of literacy. A variety of media provides students with deficits in one area an opportunity to acquire and process information another way, as well as providing practice in the deficit area.

(c) Some students absorb print better than oral instruction, others the reverse (Dunn, 1990; Burke Guild, 1989). This is particularly true of learning disabled students. Students have been shown to remember significantly more material when it was introduced through their perceptual preference (Dunn, 1990). Griggs (1990) suggests that it is also possible to help students develop effective study skills related to their learning styles, and provides case histories to illustrate her points. Providing instructions in both print and oral format makes it possible for students to acquire information in the manner that they learn best. Mr. B used handouts, but also explained them.

(d) Handouts not only let you present your material in both verbal and graphic visual form, but also give you an opportunity to graphically reflect the intellectual process which the students must follow to absorb the content. Clarke (1991) argues for using what he calls *visual organizers*, graphic representations of various thinking processes in the form of diagrams such as time lines, concept maps, causal chains, and flow charts (see Chapters 3, 8 and 10, this volume, for examples). He argues that such organizers give the students an opportunity to represent what they know and to practice higher level reasoning. Several examples should be provided which are appropriate for various kinds of material.

The way handouts are laid out can be very important. Any student may have difficulty making sense of handouts that are crowded and poorly organized. Information set off in white space always stands out better (Hartley, 1985). Make sure that material you give to students is legible, and arranged so that information can be readily extracted. Hartley's book, *Designing Instructional Text*, provides many suggestions for making instructional materials more understandable. Jeff tells us that Mr. B. added drawings and cartoons, which would certainly stimulate interest, but it is very probable that the information was well spaced, clearly legible, and uncluttered, as well.

(e) Students learning to take notes need help to do this in an organized fashion. One way is to provide them with a list of headings for the topics you will cover in any given lecture, as Mr. B did, or for an upcoming assignment. Such advance organizers can serve to clearly introduce the lecture or assignment so that the students take clearer notes and learn the information better (Lenz, Alley, & Schumaker, 1987). Research has shown that students often try to record material verbatim and, as a result, take notes that are relatively incomplete (Kiewra, 1987). Instruction in notetaking that clarifies the process and function of notetaking can assist students in capturing the main points of a lecture and encourage them to integrate and reorganize the material at a later date. Kiewra suggests that instructors should organize their presentations to facilitate notetaking, while considering the individual differences among students. Instruction in notetaking will be useful for all students, but may be particularly helpful for a student with auditory processing difficulties. Providing the student with a structure and format within which to place his/her notes may free up valuable processing capacity to permit the student to reflect on the material (see Chapter 3 of this volume for information about notetaking instruction).

(f) It is impossible to process and remember information effectively if we cannot see the underlying patterns. Even when the pattern is clear to the instructor, many students may not pick it up unless specifically shown. If I ask you to memorize an 11-digit number (say 19028672469), it is unlikely that it will stay with you very long. However, if I tell you that these 11 digits represent a phone number, which leads you to break them into smaller "chunks," they become easier to remember (1-902-867-2469) (Miller, 1956). And if the area code or exchange is meaningful, perhaps your own calling area, then you will remember this number for much longer. Johnson (1975) said that "meaningfulness is potentially the most powerful variable for explaining the learning of complex verbal discourse" (pp. 425-426). By giving meaning to the information that the students are trying to process, we make the task easier. By providing pattern and structure it becomes easier to remember the facts because the facts now fit within that structure. This is done by repeating themes with different material and expecting them to apply the themes to new material. Jeff's English teacher provided a framework for understanding stories which he then helped students to apply to many different readings. This became such a well-learned pattern that even Jeff was able to store it for permanent use.

(g) A major problem for many learning disabled students is organization. Successful study skills depend on organization (Smith, 1991). Britton and Tesser (1991) have shown that short-range planning skills and attitudes toward time were better predictors of cumulative grade point average than Scholastic Aptitudes Test (SAT) scores. Further, Weissberg, Berentsen, Cote, Cravey, and Heath (1982) found that two-thirds of their sample of undergraduates believed that their most important need was to learn effective time management methods. Similarly, Cowen's (1988) study of coping strategies of college students with learning disabilities found that time management and scheduling, along with regular class attendance, were important to the success of these students. At times, poor organizational skills may be a student's only apparent problem. This is the student who pulls out a homework sheet rumpled and covered with jam, or has lost it; who forgets that the assignment was due today; whose notebook is in tatters, with papers peeking out on all sides; who does only part of an assignment and forgets the rest; and who is frequently late. These individuals need to be taught how to structure their time and their activities. For example, they may not know enough to make lists, or to check off completed activities. They may not have enough sense of the passage of time to understand that it will be impossible to fit all they have planned into the day. Instruction in organizing a calendar of activities is invaluable for these students, and should help any student who needs to improve time management. In addition, it is important that you model good organization so that they can see it in action.

Working with Specific Students

This section will describe some of the learning disabled university students who are coping successfully with the academic tasks required of them. Each has a different type of learning problem, and each has derived different ways of dealing with his/her problems. What links them is the use of their strengths to help them conquer the difficulties created by their weaknesses. Their deficits cannot be removed, but they can perform adequately when they develop a correct strategy.

Margie has similar problems to Sherry who was described earlier. She is dyslexic but a gifted musician. She was interviewed while working toward a B.A. in Music and hopes to have a career as a jazz musician, both composing and performing. Her performance classes have been no problem for her, but she has experienced great difficulty with courses such as History of Music, and with elective courses which require a great deal of reading. With the help of a campus counsellor who became a valuable ally, she has evolved several strategies to help her with these courses. One advantage she has is an excellent memory for material presented orally (good auditory memory). She uses that memory in reviewing her class notes as soon as possible after class so that she can fill in areas where her notes are sketchy. She then uses the notes to guide her reading, searching out expressions and terms used by the professor in the lecture. Often she reads material aloud to herself because she finds that it will make more sense than if she reads silently. When the material she must read is complex, and she is having a particularly difficult time making sense of it, she has two friends who are willing to read it into a tape recorder so that she can hear the words while she looks at the text. She also checks the notes she makes from readings with someone in the same course to ensure that she has not radically misunderstood what she read.

Her most interesting strategy involves using her knowledge of music. Because she has difficulty remembering information that she has read, she tries to develop mnemonics that link the information to music. One example was her habit of tying a string of facts to melodies which she created from the first letters of key words signifying items in a list of facts she had to recall for a test. When the time came to reproduce the information the topic name would trigger the melody, and the individual notes would trigger the key words which she was then able to use to develop the points she wished to make. Music has been shown to be an aid to memory for average subjects (Chazin and Neuschatz, 1990). Both their younger and older subjects were able to remember information about minerals presented in song better than when the same information was presented in a lecture. Margie's mnemonic strategy is similar to the first-letter mnemonic discussed in Chapter 2 of this volume. Further information on mnemonics developed for use in special education is provided by Scruggs and Mastropieri (1990). Music also helps Margie if she has to deal with complex ideas with many layers of interaction. She relates them to complex musical structures which she has no difficulty understanding, linking the levels of meaning to the levels of theme development in the music. But using music is not the only way that Margie has helped her situation. With the help of the counsellor she has become an advocate for herself and was able to arrange for extra time for exams to compensate for her reading difficulties. In some courses, she was able to have the exams read to her so that she could take advantage of her strong auditory memory.

Kevin also has a reading problem, although not as severe as Margie's, and his writing skills are very weak. He was placed in a special reading group in second grade, tagged as "talented but lazy" in sixth grade, and placed in an Industrial Arts program (for slow learners) when he entered high school. Professional testing in tenth grade identified him as dyslexic, dysgraphic (a disabled writer), with difficulties in spelling, grammar, and spatial relations. However, his visual recognition was good, he displayed an exceptional auditory memory, and he showed an exceptional ability to integrate information from several sources. Often he could supply oral answers to other students although he could not write them himself.

Kevin was interviewed during his last year of an honors degree in political science, where he had to maintain an average of 70. He later graduated in the top third of his class. Based on his conversation, it is difficult to believe that this man would have any form of learning disability. He is extremely articulate, and talks well on many topics. He argues effectively, drawing on a wide range of learning to make his points. In class, he made a strong and effective contribution to class discussion. All his instructors expressed astonishment when they saw the first piece of written work that he produced for their classes. In many cases it was almost unintelligible. We found it hard to accept that a person who could manipulate ideas so well orally could have so much trouble putting those ideas in good, grammatical, written words. Probably Kevin's most effective strategy has been to use his 'gift of the gab' effectively to become an advocate for himself. Once he established that he could keep up with the work and understood the ideas and issues in a class, he would approach the instructor to explain his difficulty. He was often able to successfully negotiate oral examinations and altered assignments which still challenged his intellectual abilities but did not require so much writing. Where writing was required he would ask to submit an early draft and do so well ahead of any deadlines. Sometimes he was able to do this more than once.

In order to get his ideas organized for a paper, he would do what he called a "dump." After reading (sometimes aloud) as many sources as he could for the topic, he would be "jammed up with ideas" and "talk them into a dictaphone." He'd then have this transcribed into a word processing program to make the basis for his paper. Once he had amended this document into a form he thought was acceptable, he recruited help from fellow students and friends to go over his grammar. The use of the computer permitted the correction of his many errors without extensive retyping, and allowed him to take advantage of spell-checking programs. His honors degree required that he write a thesis in his senior year. His advisor has commented that Kevin's document is probably the worst written thesis in the history of that department, but that it contains the most complex and challenging treatment of issues that anyone has yet presented.

Kevin's ability to draw on the abilities of his fellow students points up the value of using the strength of other students to help those who have learning disabilities. Johnson and Johnson (1982, 1985) have shown that increased productivity and positive attitude change results from placing students of varying abilities in cooperative groups. They suggest that both social and cognitive development are maximized through association with a broad range of peers. Peer tutoring is another strategy which has been found useful to help individualize instruction in the classroom (Good & Brophy, 1984). Both Margie and Kevin were able to draw on the superior skills of their friends in areas where each of them was weak. The evidence is that the both the tutor and the tutored student benefit from this interaction (Good & Brophy, 1986). Kevin's use of the dictaphone or tape recorder, and the transcription to a computer to get his many thoughts on paper, shows the value of being alert to the many ways which technology can be of help to these students. Sitko (1986) has discussed developments in computer technology and how they can assist the special student, and provides an extensive checklist for evaluating computer software for classroom use, as well as a valuable list of references on the use of computers with special needs students.

Our third student is John. He failed fifth grade and was placed in a resource program with little change in his performance. He then moved to a different school, where reading problems were identified, and was put into a reading resource program. At the same time he was identified as being hyperactive and for a brief period was medicated. There was some improvement although it was not maintained. He managed to barely pass each year but received no extra help until twelfth grade, after formal testing near the end of the previous year had identified him as learning disabled. In his last year of high school he received individual tutoring from a resource teacher and was permitted to use a note-taker in class. His grades improved enough that he was accepted into college on a trial basis. Our conversation took place during his second year.

John still has difficulty maintaining attention and is easily distracted. In addition, he finds it difficult to keep his notes organized when he has to listen and write at the same time. He often cannot remember the material well enough to clarify the notes later. Because of these difficulties, he continues to use a note-taker: a person who is enrolled in the same class, using special forms that automatically create a second copy. This permits John to concentrate on what the lecturer is saying. When he can focus his attention his auditory memory is quite good. He also has his textbooks read to audiotape, a service provided by a nearby university. He is then able to listen and read (both receptive skills) at the same time, a combination that helps him to focus his attention. In some classes, such as English and Philosophy, he combines listening and reading to mark his textbook as the instructor emphasizes material. In order to remember the ideas and issues, he makes a point of discussing them with his friends in the same classes. He remarked that several friends have come to "appreciate these talk sessions as ways of getting a better handle on the material." John speaks well and is learning to be an advocate for himself. He was able to negotiate a paper instead of a multiple choice exam in his first-year psychology course. John's circumstances again point up the advantages of using available technological advances to bypass weaknesses. In addition, his strategy of discussing ideas with his friends finds support from cognitive psychologists such as Craik and Tulving (1972) who tell us that the more deeply information is processed, the better it is remembered. Activities such as expressing one's thoughts on paper and discussing or explaining them to others leads to deeper processing and aids memory.

Something which stood out in all the students interviewed was how conscientious they were and how hard they had to work to keep up. John's schedule has him in the library studying five nights a week and most of Sunday. He works between classes and usually takes a one-hour nap before supper because he tires very easily. Kevin must work well ahead of deadlines to submit material for previewing by the instructor. When reading is a problem, extra time is required to get through the necessary readings, and to read and reread the material. Repeated editing takes a great deal of time. Although some faculty suggest that these students just want the courses to be watered down for them, there was no evidence of this in the students interviewed. They all put in many more hours than the normal student to maintain their grades and were willing to work extremely hard to demonstrate their capability.

It should be noted that often these students become very adept at course selection, choosing those courses which permit them to use their strengths and minimize their weaknesses. Ken, with his auditory processing difficulties, would be wise to avoid large lecture classes, or try to arrange for assistance which will help him to cope with the specific demands of such courses. Similarly, a dyslexic student will probably have special difficulty reading multiple choice questions and might for that reason avoid large lecture classes or, like John, negotiate a written paper instead of a multiple choice exam. A student with speaking difficulties will probably avoid seminar classes, where a major part of the grade will require presentations in front of other students. All students naturally select courses that suit their interests or skills, but for learning disabled students, it is essential that they do so.

Advocacy

There was a second thread which ran through the lives of all these students. Each and every one interviewed mentioned that somewhere in the past was a person who believed in them and acted as an advocate. Many said that it was unlikely that they would have reached college without this support. They describe being confused, depressed, withdrawn, and threatened by circumstances that they did not understand. They could not understand why some teachers seemed to believe that they were lazy, disinterested, or slow when they knew in their hearts that they understood but somehow could not express that comprehension. One student described a learning disability as a "silent killer." "It leaves you uncertain and defeated." "You begin to believe all the stuff they are saying about you." "You stop trying. Nothing you do makes any difference."

For each of these students, a person appeared whose willingness to fight the system for them demonstrated a faith in their abilities. Not only did Jeff's mother provide consistent, and persistent, tutoring in his weakest areas, but she fought decisions that put him in poor academic situations. She constantly sought and found ways for him to acquire and demonstrate his knowledge. She was finally able to convince the system that his problem was specific to certain areas but that he could learn and progress in a normal classroom. Without her conviction in his capability, he believes, he would have become a serious troublemaker. Mr. B.

was the second advocate for Jeff, appearing when he was feeling almost defeated by the transition to secondary school. It was Mr. B's faith in his ability to perform that gave him the confidence to accept the challenges of proving himself.

Another parent would not accept the school's position that his child was retarded. He fought the school board to prevent placement in a special education class, and argued long and hard for professional testing. The tests showed that the student had well above average intelligence and vindicated the parent's position. It was at that point that the student began to believe in himself.

John found support from a resource teacher in his first year of secondary school. This teacher expressed faith in John's ability and shared this with other teachers, at the same time encouraging John to think of going to college.

Kevin remembers a secondary school teacher who would spend 10 or 15 minutes with him after school, encouraging him to keep trying. It was this teacher that encouraged Kevin to try coaching baseball. He is not well coordinated, has poor spatial ability, and therefore does not do well at any sports, but he understands the game of baseball very well. The teacher helped him get started and Kevin has been coaching and managing Little League baseball since that time. He commented on what a boost that gave to his self-confidence and self-esteem, in part because he acquired some prestige with his peers.

When asked what is important about having an advocate, the students said things such as, "He told me I was okay," "She helped me understand that I wasn't really dumb," "He made me feel as good as everyone else." It is clear that the role of an advocate includes having faith in the student's abilities and expressing that faith. It also means being willing to persuade others of this conviction. It acts as a mentoring role and those advocates who were contacted expressed great satisfaction in having been able to assist these students.

Unfortunately, there is little research into the value of such advocates, but there is substantial investigation on the value of self-advocacy, which is a skill that all the students interviewed have acquired to varying degrees. Brinckerhoff (1993) has called self-advocacy a "critical skill for college students with learning disabilities" (p. 23). He has argued that as students empower themselves they shift from protected child to responsible adult. McGuire (1991) has argued that college-bound students with learning disabilities need instruction in self-advocacy skills. Other researchers have developed programs to assist high school students in making the transition to post-secondary institutions (Aune, 1991; Durlak, Rose, & Bursuck, 1994; Phillips, 1990). Some of these would be useful resources for teachers wishing to empower their learning disabled students.

The approaches discussed in this chapter were designed to provide a framework for assisting students who have specialized learning problems. Although specific strategies are mentioned, it was emphasized that the fundamental principle is to use each individual student's strengths to bypass his/her weaknesses. Examples of strategies that students have developed with the aid of important teachers and counsellors were provided. Many of the techniques offered in the other chapters of this book will be appropriate in certain content areas. What matters is that the student learn what works for him/her. By being observant, by examining the most challenging and productive areas of endeavor with the student, and by expressing your faith in his/her abilities, you can encourage that process.

Additional Reading

Alley, G., & Deshler, D. (1979). *Teaching the learning disabled adolescent: Strategies and methods.* Denver: Love Publishing Co.

Bachor, D.G. & Crealock, C. (1986). *Instructional strategies for students with special needs.* Scarborough, ON: Prentice-Hall Canada.

Flippo, O.F., & Caverly, D.E. (Eds.) (1991). *Teaching reading and study strategies at the college level.* Newark, DE: International Reading Association.

Pressley, M., Harris, K.R., & Guthrie, J.T. (Eds.) (1992). *Promoting academic competence and literacy in school.* San Diego, CA: Academic Press.

REFERENCES

Alley, G., & Deshler, D. (1979). *Teaching the learning disabled adolescent: Strategies and methods.* Denver: Love Publishing Co.

Aune, E. (1991). A transitional model for postsecondary-bound students with learning disabilities. *Learning Disabilities Research and Practice, 6,* 177-187.

Brinckerhoff, L.C. (1993). Self-advocacy: A critical skill for college students with learning disabilities. *Family and Community Health, 16(3),* 23-33.

Britton, B.K., & Tesser, A. (1991) . Effects of time-management practices on college grades. *Journal of Educational Psychology, 83,* 405-410.

Burke Guild, P. (August, 1989). Meeting students' learning styles. *Instructor,* 14-16.

Chazin, S., & Neuschatz, J.S. (1990). Using a mnemonic to aid in the recall of unfamiliar information. *Perceptual and Motor Skill, 71,* 881-882.

Clarke, J.H. (1991). Using visual organizers to focus on thinking. *Journal of Reading, 34,* 526-534.

Cowen, S. (1988). Coping strategies of university students with learning disabilities. *Journal of Learning Disabilities, 21,* 161-164.

Craik, F.I.M., & Tulving, E. (1975). Depth of processing and the retention of words in episodic memory. *Journal of Experimental Psychology: General, 104,* 268-294.

Dillon, R.F. (1986). Issues in cognitive psychology and instruction. In R.F. Dillon, & R.J. Sternberg, *Cognition and instruction.* Orlando, FL: Academic Press.

Dunn, R. (1990). Understanding the Dunn and Dunn learning styles model and the need for individual diagnosis and prescription. *Reading, Writing, and Learning Disabilities, 6,* 223-247.

Durlak, C.M., Rose, E., & Bursuck, W.D. (1994). Preparing high school students with learning disabilities for the transition to postsecondary education: Teaching the skills of self-determination. *Journal of Learning Disabilities, 27,* 51-59.

Garner, R. (1992). When children and adults do not use learning strategies: Toward a theory of settings. *Review of Educational Research, 60,* 517-530.

Good, T., & Brophy, J. (1984). *Looking in the classroom* (3rd ed.). New York: Harper & Row.

Good, T.L., & Brophy, J.E. (1986). *Educational psychology* (3rd ed.). New York: Longman.

Greenfield, P.M. (1987). Electronic technologies, education, and cognitive development. In D.E. Berger, K. Pezdek, & W.P. Banks (Eds.), *Applications of cognitive psychology: Problem solving, education, and computing.* Hillsdale, NJ: Lawrence Erlbaum.

Griggs, M. (1990). Counseling students toward effective study skills using their learning style strengths. *Journal of Reading, Writing, and Learning Disabilities International, 6,* 281-296.

Hartley, J. (1985). *Designing instructional text* (2nd ed.). London: Kogan Page Ltd.

Johnson, R.E. (1975). Meaning in complex learning. *Review of Educational Research, 45,* 425-460.

Johnson, D.W., & Johnson, R. (1982). Effects of cooperative, competitive and individualistic learning experiences on cross-ethnic interactions and friendships. *Journal of Social Psychology, 118,* 47-58.

Johnson, D.W., & Johnson, R. (1985). Cooperative learning. In R. Ames & C. Ames (Eds.), *Research on motivation in education* (Vol. 2). Orlando, FL: Academic Press.

Kiewra, K.A. (1987). Notetaking and review: The research and its implications. *Instructional Science, 16,* 233-249.

Kirk, S. (1976). *Teaching children with learning disabilities: Personal perspectives.* Columbus, OH: Charles E. Merrill.

Krupski, A. (1986). Attention problems in youngsters with learning handicaps. In J.K. Torgesen, & B.Y.L. Wong, *Psychological and educational perspectives on learning disabilities.* Orlando, FL: Academic Press.

Lenz, B.K., Alley, G.R., & Schumaker, J.B. (1987). Activating the inactive learner: Advance organizers in the secondary content classroom. *Learning Disability Quarterly, 10,* 53-62.

McGuire, J.M. (1991). A field-based study of the direct service needs of college students with learning disabilities. *Journal of College Student Development. 32,* 101-108.

Miller, G. (1956). The magical number seven, plus or minus two: Some limits on our capacity for processing information. *Psychological Review. 63,* 81-97.

Morgan, C.G. (1983). Adapting a college preparatory curriculum for dyslexic adolescents: III. Applications for the classroom. *Annals of Dyslexia, 33,* 251-267.

Phillips, P. (1990) A self-advocacy plan for high school students with learning disabilities: A comparative case study analysis of students', teachers', and parents' perceptions of program effects. *Journal of Learning Disabilities, 23,* 466-471.

Powers, S.I., Hauser, S.T., & Kilner, L.A. (1989). Adolescent mental health. *American Psychologist, 44,* 200-208.

Rawson, M.B. (1978). *Dyslexia and learning disabilities: Their relationship.* Bulletin of The Orton Society, XXVIII, Reprint No. 76. Baltimore, MD: The Orton Dyslexia Society.

Scruggs, T.E., & Mastropieri, M.A. (1990). The case for mnemonic instruction: From laboratory research to classroom applications. *Journal of Special Education, 24,* 7-32.

Sitko, M.C. (1986). Developments in computer technology: Implications for the special student. In D.G. Bachor & C. Crealock, *Instructional strategies for students with special needs.* Scarborough, ON: Prentice-Hall Canada.

Smith, C.R. (1991). *Learning disabilities: The interaction of learner. task. and setting.* Needham Heights, MA: Allyn and Bacon.

Weissberg, M., Berentsen, M., Cote, A., Cravey, B., & Heath, K. (1982). An assessment of the personal, career, and academic needs of undergraduate students. *Journal of College Student Personnel, 23,* 115-112.

Author Index

Subject Index

About the Editors

Eileen Wood is a developmental psychologist at Wilfrid Laurier University. After earning her Ph.D. in Instructional Psychology from Simon Fraser University, she first taught at the University of Western Ontario. Both her B.A. and M.A. were obtained at the University of Western Ontario, where her specialization was developmental psychology. Currently, her research interests combine both developmental and educational issues: for example, she examines memory development and how it affects strategic interventions within the classroom.

Vera E. Woloshyn is an Assistant Professor in the Faculty of Education at Brock University. Her research interests include the development and implementation of strategy programs, particularly those that provide student with explicit multiple strategy instruction. She currently holds a grant from the Social Sciences and Humanities Research Council (SSHRC). Professor Woloshyn has also co-edited the text *Cognitive Strategy Instruction that Really Improves Children's Academic Performance*, in which she also appears as an author.

Teena Willoughby is completing her second year of a postdoctoral fellowship at the University of Waterloo and the University of Toronto. She received her B.A. from the University of Western Ontario and her M.A. and Ph.D. degrees from the University of Waterloo. Her research examines the developmental aspects of memory, strategies, and self-regulated learning. In addition, she is investigating teaching practices that promote self-regulated thinking in the classroom and how educators' attitudes influence these teaching behaviors.